Techniques of
Program and System Maintenance

Section I

Maintenance: The Problem and Perspective

. . . The main problem in the maintenance business is that you cannot just do maintenance on a system which wasn't designed for maintenance. Unless we design for maintenance, we'll always be in a lot of trouble after a system goes into production. . . .

Gerald M. Weinberg
March 14, 1978

Techniques of
Program and System Maintenance

Edited by Girish Parikh

Foreword by Gerald M. Weinberg

Library of Congress
Catalog Card Number: 79-54410

ISBN: 0-933950-58-6

Readers are invited to comment on this book, or the techniques they have developed to cope with the maintenance problem, by writing to Parikh at Shetal Enterprises, 1787 B West Touhy, Chicago, IL 60626.

P.O. Box 6627, Lincoln, Nebraska 68506

10 9 8 7 6 5 4 3 2 1

To my dear friend, guide, and former boss

Jon C. (Cris) Miller

Contents

Section IV: Structured Technologies and Maintenance

Section V: The Future of Maintenance

Foreword

Gerald M. Weinberg

"We often mistake the end of an illusion for the beginning of a crisis." These wise words could be applied to the energy crisis, the population crisis, the crisis of middle age, or the computer program maintenance crisis. In fact, the computer program maintenance crisis may be a composite of the other three.

1. The Energy Crisis: all those times the programmers lacked the energy to finish the documentation and all those other "nuisances" of program development.

2. The Population Crisis: the population of programs has an increasing birth rate, but almost zero death rate—which must inevitably lead to unchecked growth of an old and aging program population.

3. The Crisis of Middle Age: a) the programming business is just coming out of its irresponsible youth, and now must pay for the sins and excesses it enjoyed; b) the programmers themselves, as they grow older, are leaving for other jobs and have to live with the programming sins of their youth.

Program and system maintenance need not have been a crisis. Even a decade ago, a few small voices were crying in the wilderness, warning us of the great illusion of development. In private conversations, the subject was frequently discussed, though often in hushed tones. In software conferences, several brave souls risked reputations to give speeches on the subject. And once a year or so, an article appeared in the trade press. As the form of communication became more public and permanent, the willingness to mention "the maintenance problem" diminished. It was as if everyone thought the problem would vanish with advancing technology, like the problem of paper tape or the problem of Williams tube memories.

To be fair, the name "maintenance" isn't what I would have chosen for this subject, but it is the name that has grown upon us. And it has certainly grown, make no mistake. There may be no other reading on maintenance, but many of us are spending most of our time *doing* maintenance. Could it be that the reason we spend so much time doing maintenance is that we've never spent much time reading about it? After all, isn't most of the maintenance the result of the confusion caused by the great swarm of books on design and development that we've read over the past ten years?

Whenever I think of program maintenance, I conjure up a picture of the Great Dust Bowl of the '30s. We've seen thousands of stirring films on "How The West Was Won," but who wants to see a film on "How The West Was Made Liveable After It Was Won"? There was one such film, *Grapes of Wrath,* from the book by Steinbeck. Pretty depressing, too.

I think that our own time in computing will become known as the Great Dust Bowl of data processing. Ours is the time when everyone is choking on the dust left by a generation of pioneers who plowed too deep and thought too shallow. *Techniques of Program and System Maintenance* is the first of a long line of "conservation" books. Conservationists like its author-editor, Girish Parikh, will show us how to tame the Dust Bowl, just as other conservationists did during the Great Depression.

Make no mistake. I'm not predicting that we're going to turn the Dust Bowl into the Garden of Eden. I'm not predicting that the work will be free of dirt and toil. Nor will it generally be elegant or mathematically sophisticated. I do think, however, that the crude name, "maintenance" doesn't do this noble task justice. I would have preferred that the book be entitled, *Techniques of Program and System Rework, Redesign, and Redevelopment.* That would be a more accurate representation of its contents and its mission.

As author, I know that the time has come for this book on maintenance, whatever we happen to call it today. As publisher, it's a bit scary to back that judgement with cash and labor, but that's no more than any reader is asked to do. As programmer and consultant, I find it impossible to imagine anyone in the business of program and system development or maintenance who won't benefit from this book.

Introduction

Girish Parikh

Every adversity has the seed of a greater benefit.
*Napoleon Hill and W. Clement Stone**

In 1976, while working on some of the most depressing maintenance assignments of my career, I started work on an original book on software maintenance. I did some research, put together some of my experience, talked with some professionals and outlined the book.

After about a year's part-time effort, I condensed and published a section of it in the form of a report "Improved Maintenance Techniques." It attempted to answer the question: "How can the Improved Programming Technologies be used to maintain existing systems?"

That report became the first in the series "Programmer Productivity Reports." To date, I've published four more reports. There are currently ten titles in the series.

However, the subject of software maintenance largely remained unaddressed. I had already done some research on the subject. I decided to do a further literature search and compile a book. To my knowledge, this is the first and only book devoted to program and system maintenance in computing literature.

Software maintenance is an extremely important subject. According to one study, (Boehm, 1976), about 45% of the overall hardware-software dollar is going into software maintenance. The same study further reveals that this number is likely to grow to about 60% by 1985. And it is expected to continue growing for a long time, as we add new code to our inventory faster than we discard the old code. The on-going maintenance, where most programmers spend 50%, and in some cases 80% of their time, is clearly a significant burden to the data processing industry.

The main purpose of this book is to present programming as well as managerial techniques of software maintenance gleaned from the vast computing literature. The book is a compilation of important and useful material on software maintenance, published in the computer periodicals, conference proceedings, reports, books, as well as some original material.

The book is divided into seven sections. Through some chapters cover several topics, this broad classification will guide the reader in his study. For particular topics, the reader should consult the index.

The first section introduces the problem of maintenance and provides some perspective. The second section covers "how to" aspects for a maintenance programmer. Techniques for managing maintenance are presented in the third section. The application and impact of structured technologies on maintenance are described in section four. Section five, an extension of section four, indicates possible future developments in this vital area. It includes a chapter related to "structuring engine," a software package that automatically transforms an unstructured program into a structured program.

Section six is an extensive, annotated bibliography, containing works on software maintenance, as well as works in related areas such as software testing and debugging, software tools, and structured technologies. Section seven is the index.

The final chapter "Structured Programming Perspective," though not covering software maintenance directly, is included as a prelude to the emerging, and now rapidly spreading, structured technologies. As I see it, the major purpose of structured technologies (comprising structured analysis, structured design, structured programming, and related productivity techniques) is to help develop more maintainable and reliable software.

Presented here are techniques, guidelines, case studies, ideas, and sources providing a perspective on software maintenance. I hope this book will help reduce some of the burden of software maintenance. I believe it can also be useful as a text or as supplementary reading for computer science or software engineering courses.

* From *Success Through a Positive Mental Attitude* by Napoleon Hill and W. Clement Stone, © 1960 by Prentice-Hall, Inc., Englewood Cliffs, New Jersey.

Acknowledgements

I am grateful to Gerald M. Weinberg, my programming guru, for criticizing and helping with the manuscript, and for writing the foreword. His encouraging letters kept me going during the darkest hours when this project seemed almost impossible. He also made material on maintenance from Ethnotech publications available and gave generous permissions to reprint. I thank Jon C. (Cris) Miller for reviewing my original works critically and for making some excellent suggestions. I also thank him for contributing an original article. For helping me in the research, I thank Malcolm Peltu, past editor of the London-based *Computer Weekly;* Tom Gilb, an Independent EDP Consultant; Guy de Balbine, technical director for Caine, Farber & Gordon, Inc.; and Arnold E. Keller, editorial director for *Infosystems.* I am grateful to Gordon W. Terrill, former education specialist for Montgomery Ward Corporate Systems Division, for encouraging me to study structured technologies (that eventually led to this project), while taking Deltak video courses on structured programming featuring Edward Yourdon. I thank all the publishers/authors for giving me permission to reprint articles, excerpts, or quotations from their publications. I thank the Ethnotech staff, including Sally Cox, Linda Hollcroft, Lorri Campbell, Barbara Stock, Linda Knopp, Timothy Gill and Michael Lyons, for creating an excellent book from the manuscript made up of pasted clippings and sheets. I thank all the others who directly or indirectly helped in the project; (their names couldn't be included due to space limitations.) In preparing the manuscript my wife Hasu and daughter Sharmila gave invaluable help. I must thank my wife Hasu, without whose encouragement and patience I could not have completed this book.

Girish Parikh
Chicago, Illinois
December, 1979

The Mid-City Triangle

Gerald M. Weinberg

You've heard of the eternal triangle—the perpetual intertwining of human libidos and marital arrangements. You've heard of the Bermuda Triangle—the unending mystery of ghost ships and ghoulish seamen. But until now, only I have known of the curious circulation of programmers amongst the big three of Mid-City, USA.

I was visiting Mid-City for the third or fourth time when I became aware of a peculiarity shared by many of the programmers I had met on previous visits. Mid-City has three principal data processing installations: Amalgamated Egg Sucking, Central Cane Testing, and United Cigar Rental. Among them, they employ seventy or eighty percent of the programmers in Mid-City, perhaps six hundred in all. Of the programmers I met, those with ten or more years of experience seemed to have worked at all three installations. Some, indeed, were on their second time around what I came to call the Mid-City Triangle.

In a larger city, I would never have noticed the phenomenon because the programmers' choices were too varied. In a smaller town, it always seemed to be work at Big Daddy's or move out. In Mid-City, though, the cycle was pure and perfect.

It went something like this: Brent Bleary graduated from college and joined the new employee training program of Amalgamated, though it could equally well have been one of the others. Having completed his six-month COBOL course, he was given a small application program to write. He was challenged, but he was happy. All day long he coded, submitted jobs, pored over bugs, and wove in changes. Finally, only a few weeks after the scheduled date, he delivered his masterpiece, and the boss was pleased mightily.

Brent was rewarded with an even more challenging new application, and he set to work whistling to himself with joy. But a few weeks into the new project, he was interrupted with a minor annoyance—someone wanted a small change in his first program. But Brent took it in stride, even though his documentation had gone cold on him, and soon was back to application two. In the following months, these little interruptions came more or less regularly, but never amounted to more than an irritating diversion from the main task.

When application two was delivered only a week late, Brent was praised a thousand times and raised a thousand dollars. He even rewarded himself by taking a short vacation in a cabin on a nearby lake. Unhappily, his vacation was cut short when an old geezer brought him an urgent telegram from town—one of his applications had crashed!

Yet even then, if Brent had regrets about his abbreviated vacation, they were drowned in the importance he felt at being the center of attention while the problem was being fixed. And, when he was given application three—the very job he had been hoping for—all thoughts of vacation dissolved, past, present, and future.

The work on application three went well—at least it did when Brent wasn't being interrupted by little fixes and enhancements and questions and clarifications and hand-holding on applications one and two. When his manager inquired about the schedule, Brent answered with a query of his own. When was he going to be relieved of some of this pesky maintenance work, so he could concentrate on the important job at hand? It wouldn't be long, he was reassured. Just as soon as one of the new trainees completed the COBOL course.

But the course ended and no trainee was forthcoming. There were urgent jobs to be handled, and not enough time to have Brent turn one or two over to someone inexperienced. Indeed, it would take Brent less time just to handle the few requests by himself than it would to teach some trainee all that he knew about the subtleties of these applications. Brent had to agree with that argument, for he was certainly too busy with application three and his maintenance chores to find time to train some greenhorn.

And so another year passed, and Brent was now the proud father of quintuplets—applications one, two, three, four, and five. He had an application six on the way, but its gestation period was getting longer and longer, since Brent had less than a few good hours a week to work on it. Several times, his manager had promised relief from the maintenance. Once it had been very close, but then his manager got promoted, and the new manager just couldn't afford any risks until things had settled down.

Then, one evening, at the meeting of the local chapter of the Society for Computers and People, Brent heard that Central Cane was desperate for some experienced programmers to work on an exciting new development project. He made a few inquiries, arranged an interview, and took his Programmer Aptitude Test. He was offered a job, at a moderate increase in pay, but with the greatest fringe benefit of all. If he worked at Central Cane, he wouldn't have to maintain any of the Amalgamated programs any more. All he would have to do is develop a wonderful *new* program. It was like replacing the old jalopy with a brand new sports car—at reduced monthly payments!

But if Brent was anything, he was loyal, so he gave his manager one last chance. And, indeed, the manager was overflowing with sympathy for Brent's plight, welling with confidence that relief was coming in a few months, and brimming with news of the fat raise he had just negotiated to keep Brent happy in the interim. Brent thanked his manager for the raise, quietly left his office, and immediately called the personnel manager at Central Cane to accept the offer. When his manager found out, he was completely befuddled. How could someone quit just when they got such a nice raise and such warm sympathy?

Well, to make a long story short, Brent's stay at Central Cane pretty much followed the same script as it had at Amalgamated. After a glorious honeymoon with his virgin application, he was soon saddled with an ever-fatter nagging burden of maintenance of his previous triumphs. Eventually, he heard that United Cigar was getting into new territory, and after a few formalities, found himself across town in a freshly painted office, freed forever of the oppressive programs and management at Central Cane.

But after two years, when the cycle had come another turn, Brent had run out of places to go in Mid-City. In Gotham City, he might have kept on going to new firms forever, but here—what was he to do? As the months wore on, he began to despair—even considering a career in some new area, like calf roping. Then, by chance, he ran across his old manager from Amalgamated.

Brent was worried that there might be some residual bitterness, but in almost five years, all had been forgotten and forgiven. Besides, Amalgamated was just in the process of automating several large, new applications, so the manager wasn't in any position to offend anyone with programming experience. In a short time, Brent had packed up his templates and his job control decks and shipped them back to Amalgamated. Not to his old desk, though, for now he was a very senior programmer, and had a semi-private office to hang out in. But even more important, nobody even remembered that he had anything to do with applications one through six, oh, those many years ago. Or at least they were too polite to say anything about them.

I stayed a few extra days in Mid-City, just to interview some of Brent's contemporaries, like Sue, Harry, Betty Anne, Irma, Wolfgang, and Thelma. With minor variations, all had the same story to tell. Wolfgang, in fact, had been around the Mid-City Triangle twice, and was in the process of negotiating his third circuit. Where would it all end?, I wondered on the plane back. What would it take to break the grip this iron triangle had on so many lives? Or was it these people who had the grip on the triangle? As I recalled each interview, I realized that these were all happy programmers, perhaps far happier than the average. I wonder who's getting stuck with all that maintenance?

The World of Software Maintenance

Girish Parikh

Welcome to the world of software maintenance!

Let me ask you: Do you really like the world of software maintenance? If you know this world already, I'm confident your answer is a definite no. A few of you may be exceptions, however, you who can see maintenance as a challenge (usually unappreciated), or as job security (though it's a myth), or even find it easier than new development (once you know the system). Whether you like maintenance or not, it's a fact of life in data processing. Someone, perhaps you, must do that dirty work—until the mess is cleared and replaced by more maintainable systems developed using structured technologies. Maintainable systems make maintenance programming a decent job.

This article focuses on software maintenance as an important part of software engineering. It outlines different aspects of software maintenance, and presents a case for collection and development of "software maintenance technologies."

Software engineering and its functions

Software engineering, simply defined, is a collection of methodologies, both technical and managerial, for development and maintenance of software. (Canning 1978) The word "maintenance" is used here in its broadest sense, to include error corrections, changes (also called modifications or amendments), enhancements, and improvements to the existing software.

The field of software engineering includes technical as well as managerial functions for the equally important functions of software development and software maintenance, as shown in figure 1.

The two branches (or functions) of software engineering, i.e. software development and software maintenance, can also be called "software development engineering" and "software maintenance engineering." However, the shorter terms are already in use, and it appears that their use will continue.

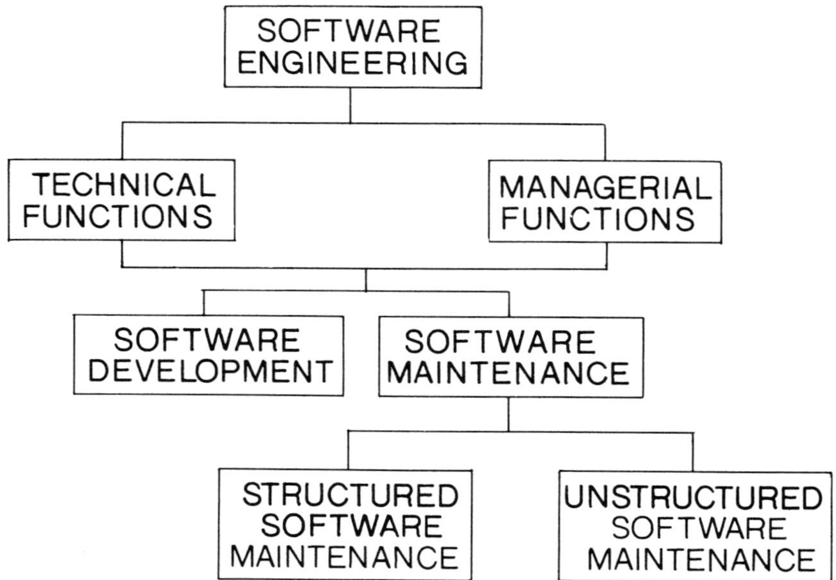

Figure 1. The Functions of Software Engineering

We can further divide software maintenance into "systems software maintenance" and "applications software maintenance." However, in this article, software maintenance includes maintenance of both.

Software maintenance includes both "structured software maintenance" and "unstructured software[1] maintenance." We will take a closer look at them later in this chapter.

Software maintenance: extremely important but neglected topic

Traditionally, computing literature has focused on software development. Software maintenance has been almost always neglected.[2] This imbalance is like trying to fly with only one wing!

According to one study, about 45% of the overall hardware-software dollar is *currently* going into software maintenance. The same study further reveals that this number is likely to grow to about 60% by 1985; and is expected to continue to grow for a long time as we add new code to our inventory faster than we discard the old code. (Boehm, 1976) The on-going maintenance, where most programmers spend 50%, and in some cases 80% of their time, is clearly a significant burden to the DP industry.

The structured technologies and maintenance in the future

The proper use of structured technologies (comprising structured analysis, structured design, structured programming; and the productivity techniques such as top-down design and development, walkthroughs, team operations, development support libraries) during software development helps produce more maintainable systems and programs, reducing the future burden of software maintenance.

Software maintenance

Software maintenance includes maintenance of all software, including "structured software" (software developed using structured technologies), as well as "unstructured software" (software developed without using structured technologies).

Structured software maintenance

The maintenance of structured software can be called "structured software maintenance," or simply "structured maintenance." However, the former term is preferable, as the latter is already used in connection with maintenance of unstructured software. (For example, see Yourdon, 1977.)

Ideally, structured software maintenance is a process of continued development. We do need, however, techniques for structured software maintenance.

The current focus in software engineering is on new systems development. The systems developed using the structured technologies need techniques for structured implementation and maintenance. The objectives of these techniques are twofold: 1) minimization of the distinction between testing, integration, and installation, and 2) preservation of the structural integrity of the initial systems design, while doing maintenance.

Unstructured software maintenance

The maintenance of unstructured software can be called "unstructured software maintenance," or simply "unstructured maintenance;" however, the former term is preferable.

Until unstructured software is given a partial or full "face-lift," (described later in this chapter), or, partially or completely rewritten using structured technologies, it may continue to be a major burden. The need for collecting (and even developing) techniques to handle such software maintenance is even greater than that for structured software.

Some techniques common to both kinds of software maintenance

Many techniques may be different for the two kinds of software maintenance. It is likely that some techniques are common to both kinds of maintenance. For example, the techniques for face-lift can be applied to the structured software also.

The collection of techniques for both kinds of software maintenance can be called software maintenance technologies.

Maintainability of unstructured software

The maintainability of unstructured software can vary in degrees, from easily maintainable to almost unmaintainable. Several factors such as the structure of the unstructured software, the quality of available documentation, the experience and application knowledge of maintenance programmers, the extensiveness and types of maintenance, and the management attitude, should be considered in estimating the maintainability of software. Again, maintainability may be relative to the criteria established, and it may vary for the different components of the same software package.

Types of maintenance

Maintenance can be classified into three types: "Corrective maintenance" to take care of processing, performance, or implementation failures; "adaptive maintenance" to satisfy changes in the processing or data environment; and "perfective maintenance" for enhancing performance or maintainability. (Swanson, 1976)

Techniques for unstructured software maintenance

Little has been written on "how to" aspects of unstructured software maintenance. Nevertheless, while each such system may have its own problems, some common techniques, based on experience and study, can be collected and/or developed.

Some of the structured technologies, such as a human librarian, walkthroughs, chief programmer teams, can also be used to maintain unstructured software.[3]

Techniques for a software face-lift

These techniques essentially improve the appearance of software. Reformatting of programs (which can be automated) may dramatically improve maintenance programming productivity.

The restructuring of programs (possibly automated) can also increase maintenance programming productivity; however, it may have limitations depending on the structure of the original software.

Software tools in maintenance

Available software packages, such as automated libraries, preprocessors including reformatting packages and structuring engines, file compare utilities, and online testing and debugging packages, can be efficiently used to increase maintenance programming productivity. This subject needs to be explored.[4]

Conclusion

Software maintenance technologies, collected and organized, can help manage maintenance better, and help reduce some of its burden. I hope that this chapter, briefly covering the range of software maintenance ideas, generates further interest in this vital subject.

Notes

[1]The term "unstructured software" in this chapter is used to represent the software developed without using structured technologies. However, the qualifying term "unstructured" might be misleading, since there is more of a continuum between the two polar extremes of structured and unstructured, and very little work is *completely* unstructured. The term, though imprecise, is used in this chapter (instead of "software developed without using structured technologies"), since it seems that it is currently in use to represent such software (e.g., see the use of the term "unstructured program", Yourdon 1979: 3).

[2]In recent programming literature, however, software maintenance has been receiving increased attention. See, for example, *High Level COBOL Programming* by Gerald M. Weinberg, *et al,* containing a whole chapter on maintenance, and *Techniques of Program Structure and Design* by Edward Yourdon.

[3]See Girish Parikh, "Improved Maintenance Techniques" in the series "Programmer Productivity Reports," (Chicago: Shetal Enterprises).

[4]For a study of COBOL preprocessors in maintenance (and new developments) see Girish Parikh, "How to Increase COBOL Programming Productivity Using a Preprocessor" in the series "Programmer Productivity Reports," (Chicago: Shetal Enterprises).

Software Maintenance

Barry W. Boehm

Scope of Software Maintenance

Software maintenance is an extremely important but highly neglected activity. Its importance is clear from figure 1: about 40% of the overall hardware—software dollar is going into software maintenance today, and this number is likely to grow to about 60% by 1985. It will continue to grow for a long time, as we continue to add to our inventory of code via development at a faster rate than we make code obsolete.

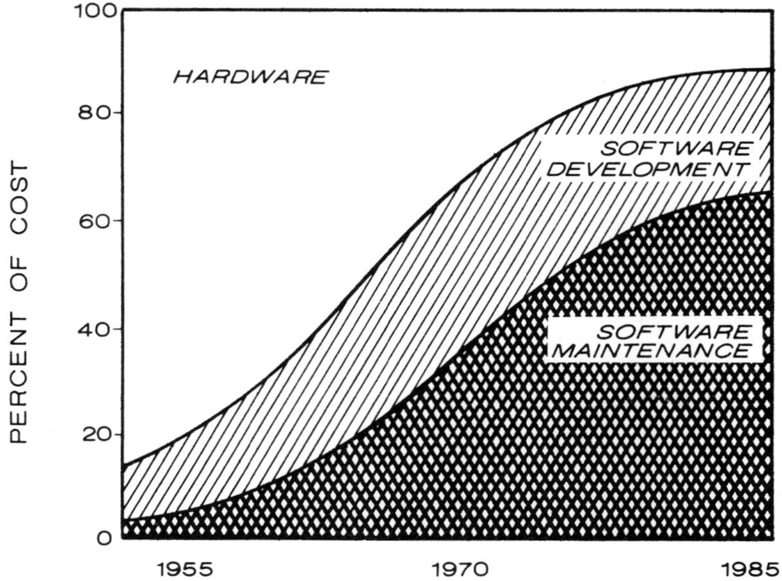

Figure 1. Hardware-Software Cost Trends

The figures above are only very approximate, because our only data so far are based on highly approximate definitions. It is hard to come up with an unexceptional definition of software maintenance. Here, we define it as "the process of modifying existing operational software while leaving its primary functions intact." It is useful to divide software maintenance into two categories: software *update,* which results in a changed functional specification for the software, and software *repair,* which leaves the functional specification intact. A good discussion of software repair is given in the paper by Swanson (1976), who divides it into the subcategories of corrective maintenance (of processing, performance, or implementation failures), adaptive maintenance (to changes in the processing or data environment), and perfective maintenance (for enhancing performance or maintainability).

For either update or repair, three main functions are involved in software maintenance (Boehm, Brown, Lipow, 1976).

Understanding the existing software: This implies the need for good documentation, good traceability between requirements and code, and well-structured and well-formatted code.

Modifying the existing software: This implies the need for software, hardware, and data structures which are easy to expand and which minimize side effects of changes, plus easy-to-update documentation.

Revalidating the modified software: This implies the need for software structures which facilitate selective retest, and aids for making retest more thorough and efficient.

Following a short discussion of current practice in software maintenance, these three functions will be used below as a framework for discussing current frontier technology in software maintenance.

Current Practice

As indicated in fig. 2, probably about 70 percent of the overall cost of software is spent in software maintenance. A recent paper by Elshoff (1976) indicates that the figure for General Motors is about 75 percent, and that GM is fairly typical of large business software activities. Daly (1977) indicates that about 60 percent of GTE's 10-year life cycle costs for real time software are devoted to maintenance. On two Air Force command and control software systems, the maintenance portions of the 10-year life cycle costs were about 67 and 72 percent. Often, maintenance is not done very efficiently. On one aircraft computer, software development costs were roughly $75/instruction, while maintenance costs ran as high as $4,000/instruction (Trainor 1973).

Despite its size, software maintenance is a highly neglected activity. In general, less-qualified personnel are assigned to maintenance tasks. There are few good general principles and few studies of the process, most of them inconclusive.

Further, data processing practices are usually optimized around other criteria than maintenance efficiency. Optimizing around development cost and schedule criteria generally leads to compromises in documentation, testing and structuring.

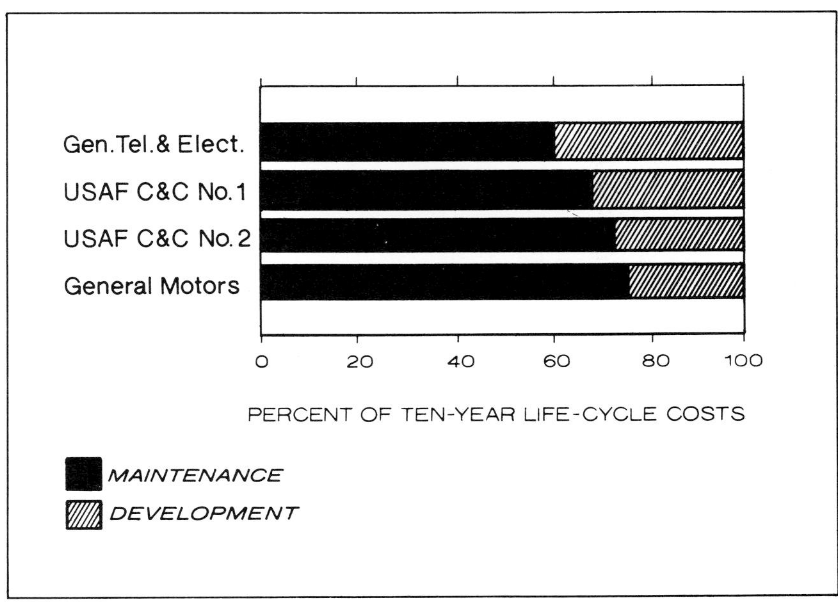

Figure 2. Software Life-cycle Cost Breakdown

Optimizing around hardware efficiency criteria generally leads to use of assembly language and skimping on hardware, both of which correlate strongly with increased software maintenance costs. (Boehm, 1973)

Current Frontier Technology

1. Understanding the Existing Software: Aids here have largely been discussed: structured programming, automatic formatting, and code auditors for standards compliance checking to enhance code readability; machine-readable requirements and design languages with traceability support to and from the code. Several systems exist for automatically updating documentation by excerpting information from the revised code and comment cards.

2. Modifying the Existing Software: Some of Parnas' modularization guidelines (Parnas 1972) and the data abstractions of the CLU (Liskov, Zilles, 1974) and ALPHARD (Wulf 1974) languages make it easier to minimize the size effects of changes. There may be a maintenance price, however. In the past, some systems with highly coupled programs and associated data structures have had difficulties with data base updating. This may not be a problem with today's data dictionary capabilities, but the interactions have not yet been investigated. Other aids to modification are structured code, configuration management techniques, programming support libraries, and process construction systems.

3. Revalidating the Modified Software: They include primarily test data management systems, comparator programs, and program structure analyzers with some limited capability for selective retest analysis.

4. General Aids: On-line interactive systems help to remove one of the main bottlenecks involved in software maintenance: the long turnaround times for retesting. In addition, many of these systems are providing helpful capabilities for text editing and software module management. In general, a good deal more work has been done on the maintainability aspects of data bases and data structures than for program structures; a good survey of data base technology is given in a recent special issue of ACM *Computing Surveys* (Sibley 1976).

Trends

The increased concern with life cycle costs, particularly within the U.S. DoD (*Defense Management Journal 1975),* will focus a good deal more attention on software maintenance. More data collection and analysis on the growth dynamics of software systems, such as the Belady-Lehman studies of OS/360 (Belady, Lehman, 1975), will begin to point out the high-leverage areas for improvement. Explicit mechanisms for confronting maintainability issues early in the development cycle, such as the requirements-properties matrix (Boehm 1974: 192–197) and the design inspection (Fagan 1974) will be refined and used more extensively. In fact, we may evolve a more general concept of software quality assurance (currently focussed largely on reliability concerns), involving such activities as independent reviews of software requirements and design specifications by experts in software maintainability. Such activities will be enhanced considerably with the advent of more powerful capabilities for analyzing machine-readable requirements and design specifications. Finally, advances in automatic programming (Balzer 1975), (Martin, Bosyj, 1976) should reduce or eliminate some maintenance activity, at least in some problem domains.

A Glimpse into Program Maintenance

Richard E. Gunderman

The observations, concepts, suggestions, and comments which follow are a glimpse of the important though somewhat neglected subject of program maintenance. Since I was first assigned the "onerous" task of determining maintenance support requirements in what I considered a dull, unrewarding, dead-end subject, I have been steadily and happily amazed to find that it is a vast, relatively untouched source for all kinds of interesting projects—at least for me. The intent of this article is not to present an exhaustive treatment (which all too often exhausts all but a special few), nor to dissect the subject into (meaningless) segments, nor to introduce myself as the Great Pontificator (although the title does have a certain ring to it); rather, it is as the title states—a glimpse.

Whether it be called a bug, error, enhancement, repair, or correction, and whether it be performed by a maintenance programmer, maintenance specialist, programmer, or even a program mechanic, it all pertains to a very important and essential activity within large, computer-based systems—program maintenance.

Estimates of its costs are frequently given in terms of initial development costs and range from approximately 50% to well over 100% (would you believe 200%?). Data on the "error-occurrence-to-repair" times range from minutes to days, with the emphasis on days. The nature of the errors and typical types varies with the particular program system and installation. (I/0 problems might be considered a leading candidate for No. 1 offender.) It is, in effect, a large and continually growing area of activity, which is taking its toll in time, money, manpower, computer use, profits, etc., mainly because of its being ignored and considered an overhead operation and secondary service.

Traditionally, program maintenance has been viewed as a second-class activity, with an admixture of on-the-job training for beginners and of low-status assignments for the outcasts and the fallen. However, because of the increasing demands of time, cost, personnel, and machine power and the complexity inherent in large, modularly programmed information systems, it is essential that this wasteful and outmoded view be replaced by a more efficient and effective approach. Do I have the solution? No! But I do have some suggestions, techniques, and concepts which may aid in the necessarily customized implementations of maintenance philosophy.

Hard facts and soft facts are terms I recently encountered in an article in *Newsweek* by Stewart Alsop, and they seem very appropriate for the following observations, experiences, and findings. A soft fact is something you "believe" to be true but can't prove, whereas a hard fact can be supported.

1. Considerable programmer time can be (and all too frequently often is) consumed in program maintenance.
2. Major or large programs are virtually never completely debugged; also, many programs acquire "maintenance-incurred" bugs.
3. The enormous number of system elements inherent to a large system introduces and promotes maintenance problems—that is, programs, records, files, load modules, libraries, program documents, design specs, etc.
4. Substantial skill and experience are required of a maintenance programmer, yet no prestige or recognition is associated with the task—even the salary level reflects this attitude.
5. The importance (or lack) of efficient maintenance techniques is brought to our attention during system downtime.
6. Program maintenance is generally practiced as a personal and individualized activity—often insuring job security but seldom furnishing usable documentation.
7. Quite often the urgencies accompanying maintenance and the putting out of one fire and then another leave maintenance personnel with little time (and inclination) to furnish meaningful documentation.
8. A "simple" bug does not necessarily imply a simple change, especially in an extensively interrelated and modularly programmed system.
9. Hardly anything of substance and utility is published or available concerning program debugging.
10. Minimum, effective documentation remains to be defined in terms of the maintenance programmer's requirements.
11. In practice, "informative and meaningful" comments within a program are often either skimpy or superfluous.
12. During a major downtime, the clock seems to run too fast and the maintenance programmer not fast enough.

Consider a large application system that might consist of:

3 subsystems,
40 runs,
275 programs,
80 record types,
75 files,
40 tables,
345 test procedures,
70 output reports,
1,000 system documents,
extensive JCL,

95 load modules (a module equals one or more linked programs), as well as other system elements.

Assume that an error has occurred during processing and is detected in an entry; within a column of figures; in a given output report; by a non-edp end user, who is knowledgeable in the subject area of the report's contents; and where the entry should have been no greater than 7.257 but was 7.657.

The trouble is reported on the standard Trouble Report form and sent to the maintenance control center, where the problem is assigned to a maintenance programmer, who then utilizes resources at hand, namely: program description, listing, flowcharts, etc.; run books; load module folders; vendor documents; console log; vendor and in-house diagnostics; administrative procedures and controls; design specs; plus other, related documents and facilities.

The error source could be caused by a bug in a program or routine that handles formatting, calculations, editing, validating, file update, data entry, or other common function; or by one that accesses changed or updated files, tables, or programs: or could be caused by an out-of-date document.

At this point in time, the maintenance programmer is confronted with at least the following prime factors:

1. A general error description.
2. Extensive resources and documents.
3. Limited amount of time to effect repair.
4. Possibly, several versions of the application system.
5. Current system-maintenance status, especially of the programs.
6. Interrelationships and interactions of system elements.
7. Best approach for searching and localizing error sources.
8. Program test outlines and test data.
9. Documents that must be revised to reflect changes.

What the maintenance programmer could use at this state of the situation is a system or a capability that would provide him with: 1) a basic, problem-oriented input procedure that produces a solution-oriented output; 2) a rapid, thorough, and automatic search-and-locate function; 3) an organized, integrated arrangement of system elements and resources. For effective maintenance support, it is recommended that these three features be combined into a maintenance-support facility, wherein the special skills and the computer's capabilities can be fully utilized to locate the error sources and aid in their elimination. Also, such a facility must be able to indicate the ramifications resulting from any changes to the system elements that caused the error, as well as be able to furnish a list of documents that might require revisions because of these changes.

The following collection of concepts, techniques, and suggestions is offered as a basis upon which to establish an individual maintenance-support facility. Essentially, it reflects what appears as a natural outgrowth or development dictated by the common needs in maintenance programming.

Maintenance specialist. Within the current edp environment and its operational requirements, there is a growing need—a maintenance specialist. This need is suggested by the:

1. Extensive and intensive maintenance demands imposed by the large, modularly structured complex of program elements within a medium or large program system.
2. Increased cost, importance, and activities of system maintenance.
3. Critical impairments to company operations caused by system downtime and failure.
4. Need for more maintenance knowledge and better debugging methods.
5. Length of time required for a maintenance programmer to become effective.

As to just what a maintenance specialist would do and how such a specialty would be best used, consider the value of his participation in and contributions to:

1. Isolating, defining, and classifying system and general program-bug types.
2. Developing new and improving current debugging techniques and tools.
3. Providing error-diagnostic services for difficult error conditions or problems on a consultative and/or operational basis.
4. Furnishing program designers with valuable feedback in the form of maintenance-oriented design features for enhancing the maintainability of programs to be designed.
5. Participating in the development of maintenance-training curricula and in class lectures and workshop sessions.

Bug types. The classification of bug types and their correlation with program sequences, routines, and/or instructions affords a basis of relationship between error source and error diagnosis that can be applied to the solution of error conditions that arise.

Program definition. Programs can be succinctly and uniquely defined in terms of an abbreviated and established set of simple verbs. These definitions can serve both the programmer's needs for meaningful information and a computer-based error-search-and-locate scheme.

Maintenance history. Upon completion of a maintenance task, the maintenance programmer (or a software documentor) should prepare a "maintenance history" of the pertinent events and action taken, including any opinions and relevant suggestions. Its contents could be guided by means of a pre-established set of guidelines and fill-in directions. An organized collection of these histories would be very valuable during maintenance, especially since it could eliminate much duplication of effort.

Documentation. Program documentation has been propelled into importance by sheer necessity. However, it still suffers from glowing tributes but inept implementations. One of the basic elements of good program documentation is an effective program listing.

Software documentor. A software documentor "should" possess that rare literary mystique, coupled with genius, intermixed with a deft dab of tact and diplomacy, permeated with saintly patience, and reinforced with an intensive and extensive knowledge of the entire field of edp and data communication. If he is also endowed with ESP and financially independent, it will serve him well. However, if reality must be considered, we could settle for much less; namely, a person with the ability to organize and to clearly and accurately write a given document about a subject in which he is experienced and for a specific type of reader.

Maintenance data and statistics. Closely related to the hunt for the bug and its ultimate classifications by type and occurrence is the accumulation of maintenance data and statistics from the maintenance activities themselves. Such data could be reviewed, analyzed, interpreted, and organized into a body of valuable debugging guidelines, as well as contribute considerably to basic program-system design techniques. One immediate application that suggests itself is the use of the data to design "scenarios" for on-the-job debugging examples for new maintenance programmers, thereby giving them valuable experience in a quasi-real trouble-environment.

That is a glimpse of—or a quick entry into—the dense jungle of program-system maintenance. There, under the overlapping foliage of time, cost, manpower, paper, etc., is where there is need for planned, directed, meaningful action.

A Look at Software Maintenance

Chester C. Liu

Analysts and programmers generally view the maintenance function as an inferior, noncreative, nonchallenging activity. They see it as a job requiring no more than average intelligence, and definitely not for "super" analysts or programmers. And yet, it is probably true that most programmer/analysts with ten years experience have spent at least 60% of their time in maintenance.

This low opinion of systems maintenance is reflected in commercially available short courses such as those given by the AMA or AMR, as well as offerings from DPMA and ACM. If not ignored entirely, a course such as one on systems analysis and design would devote at most about 5% of the time to the subject. Yet many dp installations, especially those specializing in business applications, apply at least 70% of the time of their systems analysts and programmers to the maintenance function. At some installations the percentage can reach as high as 95%.

There are large sums of money spent on systems maintenance, yet there is little attempt to present general guidelines on how this money should best be spent. And just what specifically is systems maintenance?

Traditionally, systems maintenance refers to modifying a program to generate new reports, to changing processing logic to incorporate a new feature, to expanding masterfile records, to adding new files, etc. Most generally, it is the process of adaptation, i.e., updating existing systems functions to reflect new constraints or additional features. Table 1 lists some typical maintenance as well as development activities.

From the list in Table 1, it would seem that the differences between development and maintenance are not really that significant. The development function requires no more "superior" or creative person than does maintenance. Much of the basic work is similar in concept. If one does not like the term systems maintenance, he could just as easily use "systems support," "systems enhancement," or "systems continuation."

It should also be noted that it is not the magnitude or complexity of the project which determines whether it is a function of maintenance or of development. It is rather the point at which a project is initiated which indicates which type of function

Table 1

ACTIVITY	FUNCTION
1. Design OS, VS, DBMS, etc.	Development
2. Generate OS, Compliers, HASP	Maintenance
3. Implement a DBMS for an existing application system	Maintenance
4. Any type of conversion, e.g. from 7010 to 370	Maintenance
5. Add three new programs to the billing system for new options	Maintenance
6. Design a Personnel system and adopt three modules from Payroll system	Development

it is. One important distinction between maintenance and development is that the former usually has some supporting documentation. This could be systems manuals, program specifications, module listings, or some other reference aid which will help start the project. In a development phase, there are, of course, no such references.

To understand more fully the function of analysts and programmers in a maintenance environment, it is helpful to review the manner in which a system is developed and what types of information are available.

Normally, the implementation of a computer based information system reflects in varying proportions the following general characteristics:

1. Management philosophy and strategy in dealing with broad changes, such as new government or industry regulations, as well as long term plans;
2. Department operating procedures;
3. Organizational structure in various users' departments;
4. Systems designers' concepts and constraints;
5. Programmers' skills and particular approaches to programming problems;
6. Hardware and software configurations.

At some installations, the information required for system development is relatively easy to collect since few people are involved. At large installations, however, system development usually consists of countless meetings, interviews, and special studies. The results finally are numerous functional specifications, design guidelines, program and module specifications, and ultimately, the programming.

To see how an analyst/programmer functions in the *maintenance* activity, a safe assumption would be that the maintenance staff is not the same as the original design staff. While what documentation is available certainly helps, the maintenance people normally have a difficult time understanding some of the broader background issues, such as problems that arise due to government or industry regulations, or long term departmental plans. Much of this valuable background information which could influence proper maintenance decisions has been defined and discussed in the conference room. If minutes were taken, they are unfortunately not made available to the maintenance staff.

Documentation standards at well-organized dp departments are generally stringent. As a result, important documents such as project planning and control charts, conceptual design guidelines, data gathering reports, and feasibility studies are readily available. On the other hand, in an amateur dp shop managed by an accounting manager, financial controller, or political appointee, systems documentation inclines to be slack and loose. This situation has little to do with competence or incompetence. The reason is that these people are primarily result-oriented; they are more interested in a correct computer report than in a quality system.

The age of a system in itself is not that important as far as systems maintenance is concerned. A two-year old system will obviously have more valuable, timely, and meaningful information available than a seven-year old one. But by no means does this imply that an old system is always more difficult to maintain than a newer one.

What may cause problems with the passage of time is when the original design concept and documentation no longer reflect the present system status, and conflicting logic has occurred as the cumulative result of constant updates. It is for this reason that most systems professionals believe that any application system has a finite life. Regardless of how carefully maintenance projects are planned and executed, the system will eventually be replaced by, or consolidated into, another system which reflects a newer design concept of hardware/software constraints. (Various ways to prevent the deterioration of a system will be discussed later.)

In numerous dp installations, the program specifications, source listings, and JCL are the only reliable maintenance information. At times, unfortunately, program specifications may not be available, particularly if the system designer happens also to be the programmer. Then it is the program listing—which is the product of his design concepts, programming skills, and particularly programming approach and style—that becomes the only working document. It is easy to envision what becomes of maintenance in these circumstances.

Typically, the maintenance function can be summarized as follows:

1. The capacity, function, and logic of the existing program or system must be understood thoroughly.
2. New logic to reflect the new request or additional feature must be developed.
3. The new logic must be incorporated into the existing one.

In addition, project management techniques commonly exercised in the system development phase should also be applied to maintenance jobs. These would include the systems survey, project planning, PERT/CPM, and Gantt Charts.

There are several possible results that maintenance can achieve:

1. While implementing the new logic or modifying the old one, a conflicting situation in the system is created.
2. The new logic is implemented while the old one is left intact, with future problems a strong possibility.

3. Both the new and old logics are combined and implemented as an integrated function for the system.

It is strongly recommended that the system practitioner have the third possibility as his goal.

It should be clear now that maintenance can be as challenging and complicated as pure development. The analyst/programmer should make certain not only that the new logic is functionally correct, but also that the unmodified portions of the system are not inadvertently affected or disturbed. What would make systems maintenance less than completely rewarding, however, is the emergency or crisis situation normally associated with it.

Documentation is a critical issue of systems maintenance. A set of quality documentation certainly helps make maintenance jobs much easier, but no experienced dp person should assume that every dp department has kept a decent level of systems documentation.

It has traditionally been the responsibility of the analyst/programmer to produce the necessary documentation. Since the results have apparently not been completely satisfactory, dp managers have recently been using technical writers for the task.

There are distinct differences in the documentation prepared by these two groups. Documentation written by dp people is generally sloppy and disorganized, and the English language is used as though it were a programming language. However, if less readable, it is usually more substantial in content. Documentation prepared by technical writers is usually more readable, understandable, and very well organized. However, the basic problem is that they normally do not provide enough information on the essential guts of the system. This is because the technical writer is neither dp-oriented nor user-oriented. Thus, in preparing the system documentation, the information flow between systems people and technical writers is substantially reduced. Consequently, conflicting and noncommittal statements can be located throughout the documents—and essential ones may have disappeared.

A number of fundamental misunderstandings of documentation technique exist. First, it is devoted almost completely to "what has been done" instead of "why it has been done." (Think how often, for example, dp managers instruct their people to document everything, but the "why's" are completely ignored.) As a result, the quality of system documentation is seriously impaired.

Secondly, system documentation is written from the writer's point of view (whether it is the analyst/programmer or technical writer), rather than from the user's point of view. It is the writer who determines what type of information goes into the documentation; what the maintenance staff needs receives little consideration. As already noted, information required in the maintenance phase is in many respects distinctly different from that in the development phase. Information not documented because of its obviousness in the development phase may be extremely valuable for the maintenance group—and it is often lost.

The systems documentation that emerges at many dp organizations falls then into one of three categories: no documentation, insufficient documentation, and misleading documentation.

The problem of no documentation is most critical at the management level. A successful system not only has to perform the specified functions, it must also be flexible enough to accommodate additional features, as well as future modifications. If the maintenance staff is unaware of management's long term planning, it cannot gear the system accordingly. Furthermore, the flexibility and expandability originally designed into the system might be seriously undermined. This situation is common in data processing, regardless of development or maintenance environment. It is especially true when management has adopted a closed door policy. Any business manager will appreciate the reasoning that in order to compete and survive in a complicated business world, some secrecy concerning the company's strategy and future action is required. However, to expect dp people to maintain the system at the maximum efficiency without a general guideline for future planning is irresponsible and undesirable, and results in money wasted and mass confusion. This wasteful process can be avoided only when management's policy and practice are properly documented and become available to systems people.

Insufficient documentation can be seen at all levels: Management, systems and programming, and users. Several factors contribute to the situation, including improper systems planning, lack of budgeted funding, insufficient time, etc. The foremost factor is the setting of standards for adequate documentation. The basic question is "What is adequate documentation?" Each individual has his own answer, and nobody really can give an enforceable guideline for how detailed a system of program specification should be. As a result, a frustrating situation is developed whereby analysts/programmers go through the specifications repeatedly, and still cannot understand the logic or obtain the information they are seeking.

When insufficient documentation extends to an extreme, misleading documentation develops. This is the worst kind of documentation and usually is the result of oversight, neglect, and ignorance. It occurs most frequently when a new analyst/programmer is introduced to a maintenance team while no proper orientation is given. It is not uncommon that many systems people working on a project team for months are still not aware of how many documents are available in the project group.

Under such circumstances, analysts/programmers understandably develop an unwillingness to trust any documentation. A direct consequence of this is a further degeneration of documentation activity. If no decisive action is taken, eventually all documentation becomes a stockpile of garbage.

It is critical to know the right time to start documentation activity. Traditionally an analyst/programmer arranges the documentation as the last activity in system development. Surely there are logical considerations involved in this arrangement. If a system is not completely tested and finalized, it would be extremely difficult to write operation instructions, and error and recovery procedures. But, when a programmer develops his program first, and then documents the processing logic, documentation merely becomes a translation and summary activity.

From the systems maintenance point of view, documentation activity should commence the moment the project is initiated and should remain a continuous process for the duration of the project development. Minutes of meetings, correspondence, memoranda, systems proposals, management decisions, and systems planning are all valuable information for the maintenance staff.

From the discussion so far, as well as from general experience with the problem, here are some suggestions for improved documentation:

1. Start documentation activity the moment the project is initiated.
2. In addition to "what has been done," document "why it has been done."
3. Consider management's policies, practice, and long term plans as essential parts of documentation, and make them accessible to analysts/programmers.
4. Document for the "poor guys" in the maintenance group as well as for system development and control.
5. Document not for formality, but for reality, especially if a technical writer is employed.
6. Document for the communication gaps rather than communication clusters. In other words, try to establish cross references, indices, a dictionary, as well as the traditional program specification, systems manual, and operating instructions. Further, describe all documentation available and make analysts/programmers aware of them.
7. Make documentation an auditing criterion in evaluating the system's integrity.

For a maintenance group, it is crucial to have complete documentation containing all pertinent information. Nevertheless, overdocumentation, aside from being unnecessary, could consume a great deal of valuable resources and budget.

In a development environment, systems testing has been estimated to consume approximately 20–50% of the total project schedule, depending upon the complexity of the system. In the maintenance phase, however, the extent of systems testing varies greatly; there is no general guideline available. In some dp departments extremely stringent testing procedures sometimes consume as much as 80% of the maintenance effort.

On the other hand, many other dp departments do not exercise any systems testing procedures; the choice to do so is left completely to the analysts/programmers' discretion. In these instances, the meaningless terminology of "major" or "minor" changes is widely used, resulting in what is called "production-testing." That is, when a program change causes a production failure, it is considered as "testing"; otherwise it is production!

It is strongly urged that every systems department establish a strict testing procedure, and see that the rules or regulations are faithfully carried out. The establishment of a socalled quality assurance group to perform the functions of total systems and production control can be effective only when a standard testing procedure is available.

It is important to understand the analysts/programmers' attitudes toward system testing. In their daily work of systems maintenance, they tend to see themselves as constantly—and anonymously—fighting fires. The systems test presents them therefore with an opportunity to show "superior" work, since they can see the results directly. Consequently, an interesting situation develops. The analysts/programmers concentrate their testing effort on changes they make, and tend to ignore the unmodified portions. They look at the test results where they feel most confident of success, and disregard parts where certain "peculiar" conditions may exist. Needless to say, this distortion of interest and attention to certain portions in the systems testing procedure creates a major problem for the maintenance staff.

A complete psychological transformation of the analyst/programmer must be achieved. He should be trained to place the priority of steps in the systems test in the following order:

1. Test for system failure first.
2. Test the unmodified portion of the system or program.
3. Test the modified portion with all imaginable conditions.
4. Aim at the few most representative situations which constitute a major portion of the system.
5. Finally, test the documentation.

The acceptance test is probably one of the greatest inventions in system maintenance. The original concept was well intended: to get the user to participate in testing activity, and to bring the dp operation closer to the real world so that the so-called professional bias could be prevented and the communication between users and systems designers could be enhanced.

It is sad to see that the concept often becomes a tool for abuse—for passing the buck back to the user. The practice is simple and effective. Since most users are not dp-oriented, it is quite a simple task to take away the unfavorable effect of the systems test from analysts/programmers and give it to users. As a result, the traditional analysts' responsibility is transferred to the users. Because he is an innocent party in a complicated dp world, the user, all at once, is placed in a critical spot where silent grievance can be seen but not heard.

Although the acceptance test is a necessity in systems maintenance, it is recommended only when the user possesses a proper and adequate orientation of the nature and function of dp activities. Only when the user thoroughly understands the concepts of data processing can the constructive side of the acceptance test be realized and the original intent achieved.

With or without adequate documentation, systems maintenance eventually ends up in program modification at the elementary level where programmers physically go to the source listing and make changes. Cumulative changes over time performed by analysts/programmers may form a uniquely peculiar pattern which could deviate from normal logical inference and common perception or comprehension. The situation can then result in a system game, a phenomenon closely associated with development activity.

Generally speaking, after preliminary research, the analyst prepares specifications based on his perception of the problem and the manner in which the problem will be solved. Similarly, the programmer will perform his function based on his comprehension of the application and logic manipulation. The situation is similar to a typical college mathematical class where students arrive at identical solutions to a problem using completely different methods.

These different approaches to problem solutions can result in systems games. A typical programming game is to write a COBOL program like an assembler language program. Paragraph names have no sequence numbers; data fields have no prefix to identify work areas or actual records; data names are meaningless; peculiar instructions prevail throughout. The program does not follow COBOL conventions and appears to be without organization. On the other hand, an analyst can write specifications without indicating the purpose of the change, who requested it, or what the testing criteria are; it appears on a coding sheet and reads like a COBOL program.

A certain degree of personal variation in data processing is both understandable and tolerable. After all, if every activity is standardized, analysts/programmers will perform like accounting clerks, where no creativity is required. However, management should not allow personal approaches or preferences to cause deviation beyond a tolerable level. Otherwise, the task of system maintenance will become an endless game, where everyone pays homage to the eccentric wisdom of the original player.

There are also other factors than personal programming approach or preference that contribute to the formation of systems games. The most obvious one is inadequate training and improper orientation. More often than not, a person introduced to a maintenance group is instructed to assume the maintenance responsibility as it is, instead of first being given an orientation based on logical reasoning. This is probably because the tricky games, accumulated through the years by many individuals, are most embarrassing to mention to a new employee. Consequently, each individual is left to tackle his own problem and play his own game. The traditional method of "learning by doing" becomes a sacred cow. If lucky, an individual may pick up most of the games and enjoy the remainder of his life preaching the method of maintaining a system by game play. Otherwise, he may become a member of a mediocre society, being busy all day long and accomplishing nothing.

When discussing this situation, maintenance oriented systems managers generally agree that training a maintenance staff can be tedious and time consuming. However, they seem to agree that system games are as integral as any other part of the system which the maintenance staff has to learn to live with. Now you know why it takes three years just to train someone to assume maintenance responsibility for a large application system!

Another factor that encourages people to participate in game play is related to the productivity differential between programmers. Application experience and technical ability are important, of course, but there is a tendency to use years of experience as a sole criterion in determining the analyst/programmer's value. The basic learning curve used routinely by psychologists shows that after two or three years, additional progress in knowledge is limited and insignificant. One can always find a creative, competent programmer/analyst with two years experience who can outperform a mediocre one with ten years experience. And there is no evidence that a programmer with seven years of experience can design or write a better program than one with three years experience.

As a result, it could take one programmer five hours to write a particular program, and another, 25 hours. If the latter, for example, is given overtime or some other incentive to come up with the program, while the first programmer could have completed the program during normal working hours, a potential for frustration exists. In other words, if the more productive programmer feels he is not getting sufficient rewards, he might possibly begin to play games.

Because productivity does not depend then on years of experience, paying on the basis of experience will be considered by the more productive programmer as unfair. And this situation is likely to lead to game playing. On the other hand, by leaving a system unnecessarily complicated, the game player can more nearly insure his position and level of compensation. And thus we have reached the primary reason that contributes to the formation of systems games: job security.

In some dp departments, there exist "senior man teams," in which a senior member has charge of overall maintenance, with limited help from novices. The senior man is defined as the department member with the longest working experience with the system, regardless of capability or technical skills. The higher the turnover rate, the more indispensable he becomes due to his "proprietary" knowledge of the system, and the games which went into it.

With the advent of third generation computing technology, with large scale computer applications, and new concepts of programming structure and design, the play of systems games has been substantially reduced. Nevertheless, the general attitude still prevails, although on a lesser scale. It may still take some time before dp people recognize that real job security is not built on a foundation of systems games, but rather on a thorough knowledge of technology and capabilities.

Data base technology presents another vulnerable area for games playing. Data and system integrity are constantly emphasized in terms of protecting the data base against invalid or illegal access or alteration. Even if the ordinary programmer and analyst can be induced to stop playing such system games, we might now get a new generation of games within the data base administration.

Games developed for the various reasons stated can be classified as "intentional games." Management undoubtedly must assume most of the responsibility for the situation for allowing it to continue for so long. The following measures to combat such systems game are suggested for the dp manager:

1. Provide systems maintenance guidelines.
2. Establish systems, programming, and documentation standards.
3. Establish an enforceable system modification procedure.
4. Adopt the concept of a quality control unit, and make periodic systems audits.

5. Ecourage the flow of communication, both vertically and horizontally.
6. Emphasize team effort and contributions in addition to individual performances.

Of course, not all the systems games are developed for specific purposes or reasons; many are the result of sloppy habits, unorganized thought, or lack of professionalism. In any event, the simple fact that a majority of maintenance jobs are done on a "rush" basis reduces the analysts/programmer's concern for system integrity. These types of system or programming defects are "unintentional games," or low quality outputs that complicate the maintenance activity.

On reviewing the activity distribution of any maintenance project, a great portion of activity is usually loaded into the last quarter of the project cycle. As a result, a heavy overtime schedule develops. "Getting the job done" becomes the dominating theme, while maintaining the quality becomes secondary. It should not come as a surprise that the unintentional game flourishes in this environment.

The most effective measure to prevent unintentional games is to provide continuous education in system concepts and programming technology, as well as in project management technique. With modern dp concepts, specifically data base telecommunications, systems professionals tend to agree that traditional training in systems design and programming languages is inadequate. Emphasis should be placed upon the structure of the system and the program organization. It is ironic that after a quarter century of programming language development, systems people finally realize that a standard set of grammar in program writing is sorely needed. As far as project management technique is concerned, the maintenance staff should be trained to plan the project properly. By using PERT/CPM or Gantt Charts, the common symptom of overoptimism in time and cost estimates could be reduced considerably.

Another measure is to provide systems personnel with extensive training in their particular application. A general assumption seems to be that analysts/programmers' primary interest is in systems analysis and program development. Application knowledge then is considered secondary and is often ignored. Without proper training in billing procedures and accounting principles, for example, a maintenance staff cannot effectively maintain a billing system.

Finally, recruiting high quality analysts/programmers to participate in maintenance activity may be another desirable alternative in avoiding the occurrence of unintentional games. Although the misconception of maintenance as an inferior activity still prevails, a proper distribution of workload in maintenance and development phases will alleviate the problem.

With a short history of a quarter century, data processing is still in its infancy, at least as regards software. However, regardless how rapidly software technology will progress, we can reasonably expect that a large number of programmers and analysts will continue working in the maintenance environment. Many companies will continue to require extensive maintenance to keep systems going, and large sums of money will continue to be spent on maintenance.

To finally achieve the goal of professionalism, various misconceptions mentioned must be corrected, documentation and systems testing improved, and systems games playing ended. Data processing professionals will probably agree that a quality system is just as important as an accurate computer report.

Flashes on Maintenance From *Techniques of Program Structure and Design*

Edward Yourdon

In my opinion, there is nothing in the programming field more despicable than an uncommented program. A programmer can be forgiven many sins and flights of fancy, including many of those listed in the sections below; however, *no* programmer, no matter how wise, no matter how experienced, no matter how hard-pressed for time, no matter how well-intentioned, should be forgiven an uncommented and undocumented program.

If this seems an unreasonably venomous attack, you are invited to debug, maintain, or change someone else's uncommented program; you will usually find that it is worse than having no program at all. An abundance of comments is also imperative to test your own program quickly and painlessly. Only a fool would venture into an unknown forest without leaving trailmarkers behind. Writing an uncommented program is roughly the same as crawling blindfolded into the jungles of the Amazon. Though there are no firm rules in this area, a good guideline to follow is four to five lines of comment for every subroutine (or COBOL section, etc.), and an average of one comment for every two or three lines of source code.

Of course, it is important to point out that comments are not an end unto themselves. As Messrs. Kernighan and Plauger point out in their excellent book, *The Elements of Programming Style,* good comments cannot substitute for bad code. However, it is not clear that good code can substitute for comments. That is, I do not agree that it is unnecessary for comments to accompany "good" code. The code obviously tells us *what* the program is doing, but the comments are often necessary for us to understand *why* the programmer has used those particular instructions.

In my experiences as a programmer and programming supervisor, I have had the opportunity to hear (and occasionally use) some of the following objections (a polite euphemism for *excuses*) for not putting comments into the program:

1. I don't have enough time to put in any comments.
2. I have to do my own keypunching, and I don't type well—so I can't bother with a lot of comments.
3. I type my programs into a time-sharing terminal, and I get charged for connect

time—and since I don't type well, I can't afford to put in a lot of comments.

4. My program is self-documenting.
5. Any *competent* programmer can understand my code without comments.
6. My program is only going to be used once, so documentation is not necessary.
7. The program will certainly be changed drastically during the testing and debugging phase, so the documentation will be obsolete by the time the program is finished.
8. I understand perfectly well what my program does—so why should I have to document it?
9. I don't like to document or comment.
10. It's not good to have too many comments—it obscures the important ones.
11. If I put in too many comments, my program will take longer to compile.
12. My source program will take up too much room on the disk (or on punched paper tape on some minicomputer systems) if I have a large number of comments.
13. Who reads the documentation anyway?

Nonexistent comments are an obvious problem; a more subtle problem can exist if the program is heavily laden with comments, but:

1. The comments are redundant.
2. The comments are obsolete.
3. The comments are (and always were) incorrect.
4. The comments are vague and imprecise.
5. The comments are correct, but incomplete.
6. The comments cannot be understood by anyone else.

Indeed, it is this aspect of comments that makes them so potentially dangerous. A comment that gives incorrect or misleading information about the program statement it accompanies is probably worse than no comment at all; a comment that is redundant (e.g., a comment that says "now we are moving A to B" accompanying the COBOL statement MOVE A TO B) will probably so discourage the maintenance programmer that he won't bother looking for useful comments elsewhere in the program. Indeed, it is not surprising that some experiments have shown that it is faster and easier to fix bugs in someone else's program by first removing all the comments.

Unfortunately, many programmers seem to write comments as personal messages to themselves, that is, to remind themselves of the purpose of the particular instruction or program statement they used. The personal note, though, may be completely indecipherable to anyone else, and even the original programmer may have difficulty understanding the meaning of the comment (as well as the statement that it accompanies, of course) at some later time. An interesting example of this occurred several years ago when a lone superprogrammer single-handedly developed a FORTRAN II compiler for a well-known computer manufacturer. After he tested the compiler and turned it over to his manager, the programmer disappeared for several days, during which time the manager discovered that there were some bugs that required immediate attention. The junior programmer assigned to find and fix the bugs discovered, to his horror, that the entire compiler contained only *one* comment, which accompanied an octal constant in the following manner:

```
CONST23:     3443     ;R.I.P.L.V.B.
```

Since the superprogrammer had a reputation for brevity as well as brilliance, the junior programmer began to think that perhaps this single comment would unlock all of the mysteries of the compiler. After several hours of pondering the meaning of the comment, he finally hit on the answer—the number 3443, in octal, is equivalent to the number 1827 in decimal. Being a classical music fan and a collector of trivial information, the junior programmer happened to remember that 1827 was the year Beethoven died! As one might imagine, the programming manager was quite unamused by all of this, and when the superprogrammer reappeared, he was asked to take his inestimable talents elsewhere.

Minimize Maintenance Costs

Any program that is worth anything at all will be around for a long time. There are a significant number of IBM 1401 programs, for example, that were originally written in the early 1960s. They have subsequently been simulated, emulated, and generally beaten into the ground on IBM 7040/7044s, 7090/7094s, System 360s and System 370s, but the original form and logic has remained virtually unchanged. There are even a few IBM 650 programs, originally written in the mid-1950s, that are still running today. On the other hand, there are a few programs—often scientific and engineering applications—that are truly used once or twice and then thrown away. However, these are extremely rare and should be considered as the exception rather than the rule.

Whether you, as the original programmer, continue to maintain your program, or whether you turn it over to someone else, the fact remains that there will almost always be ongoing development and maintenance. It has been only recently that data processing organizations have begun realizing the magnitude of this effort: a recent survey showed that the average American organization spends 50% of its EDP budget on maintenance (Canning, 1972). Another informal survey taken by a major computer manufacturer in England suggested that a program written by an individual programmer was generally maintained by ten generations of subsequent maintenance programmers before being discarded and rewritten.

There are several aspects of the maintenance problem, some of which can be solved by proper design and some of which cannot. The major problems facing a maintenance department seem to be the following:

1. Programs that are put into maintenance still have a significant number of bugs; so what is called maintenance is really just a continuation of the testing effort. This seems an obvious point, but it is often ignored. What is happening is that the maintenance programmers are suffering from the sins of the original programmers.
2. There is the continuing problem of upgrading the program for new compilers,

new operating systems, and other new system software. It is not likely that this problem will cease in the immediate future.

3. Most significant programs require continuing maintenance to meet the needs of an evolving user community. There are very few programs that are so well-defined that they need never change.

4. When maintenance changes are required, the original programmer has often disappeared.

5. We face a basic problem that people generally don't like to do maintenance. It is not considered very glamorous work, often doesn't rate the same pay schedules, and suffers from the obvious frustrations of trying to fix up someone else's sloppy work.

6. A very basic problem is that most people have great difficulty understanding other people's code. Perhaps this is because most programmers seem to evolve their own personal programming style; a larger part of the problem, though, is that many programmers write their code in a relatively disorganized style.

7. The documentation that accompanies most programs is awful. Some experiments have indicated that maintenance programmers would be better off by first removing all of the comments that accompany a program, and *then* trying to find a bug or implement some improvements. Clearly, many organizations are now paying the price for poor documentation standards in the past.

It is obvious that good program design cannot solve *all* of the problems of maintenance; nevertheless, it is equally clear that such problems would be reduced drastically if we were able to design, code, and test programs more adequately. In any case, it suggests that when we write a program, we should plan things so that the maintenance work will be as simple as possible. As we do this, we should keep in mind that our program will almost certainly be maintained by someone else.

Most of the suggestions found elsewhere in this chapter and in subsequent chapters of this book should be of great help for the maintenance programmer. Presumably, if a program is easy to test and debug, it will be relatively simple to maintain—whether by the original programmer or someone else. The most important ideas in this area are the following:

1. Structured programming or some form of modular programming. It is extremely important to avoid a random program organization; it is not clear that the *original* programmer can even understand such a program, but it *is* clear that most maintenance programmers cannot.

2. Simplicity of programming style is extremely important. As you program, keep asking yourself, "Would a typical maintenance programmer understand this?" Avoid the egotistical attitude of, "Any decent programmer ought to be able to understand this . . . ." Don't forget that the maintenance programmer may not be as brilliant as you are.

3. "Document unto others as you would have them document unto you." This gem is taken from the excellent book, *The Elements of FORTRAN Style,* by Kreitzberg and Shneiderman (Harcourt, Brace, Jovanovich, 1971).

Of course, if all programmers followed these suggestions, we would have very few maintenance problems; the fact that they do *not* follow such suggestions is the major cause for maintenance headaches. This suggests that we may actually be dealing with a management problem. A program should not be accepted by the maintenance department until that department decides it is adequate. This is perhaps the greatest failing in many EDP organizations—as long as the program still has bugs in it, it might just as well be worked on by the programmers who know its characteristics, rather than dumping it on programmers who don't want it and don't understand it. Thus, before accepting a program for maintenance, there should be some verification that it has been adequately tested, adequately documented, written according to reasonable programming standards, and *accepted* by both the users and the maintenance department.

Many other suggestions concerning maintenance could be given, but they tend to fall into the category of "management suggestions," an area generally outside the realm of this book. On the other hand, it may be helpful to give some suggestions to those unfortunate programmers required to maintain a program that has *not* been adequately designed, tested, or documented. Such an activity is often referred to as maintaining "alien" code. The following suggestions may be helpful:

1. Study the program before you get into "emergency mode." Get to know it fairly well. If possible, find the original author of the program; try to get as much background information about it as possible. Ask him for any unofficial documentation that might exist.

2. Try to become familiar with the overall flow of control of the program; ignore the coding details at first. It may be very useful to draw your own high-level flowchart at this point, if one doesn't already exist.

3. Evaluate the reasonableness of the existing documentation. Insert your own comments into the listing if you think they will help.

4. Make good use of cross-reference listings, symbol tables, and other aids generally provided by the compiler and/or assembler. Make up your own tables if necessary.

5. Make changes to the program with the greatest caution. Respect the style and formatting of the program if at all possible. Don't change the program just for the sake of changing it, e.g., don't rewrite a whole subroutine just to eliminate one or two apparently useless instructions. *Always indicate, on the listing itself, which instructions you have changed.*

6. Don't eliminate code unless you are sure that it isn't used.

7. Don't try to share the use of temporary variables and working storage that already exist in the program. Insert your own local variables to avoid trouble.

8. Keep detailed records of the changes you have made, the bugs you have fixed, and the improvements you have made.

9. Avoid the irrational urge to throw the program away and rewrite it. Instead, keep good records to show the amount of effort that you have invested in maintenance, and try to extrapolate into the future. Make a reasonable effort to estimate the amount of time that it would take you to rewrite the program—and remember that your program will also require maintenance!

10. *Do* insert error-checking all around the code you are inserting, as well as around existing code wherever it looks reasonable to do so.

Flexibility—Ease of Changing, Expanding, or Upgrading the Program

Despite everyone's best intentions, most programs are changed during their lifetime. The requirements and specifications stated by the user or the customer are rarely "frozen," and you should always assume that your program will eventually have to be modified so that it will be bigger, faster, more extensive, etc.

This is a very difficult point to impress upon new programmers. Quite often, the junior programmer will argue that he is writing a "quick and dirty" program, one that he doesn't intend to keep around for any length of time. While this is sometimes true, it is nevertheless like an architect telling his client that the building he is designing is not intended to be permanent, but rather just a "quick and dirty" edifice. This analogy is not quite as extreme as it sounds: A number of shoddy wooden barracks and Quonset huts were erected during World War II and are still being used, much to the irritation of the present inhabitants.

To judge whether a program is easy to change or upgrade, you and your manager should constantly be asking yourselves, "What happens if we want to expand this table?" "What if we want to define new transaction codes someday?" "What if we have to change the format of that output report?" "What if someone decides to provide input to the program from a teletype instead of the card reader?"

In most cases, it is not difficult to discover what questions to ask; one simply has to attack a program with the philosophy that *everything* is liable to be changed, expanded, or modified. Thus, you simply have to train yourself to look at *every* program module, *every* subroutine, *every* table, and *every* data area with an eye toward its eventual revision. Of course, it may be rather difficult deciding how to best write the program with these considerations in mind. There are certainly some tradeoffs to be established, and you may need guidance from your manager or your analyst (if you find yourself completely indecisive in this area, your psychoanalyst may be of more assistance than your systems analyst) before deciding to implement an extremely general and flexible approach. On the other hand, a very large number of the problems that occur in this area could have been avoided with a trivial amount of work at the beginning of the design of the program.

The Scope of the Testing Problem

Furthermore, the number of bugs *remaining* in large programs and systems (after they have supposedly been thoroughly tested) is rather immense. It has been estimated in references (Boehm, 1973) (Yourdon, 1972) that each new release of OS/360 contains over one thousand errors; Tom Gilb, an EDP consultant in Oslo, Norway, claims to have counted over *eleven thousand* bugs in a recent release of OS! The author's studies of several vendor-supplied operating systems suggest that they retain a relatively constant number of system failures over a period of several years. (Yourdon, 1972) More quantitative studies (Shooman et al, 1972) suggest that the number of bugs in a large complex system is likely to follow an exponential decay—but it is likely that this ignores the new bugs that are constantly introduced into operational programs by ongoing maintenance and development.

Testing is also a serious problem from the programmer's point of view. Sackman's classical study (Sackman, Erickson, Grant, 1968) suggested that some programmers require as much as 25 times longer to test and debug their programs than others. Since this study was based on a rather small sample, a number of observers have been tempted to conclude that things aren't really that bad in the real world; nevertheless, the author's personal observations of many EDP organizations suggest that there is at least a factor of ten difference between the best and worst programmer in the average programming group.

A similar study described by Boehm in references (Boehm, 1973) (Boehm, 1971:42–50) has indicated that the programmer has a remarkably low chance of success when he attempts to modify a working program. If he attempts to change less than ten source statements in his program, he has approximately a 50% probability of making the changes correctly on the first attempt. If he tries to change as many as fifty statements, the probability of success drops to 20%.

If testing is difficult, it is not surprising to see that *maintenance*—which usually requires its own cycle of testing and debugging—also causes difficulty in many organizations.

Selections from *Software Engineering: Concepts and Techniques*

There is a widening gap between ambitions and achievements in software engineering. This gap appears in several dimensions: between promises to users and performance achieved by software, between what seems to be ultimately possible and what is achievable now and between estimates of software costs and expenditures. This gap is arising at a time when the consequences of software failure in all its aspects are becoming increasingly serious. Particularly alarming is the seemingly unavoidable fallibility of large software, since a malfunction in an advanced hardware-software system can be a matter of life and death, not only for individuals, but for vehicles carrying hundreds of people and ultimately for nations as well.

E. E. David and A. G. Fraser
(Pp. 77–78)

Maintenance and distribution are strongly interdependent: upon being written each program requires a certain amount of testing, the so-called field test. The field test is considered to be successful when the programs that are being tested have been allowed a reasonable number of fault-free machine runs and when it is thus indicated that they will effect the full spectrum of their intended applications. The duration of the field test depends upon quite a number of different factors, such as the amount of machine time allocated to a given program, the frequency of machine runs required, the complexity of the program, etc. Consequently the actual times for the duration of field tests should always be determined by the people actually responsible for the maintenance of a respective program; and great care should be taken to make sure that a given number of runs has been achieved during the test and that any faults recognized by the user have been properly recorded and reported to the interested parties. No one should hesitate to prolong the field test period if—during its course—it should become apparent that the number of existing program faults shows no, or only small, diminishing tendencies. On the other hand, it should not be expected that a complex program, after being given an appropriate field test, is completely free of errors. Owing to the complexity of certain programs, each user of electronic data processing equipment has at times to be prepared to deal with program failures, especially when handling more sophisticated applications.

Thus each maintenance depends upon the proper recording of programming errors by the user and upon the quality of such records. In those cases where the maintenance-center and the distribution-center constitute a single organizational unit, maintenance can operate with great effectiveness and, when distributing their programs to users, can influence all users as regards proper error reporting.

H. Kohler
(P. 71)

The economics of software development are such that the cost of maintenance frequently exceeds that of the original development. Consider, for example, the standard software that many manufacturers provide and deliver with their hardware. This product can include a basic operating system, a machine language macro assembler, an Algol, Fortran, and Cobol compiler, a sort/merge package, a file management facility, and so on. In scope this represents something in the order of more than 250 thousand lines of generated code that must be released to customers whose configurations and requirements vary a good deal, encompassing the spectrum from batch oriented data processing shops, to hybrid time-critical, time sharing and scientific shops. Producing such systems currently requires about a two- to three-year effort involving perhaps as many as 50 personnel. Maintenance of such systems is an unending process which lasts for the life of the machine; as much perhaps as eight years. . . .

Maintenance of a system is required in order to satisfy three basic problems. First, in an effort of the magnitude of that described there will be bugs in the system. These can originate from ambiguous specification and reference documentation, because of design error, or because of programmer and system checkout error. Second, design decisions and code generation cannot always result in "good" performance. In a basic operating system, for example, a code module may get executed on the average of once per 10 milliseconds while the system is operational; it is desirable to make the code as fast as possible. In the hurry to deliver an operable system it is seldom that code can be truly optimized; the emphasis is on correct execution rather than speed. Much effort is expended to improve system performance in order to remain competitive. Third, and finally, in a span of several years, new hardware is developed which must be supported and new customer needs develop which must be met. To support this a system must be extended to include capabilities beyond those that the original designer conceived. In summary, then, the maintenance process involves corrective code, improvement code, and extensive code.

H. R. Gillette
(Pp. 71–72)

Creativity Seen Vital Factor, Even in Maintenance Work

Robert R. Jones

There has been a lot said and written about the functions of effective organizations when designing and implementing a system. The approaches, pitfalls, rewards, successes and failures have all had some attention paid to them.

Notice that I did not say all have been identified; if every possible pitfall could be identified, the role and functions of a design group could well be eliminated.

There have been many courses offered and conferences held with the goal of refining the art of systems analysis in general. More specific attention has been paid to designing and implementing systems or applications.

Analyst and programming skills have been sharpened as a result of all this effort. The product of all this concern is an efficient, well-planned, successfully running, neatly documented, user satisfied *easily maintainable* system. But, invariably, the best of plans often miss the target.

At any rate, changes or fixes of some sort are going to be required in almost every system delivered. This is no surprise and is also a very crucial part of the system. The responsibility of making the necessary changes is often referred to as "maintenance."

In many shops, the maintenance group is responsible not only for correcting errors, but also for adding enhancements. It is often difficult to get good people to want to work in a maintenance group. This may be because the thought prevails that there is a lack of creativity which may be exercised on the part of the programmer/analyst working in the maintenance group.

The fact that the programmer/analyst has to "straighten out somebody else's mess" is the cry most often heard coming from the maintenance group.

The good systems analyst or programmer has an especially difficult task in finding a meaningful relationship between his creative talents and his role in a maintenance group. When attempting to solve problems in a system, he feels all creative talents he has acquired are put aside, and he sees himself functioning strictly as a program investigator.

It is uncommon for him to view this role of investigator as requiring creative talents. In actual fact, however, if he would take the time to evaluate what in fact his steps and his approaches were, he would often times find in solving a particular problem that most of what he considers creative talent had been involved and utilized.

The other things the maintenance group is often called upon to produce is add-ons or enhancements. These are often considered insignificant to many analysts and programmers because they are usually relatively small, compared with the system as a whole, and they are usually supportive in nature to the functions already operating.

If an examination of what processes are required when implementing the add-on, it would again be realized that a great deal of creativity and often ingenuity is required. For example, when an enhancement is being added, the individual who is designing the changes required must first become extremely knowledgeable in the system as it presently exists. This is to enable him to be aware of precautions he must consider such as interfacing with other subsystems and data base integrity.

He will probably be dealing with different programming styles, assuming that more than one individual designed and wrote the original system. This is not to be taken lightly; if one is to understand a given program, he should be able to examine the code and understand why that particular approach was taken.

To do this one must put oneself in the position of the author of the given task or program and adopt his style as much as possible while reviewing his work, which may be impacted by any changes made.

After a thorough knowledge is obtained on the existing situation, only then can an add-on be designed. During the design phase of the add-on, a constant vigil must be kept on the impact the addition may have on storage and timing of the system.

Data base utilization, efficiency and sizing are items that must be given the same consideration as when the original system was designed. The impact the new function may have on existing functions must also be considered. Does this new function duplicate any part of existing coding? If so, is the duplication required? Does the new function overlap or eliminate the need for coding elsewhere in the system, or does the similar coding serve another function for entirely different reasons?

Care must be exercised to ensure that destructive interference in the way of coding is not inadvertently implemented. If all of these items are given the attention needed and the user requirement is met satisfactorily, the design should be implemented efficiently.

After coding is complete, vigorous testing is required. Not only is the new function tested to determine that the goals of its intended purpose are met, but the entire system must undergo complete testing to verify that the new function does not adversely impact any other function in the system.

With this phase complete and all necessary documentation changes made and user training complete, the system is ready to run.

If all of the foregoing items were attended to with the detail necessary to accomplish a satisfactory system enhancement, an efficient, well-planned, successful running, neatly documented, user satisfied, easily maintainable system would be the result. This also describes the goal of the system as originally delivered and indicates the need for originality, creativity and ingenuity that went into the original system are also required processes for system enhancement.

It should, therefore, be clear that at least as much talent and creativity as is required in an original system development group is also required in the maintenance group. This will no longer be the case when the group that developed the original system is flawless and develops the ability to anticipate all future user requirement changes.

From Development to Maintenance[1]

In the beginning of application developments in data processing, it was commonly supposed that development was the main problem. But in only 25 years, some 75 percent of data processing personnel are already taken up with maintenance, not development. And unless radical new methods are found, maintenance will go even higher in its demands and will very nearly stifle further development. Why is that?

There are two reasons, one of simple but often overlooked logistics, one of a deeper technical nature: The logistic reason is that an application system is maintained indefinitely after a definite period of development, and with every completed development some fraction of the development team (or its equivalent) must be deleted from development and added to maintenance. For example, with a constant work force, if a fraction x of each development team must stay behind for maintenance, then in an average development period, the fraction of all personnel devoted to development goes from D to $D\ (1 - x)$. At the end of k periods, starting at $D = 1$ (all development), the fraction of development is $(1 - x)^k$, and the fraction of maintenance M is $1 - D$ or $M = 1 - (1 - x)^k$. In illustration, if $x = 0.2$, $k = 6$ (say a dozen years of 2-year projects for an enterprise), then $M = 1 - (0.8)^6 = 0.737856$, i.e., just about the 75% which is typical today. There is only one stable point in this ecology—100 percent maintenance. Only the purging or replacement of applications brings this stable point below 100 percent.

The technical reason for this high level of maintenance is that it has turned out to be more difficult to develop good systems than commonly supposed. By "good" is meant both correctness and capability. First, the difficulty of integrating and debugging systems has been severely underestimated time after time. And a large work force is used today in corrective maintenance, simply to fix software that "could have" been built correctly to begin with. Note the misuse of the words "debugging" and "maintenance." Debugging connotes the removal of errors which have been inserted by some natural process beyond control of the programmers—but it was the programmers who inserted the bugs! Maintenance connotes restoring a device to its original correct state—but the program was not correct to begin with! In both cases, these are kind euphemisms for a bewildered society of programmers. Second, there has been a consistent underestimation of the uncertainties and change facing data processing applications. For example, tax laws change, and differ from state to state—users get better ideas—operations change. So a considerable work force is required in adaptive maintenance, adding to and modifying the basic system, often until the basic system can no longer be found in the confusion caused by the modification process.

—Harlan D. Mills

Section II

Practical Tips for Maintainers

For a Friend Assigned to a Maintenance Group

The fellow who designed it
Is working far away;
The spec's not been updated
For many a livelong day.
The guy who implemented it is
Promoted up the line;
And some of the enhancements
Didn't match to the design.
They haven't kept the flowcharts,
The manual's a mess,
And most of what you need to know,
You'll simply have to guess.

We do not know the reason,
Why the bugs pour in like rain,
But don't just stand here gaping!
Get out there and MAINTAIN!

David H. H. Diamond

Maintenance Reviews

Daniel P. Freedman and Gerald M. Weinberg

What are redundant round-robins?

One example is what Harlan Mills calls a *Speed Review.* The work is divided into equal parts in some fashion, after which each individual spends a short time—say three minutes—studying each part and making notes of issues. At the end of the interval, the work units are passed around the room, with sufficient intervals being scheduled to give the desired level of redundancy.

In Mills' original description of the speed review, each participant reviewed each piece of work—in that case, one proposed solution to some classroom exercise. The object there was to feed back to each producer a series of independent impressions of the individual's work, but a speed review is very useful for certain other tasks.

For instance, suppose we want to find out if a particular module is easily understandable for maintenance. By dividing the module into pieces and speed reviewing each piece, we can collect the first impressions of half a dozen people. These impressions, taken together, will give us a much more reliable estimate of the readability of the code than we could get from any one person. Speed reviews of this type are also very effective at detecting certain types of bugs—the kind which, if it isn't seen in the first glance will probably never be seen, once the mind gets set in a certain way. With five first glances, there's five times the chance of one of them catching it.

Why are reviews required of systems already in production, since changes are usually minor in size and complexity?

It's hard to understand why many people have the impression that maintenance changes are "minor." The major expenditure in most data processing installations is for maintenance. People involved in maintenance activity are generally less experienced than people involved in development, so even simple changes may appear complex.

Maintenance staffs are usually working with systems which were designed under older technologies. As a result, maintainability was often neglected, leading to systems that were hard to maintain from the start. Since their development, these programs have been patched, repatched, modified, enhanced, patched, tuned, repatched, simulated, patched, and are now running under emulation. The people who designed these systems are long since vanished from the scene, in many cases leaving nobody in the installation having experience with the system.

To complicate matters, these are ongoing systems. The business pressure of keeping these systems running is intense, thus increasing the chance for error. When an error does occur, the consequences can be staggering, yet errors occur in more than half of the maintenance changes—even those as small as one line of code.

We don't have to look far for the source of these difficulties, even in code that was originally well designed for maintenance. If documentation was created, it certainly wasn't maintained. Sometimes we find little more than a flow chart—not of what the program does, but of what it once may have done. The maintenance programmer daily encounters vestiges of old changes, such as labels which are never referenced, variables set to values which are never used, dummy routines that branch immediately back to the point of invocation, or huge sections of code activated by long-forgotten flags unknown to anyone and not described in any documentation.

The quality of these products often creates a morale problem. In many cases, this problem is intensified by the general knowledge that a new system is being designed, so that the maintenance programmers are responsible only for keeping this beast ambulatory for "one more month" until the last few bugs are out of the new one.

The pressure on maintenance is growing more intense every day. The severe rush on maintenance efforts rarely leaves adequate time to test a patch, let alone to explore its effects on the rest of the system. Eventually, things reach the point where each patch is more likely to create errors than correct them. Before long, the programmers realize that they are not correcting today's errors, but merely transforming them into tomorrow's more difficult errors. The very procedures and methodologies used in most maintenance efforts are creating monster systems that are becoming increasingly out of control. A sorry, sorry state—not at all what you'd call "minor" in size and complexity.

But how can reviews help out in this situation, when we already lack adequate time to make maintenance changes?

Pulling yourself out of a hole can be a problem, but maintenance reviews pay off quickly. True, you now spend time reviewing, but other times are reduced to more than compensate for review time. Time savings occur in

a. fewer computer runs
b. less analysis of bad runs
c. fewer changes to changes
d. less complicated future changes
e. fewer production changes and concomitant reruns to repair files

What do we look for in a maintenance review?

In the ordinary maintenance review, there are three fundamental questions to be asked:

a. Does the proposed change do what it's supposed to do? That is, is it CORRECT?

b. Does the proposed change do things it's not supposed to? That is, is it CONSOLIDATED?

c. Does the proposed change leave the code looking patched? In other words, is it CLEAN?

Because the maintenance change is often to a small amount of code, but potentially harmful to a large amount of code, the most danger is from side effects, rather than incorrect intended effects. The walkthrough of the added code, therefore, is insufficient as a test of the change.

An excellent way to approach a maintenance review is to ask the three questions in order, using different review techniques for each:

a. CORRECT? Use a walkthrough here, comparing the test results to the specified results, which may take a relatively small part of the review.

b. CONSOLIDATED? Here an inspection may prove the best way to avoid overlooking some type of side effect. Make a checklist of the ways in which one change can affect existing code and documentation. Look for each of these side effects in order, so when the inspection is finished, you have strong assurance that nothing has been skipped.

c. CLEAN? Perhaps the best approach to cleanliness is just a generalized look at the code, or perhaps you will prefer a standards inspection. A good check is for each review committee member to show the code to an innocent bystander before the review, asking if they can locate the patch. If they can't tell which code was patched in, then it's probably clean enough to pass review.

A Checklist for Potential Side Effects of a Maintenance Change

Daniel P. Freedman and Gerald M. Weinberg

How about a checklist for potential side effects of a maintenance change?

Over the years, we've accumulated a lot of cases of "side effects"—unanticipated and usually undesired effects that were triggered by changing "just one thing." We've gathered all these things in the checklist given below. Because the list gathers material from many installations, systems, and programming languages, not all items will be applicable to your situation. To use the list, have several knowledgeable people sit down in a review, making sure that they understand each item, that inapplicable items are deleted, that applicable items are tailored to your situation, and that any omitted items are added.

Once the list has been tailored to your installation's needs, you may begin to use it in maintenance inspections. Merely inspect the proposed change for each type of side effect in succession. If the change passes this inspection, it's very likely to work correctly the first time on the machine—and not to cause any side effects.

For convenience the side effects have been divided into four categories: Code, Data, Documentation, and Miscellaneous. Don't worry too much about classification, though. It doesn't hurt to catch the same problem under two different categories, but it sure hurts to miss it because of a jurisdictional dispute.

Code side effects

Generally, code side effects are the most dramatic, though for that reason they may be detected and corrected earlier. Many of these potential side effects can be caught by a good compiler, perhaps with the aid of the linkage editor and/or operating system. You'll be better off, though, to catch most of them before compiling, since maintenance changes often require huge compilations, within which error or warning messages are often missed.

1. New error message. If you do make a compilation, make sure that no new

messages are issued, and no old ones are changed or deleted unless that was the purpose of the change.

2. Active label deleted. The deleted portion of code may have contained a label branched to from elsewhere. Compiler or cross-reference should spot this, but it's an easy manual check to trace back all deleted labels.

3. Active subroutine deleted. The deleted portion of code may have contained a performed paragraph or a closed internal subroutine which is executed from elsewhere. Should be caught by compiler if hand check misses it.

4. Active macro deleted. The deleted portion of code may have contained a macro definition used to expand code elsewhere. Under some systems, this would not be caught automatically if the name of the macro is a legal default name, leaving code with a valid interpretation of the unexpanded form.

5. Active label changed. Instead of deleting a label referenced elsewhere, the change may have placed the label in a slightly different position, or changed the code following that label which would be executed after a branch to the label. (Note that without GOTO's these label problems can be controlled.)

6. Active subroutine changed. A closed subroutine or executed paragraph invoked from elsewhere may have been changed. The cross-reference list should be used to check for this and the label possibility (point 5).

7. Active macro changed. Any change, no matter how slight, to a macro definition can cause arbitrary amounts of trouble if that macro is used in a different context. Cross-reference listings may not identify all places the macro is invoked. A macro listing from the previous compilation might help—otherwise a hand check of the source code (before macro expansion) must be made. If this list is not available, get a straight listing of the program source code.

8. Changed function. Any function whose line of execution passes through the changed statement could be changed. Walk through each different function that passes through the changed code, checking that the input and output state are as they should be in the new code.

9. Timing relationships. If the speed of execution changes—either faster or slower—and there are any time dependent operations, the change could cause you trouble. It's best not to have time-dependent code, but sometimes there's no way out. Remember that it's not just slower code that causes trouble of this type.

10. Efficiency. Although the code may be time independent, your budget may not be. All functions that pass through the affected code must be checked for important speed changes that might hurt your computing budget or performance of the entire program. Don't just check the function you're changing.

11. Access arm contention. When timing relationships are changed, new files are added, or file characteristics are changed, the result can be increased access arm contention on movable arm disk files. The function may be exactly the same, but total elapsed processing time can be raised by huge factors—100 times or even more.

12. Memory usage. If the change requires more primary storage, it may push that part of the code over its allocated memory, resulting in an error.

13. Memory layout. Even if memory usage decreases, the change may affect the layout of other parts of the program. If the original program was correct and relocatable, this change shouldn't affect it, but the original might not have been entirely correct. For instance, a data word was uninitialized in the original, but happened to fall on a word left zero by the loader. Deleting one word earlier in the program caused the uninitialized word to be laid over a non-zero word, causing the program to fail. The error was, of course, in the original, but wasn't manifest until the "foolproof" change.

14. Virtual behavior. Any change in core layout, no matter how small, could have an effect on the paging behavior of the program, resulting in a surprising and perhaps unacceptable change in efficiency or elapsed time. For example, pushing just one instruction over a page boundary (and it need not be anywhere near the changes) can double or triple the amount of paging experienced by a program. So large an effect is rare and unpredictable, so you'd better be prepared to ask if it would be possible, and to check for it in the first executions.

15. Invocation count change. Certain subroutines, including system subroutines for handling I/0 and other system functions, keep a count of the number of times they are invoked. This count may be used to control messages, priority, system aborts, and other functions. If you change the number of times a routine is entered—either increasing or decreasing—the invocation count will change and could cause side effects.

16. Change of priority. In some operating systems, priority can be lowered and/or raised dynamically by the application program or by the operating system if the program behaves in certain ways. Such a priority change could be triggered by a small change in program size, or perhaps a change in the pattern of calling some system routines, resulting in vastly altered operating times.

17. File opening. By opening a file at a different point in a program, we may accidentally give a file different characteristics. For instance, in PL/I an implicit opening can be caused by many file operations, with each operation giving different attributes. Explicit opening before first use prevents this problem, but not all programs in maintenance have followed this safe practice.

18. File closing. The program may cause trouble if it closes or causes a file to close that was open previously. This problem cannot be so easily prevented as the file opening problem. It depends, instead, on a discipline of each programmer to avoid any closing before the last possible use.

19. On unit change. In PL/I and other languages that provide for interrupts, a program change could change the "active ON UNIT"—that is, the action to be taken in case of a particular interrupt. Such a change could affect any following process that may expect to be interrupted.

20. Interrupt mask change. In systems with interrupts, certain interrupts can be "enabled" and "disabled" by program action. If a change modifies the "mask" governing enabling and disabling, any subsequent process can be affected. There can be an interrupt which was previously disabled, or a previously enabled interrupt may now be "masked."

Data side effects

Data side effects can be very subtle and related to the actual change in the most oblique ways. Many data side effects lie unnoticed for weeks or months after a change, until some user gets a funny feeling about what's happening to the output. The savings to be gained from finding data side effects in a review before they happen are, therefore, potentially enormous.

1. Flag change. If the change modifies the state of a flag, or deletes the modification of a previously modified flag, or changes the conditions under which a flag is modified, any part of the program that accesses that flag could be affected.
2. Condition change. In languages such as COBOL which have named conditions, changing a data item's value could change a condition which doesn't seem to have any obvious relationship, according to its name. Check all conditions that are based on any data item changed by the program.
3. Data value change. Any time a data item is used in more than one place, any change to that item could cause problems with any process that accesses it. Use the cross-reference listing to indicate potentially changed processes.
4. Changed allocation. When dynamic storage allocation is used, any change that allocates or deallocates storage could affect another part of the program. For instance, if an extra item is put on a stack, the stack count in other places could be out of synchronization, perhaps leaving one item unprocessed. If an item is deleted, a system error might result when the stack empties too soon. Also, the total allocation might become too large, dynamically, if additional allocations are made by the changed code.
5. Overlay change. When various data areas are overlaid, the chances for side effects escalate. Avoid overlaying whenever possible. Where it must be done, or has been done, check each and every name under which the same storage can be accessed or changed.
6. Parameter change. If a subroutine is changed, and if that subroutine now changes some parameter passed to it by reference, the calling routine can be devastated. In FORTRAN, for instance, the called routine can even change "constants." Search out all references to parameters and eliminate such changes if possible, but be sure to check out all that can't be eliminated.
7. File position change. If a sequential file is read or written, or was formerly read or written, by the changed code, any change in the number of reads or writes, or in any other file positioning actions, could disturb the behavior of other regions of code. Even on a print file, an extra line could cause disruption of line counts or break up a previously contiguous group of output lines.
8. Invalid pointer. Whenever data structures are linked together by pointers, certain operations on the pointer itself are not, of course, side effects, but operations on the referenced material may affect the pointer in non-obvious ways. If the number of items in a table is changed, the pointer to the last element may not be updated, or the table count may not reflect the change. Even moving an item, within core or back and forth to a backing store, can render pointers invalid.

9. Record layout changes. Expanding, contracting, or deleting a field in a record can change the definitions of other fields, which in turn can disrupt other programs that reference those fields, or other parts of the same program. In higher level languages, recompilations may be required, but these do not always automatically correct the problem. In some data base systems, the change of physical record layout is "transparent" to the user programs—except for possible efficiency considerations or bugs in the data base system.

10. Security alterations. In some operating systems, files and data bases can be protected with some access control scheme. If the scheme is dynamic, any change to the security level or interlock pattern could have effects on other portions of the same program, or on other programs operating in parallel.

Documentation side effects

Probably the most frequent side effect of maintenance changes is the corruption of the existing documentation. The programs change and the yet documentation remains the same. Even when an effort is made to update the documentation, subtle points are overlooked in the rush to production. Eventually, the accumulation of small errors in the documentation produces documents that nobody can rely on. After that, nothing short of a major effort to rewrite can restore the documentation to usefulness. Only by systematic review of the impact of each change on all documentation can we keep the documentation current and useful.

1. New name. When a new data name, file name, or label is created, it must be posted to all reference lists. The newest names are the ones most likely to be sought in the documentation, yet are the least likely to be found there.

2. Old name deleted. When an old name is no longer used, it should be deleted from all appearances in the documentation. If the documents are not well indexed, it may prove difficult to locate all references. Eventually, old names accumulate in a document, cause confusion, and slow down the use of that document. An excellent practice is to create a section of the document called "formerly used names." These names are kept in the index, as well, so that anyone running across a leftover name can immediately find out that the name is no longer in use. The list of formerly used names can also be helpful in avoiding the use of names recently in use, which may prove confusing.

3. Invalid index. When pages are added to or deleted from a document, the index may be rendered invalid. Without automatic production of the index which updates all later page references, such an index becomes worse than useless. It becomes misleading. One method of keeping the index valid is to use fractional page numbers for inserts. This postpones the problem of updating the index until the pages are renumbered, but then makes the job practically impossible without starting over. Also, any indexable items in the insert must be referenced—to the fractional page numbers. This kind of updating seems, at the time, to be a real pain in the neck, but if you aren't going to do it, then get rid of the document altogether.

4. Invalid table of contents. When sections are added or deleted, the table of contents becomes invalid. Usually, all this requires is a retyping of a page or two. Don't make the mistake, however, of thinking that the table of contents is the only reference list that must be updated. In general, especially for large documents, the index is a far more important starting point for information searches.

5. New error message. Of all the error messages, the newest are the ones most likely to be encountered in the use of the system, yet they are the least likely to be found in the message reference manual. "Self-documenting messages" are one solution to this problem, but few systems are willing to devote sufficient storage or time to make messages truly self-documenting. The best way to be sure that messages get into the message documentation is to have an automatic way of updating that documentation. Even then, the reviewers need to check that the programmer has taken the trouble to activate the update.

6. Deleted error message. It's not usually too serious if we forget to delete the documentation for a deleted error message. Nevertheless, it's good to keep things tidy, and to prevent the documentation from growing overly large. Also, keep a list of previous error messages so that they won't be reused. There often are old copies of documentation laying around which would give a user the wrong interpretation of the new message under the old name.

7. Error message meaning changed. Old copies of documentation make it very difficult to "spread the word" when an existing message changes meaning, even if the master documentation is updated. The review group will want to question any change of meaning or addition of new meaning to an existing error message. Usually it's best to create a new message to handle the new case. Any cost in machine resources is quickly recovered by benefitting the otherwise puzzled users.

8. Operator response changes. All the same arguments we've given about error messages apply to operator responses. In addition, if new operator responses give the operators more power, it's usually a good idea to provide training. Otherwise, the operators tend to continue as always, ignoring the new and improved ways of doing things. The review group should ask, "How will the operators learn to use these new features?"

9. Accepts new data. When input routines are modified to be more forgiving or to accept previously forbidden forms of input, failure to document and train can wipe out the value of the changes. The review group must once again ask, "How are these new features communicated to the people who prepare the input?"

10. Rejects old data. When acceptable ranges of input are narrowed, the users will ordinarily find out, even if the changes are not documented, when they try to use previously acceptable inputs. Nevertheless, their attempts to get the system to accept these data will prove costly and annoying unless they are informed in advance of the changes.

11. New data interpretation. When previously acceptable input is now accepted under a different interpretation, users will make costly mistakes unless they are most carefully and thoroughly prepared for the changes. It will generally be best for the review group to question a design which changes the interpretation of existing

inputs, rather than incur the costs of dumping such a design on the users, no matter how carefully they are prepared.

Miscellaneous side effects

Rather than debating the classification of a particular side effect you encounter, add it to this list of miscellaneous side effects.

1. Clerical procedures. Take the time to review what effects will be made before and after the computer portion of the processing. For instance, incorporating more information in a report may eliminate or change clerical operations that previously had to be performed before the former report was used. Although these short cuts may seem completely advantageous, any changes in clerical procedures can initially be expected to lead to errors unless specific provision is made to retrain those people performing the operations.

2. Forms. Changes may require new forms or new interpretations of old ones. In the first case, form printing may be the longest lead time item in the design—and the existence of a 5-year supply of old forms may generate resistance to the new system. In both cases, the review group had better check that the system will provide some information along with the first new outputs, so that users understand the new material.

3. Impact on other systems. In one case, a maintenance change increased the amount of 6-part output from an insignificant few pages to a major portion of the inventory. When it came time to run other systems using 6-part paper, the stock was quickly depleted. There's no end to such subtle effects, and no way to guarantee that all of them are caught in a review. It never hurts, though, for the review group to take a few minutes and brainstorm what areas may have been overlooked. Keep track of all cases that occur, and eventually you'll have a pretty effective checklist, including such items as:

   a. use of a shared forms inventory
   b. shared hardware resources
   c. skilled personnel needed by two systems
   d. scheduling conflicts
   e. telephone or communication line loading
   f. exclusive use of files
   g. competition for auxiliary equipment or services, such as bursters, delivery carts, and storage space.

4. Job control. Many program changes require associated job control changes. Such changes are obviously part of the "side-effects" of any maintenance change. Less obvious are the changes that make the job control procedures less efficient, though still valid. The review group must check that the previous job control is still the best for the modified system. Will there be inefficiencies? Will operating procedures become less convenient? Can we take advantage of the change to bring the system more in line with present operational standards or with newly available equipment?

5. Expectations. One of the most frequently overlooked side effects is the effect of a modification on *what people think.* The announcement of a change may make the users prepare themselves (perhaps wisely) for a rash of errors. On the other hand, the announcement of one change may lead them (foolishly) to expect that other changes will naturally accompany it, or soon follow. The net result of an "improvement" is often a mob of even less satisfied users, so the review group ought to speculate on what will happen when this change encounters the wooly world of the human psyche.

6. Success. In the past, maintenance has been so fraught with side-effect dangers and just plain errors that success was seldom achieved. Once our maintenance reviews are in full swing, however, we have to anticipate that we will in fact succeed once in a while—and we must also anticipate what that success will bring. For instance, one error-riddled system was seldom used by its several hundred potential users, so management decided to mount an effort to have the system repaired in a systematic fashion. The resulting system was so dependable and useful that usage suddenly increased by a factor of a thousand over previous usage. This increase in transaction volume made the file design of the system completely inadequate to the daily load—which soon meant that nobody could get results fast enough to be useful. The entire problem—and so many others like it—could have been avoided if the review group had only considered that unavoidable law of nature: success breeds failure. So, just when your maintenance reviews start to pay off, be prepared for the inevitable reaction. If you start making systems better, your users will want more of the same—the best side effect of all.

Some Tips, Techniques, and Guidelines for Program and System Maintenance

Girish Parikh

The following tips, techniques, and guidelines have been distilled from several years of hard-earned maintenance experience, informal talks with programmers, and study.

Have you ever worked on a storage dump and a program listing to determine the cause of the abend and got nowhere? Probably you were working with a wrong program listing. After some wasted effort you realized it, and tried to locate the right one. Obviously, someone changed the program and forgot to file the new listing. But who made the change, and when?

In case the changed program goes to end of job, there still may be a problem. If the output produced is not as expected, how do you check the program if you're not sure which program version was executed?

The following technique solves the above problems: Include the program identification line (literal) in the working storage and display (or print) it in the beginning of the procedure division.

Figure 1 illustrates an example of program identification line (literal) defined in the beginning of the Working Storage section. It is also displayed by a statement in the beginning of the Procedure Division. The program identification line (literal) in the dump will quickly give you the information that you need. Before probing the dump, you can even ensure that you're working with the right listing.

When the program does not abend, the displayed (or printed) information by a statement in the beginning of the Procedure Division provides valuable information for identifying the program that produced the particular output.

What is the use of version number? The version number is useful when the program is changed more than one time during one day, especially by the same programmer. When changed the first time, the new program has a version number of zero. Subsequent changes to the program will have version numbers incremented by one. Another approach is to use the time of day instead of a version number to identify programs.

```
 WORKING-STORAGE SECTION.

 01  PARA-ENTERED                         PIC X(32)  VALUE
            'WORKING-STORAGE SECTION'.

*****************************************************************
* NOTE - FOLLOWING IS THE PROGRAM ID COMPRISING OF (SOURCE)       *
*        PROGRAM NAME, VERSION NUMBER IN PARENTHESES, DATE OF     *
*        CHANGE, AND PROGRAMMER NAME.                             *
*        IT IS DESPLAYED WHEN PROGRAM IS EXECUTED.                *
*        PLEASE CHANGE IT WHEN RECOMPILING THE PROGRAM.           *
 01  PROG-ID                              PIC X(52)  VALUE
            ' ******P1787B   (5)   03/27/77   GIRISH PARIKH******'.
*****************************************************************


 PROCEDURE DIVISION.

      DISPLAY PROG-ID.

 BUILD-INFO-IN-POL-DATA.
      MOVE 'BUILD-INFO-IN-PCL-DATA' TO PARA-ENTERED.
      DISPLAY PARA-ENTERED.
```

Figure 1. Program identification line (literal) defined and displayed. Name of the paragraph entered moved to the working storage data name and displayed.

If a program abends, how do you know which paragraph was being executed at the time of abend? Working with the addresses in the storage dump, you can usually locate the statement that caused the problem.

A quicker way to locate the paragraph that was being executed: When you change the program, insert code to move the paragraph name in the working storage data name, as shown in figure 1. This can be done for every paragraph in the program or, while doing maintenance, only for the new or changed paragraphs. The storage dump will show the paragraph name, if a paragraph (with the paragraph name moved in) was being executed when the abend occurred. The code that moves the paragraph name to the working storage data name may remain in the program after testing is finished.

While testing the program, displaying the paragraph (especially the added or changed paragraph) by a statement in the beginning of a paragraph serves as a full or partial trace of the program.

In top-down development of enhancements to the program, when stubs are used for some functions, the displayed paragraph names containing stubs help check the program flow.

Some tips for maintenance of program and system

1. Keep new function in a program separate, and depart temporarily from the normal sequence of the original program to execute that function, then return to the normal sequence.

2. Insert additional code to print intermediate results when possible, to help you check the program and/or final results. Such code can be left in the program, making the printing of intermediate results optional, or turning the code that produces it into comments, when possible. (For example, in COBOL, insert '*' in column 7. When this code is required, '*' in column 7 can be removed. This is especially easy in on-line programming.)

3. Insert code for accumulating, and, if possible, print counts of input and output records. In COBOL working storage, insert literals such as "INPUT RECORD COUNT," "OUTPUT RECORD COUNT" before the definitions of the data names. They will help to locate the counts in the dump, if the program abends.

4. If a program has internal (hard coded) tables requiring much updating, change the program to use external tables when possible. Once you build external tables and modify the program, future table updates will be easy.

5. If you borrow job control cards from someone, make a copy and return the original deck, *as it was,* promptly.

6. Always make a test copy of the program. Make changes to the test copy. Test it thoroughly and then move it to production. Save the previous version and its program listing.

7. In some cases, with a temporary modification in the program, you can create a situation or manipulate the incoming record to test a condition. Don't forget to remove the temporary modification after testing.

8. Concentrate on program logic. Try to reduce reading dumps. By focusing on logic, you may be able to locate more errors, which may go unnoticed if only a dump is used.

9. Review involved input records thoroughly. Remember GIGO—Garbage In, Garbage Out! Don't believe if someone (even your boss!) says, "Input is OK!" Ask tactfully to see the input. Often the problem is in the input which was supposed to be correct!

10. However small a change may be, it is a good practice to test the program before moving it to production.

11. Listen to every suggestion carefully. Pay attention to even stray remarks. Casual information may lead to a solution.

Problem-solving procedure

When you discover a solution to a nasty problem or design an enhancement assignment, you may be excited to try it . . . but wait! Review it before implementing. Such a review has often saved me a test re-run, if nothing else. When possible, review the problem again the next day. You'll be more objective. Alternative solutions may also come to mind. They may not always be better, sometimes not even feasible, but such a consideration provides valuable insights into the problem, usually leading to a better solution. Reflective thinking is not always possible in a crisis. You'll have to make quick decisions, but the discipline helps.

When you write down the problem, you're forced to think. List the available facts. Try to be concise and to the point. Such a description of the problem not only documents it, but also helps in effectively communicating it. If for some reason, you're not able to work on it, another person can easily pick up from where you left off, avoiding duplication of effort.

Discuss the problem with your co-worker who thinks clearly and is understanding. You may get the answer while describing the problem or soon after that. A brief written description of the problem and a list of facts aid your discussion. Express clearly what you think the problem is. Often, while uttering the first sentence or two to my co-worker, an answer to the problem has rushed to my mind.

The technique of asking the right questions to the right persons may lead you to the correct solution to a problem. Make a list of logical questions. Don't worry if some of them may look stupid to you—one of them may have a germ of the solution! Against each question or group of questions write the name of the person most likely to have an answer. If you can't think of a right person, just guess and put someone's name . . . he may give you a lead to find the right person.

Then start doing your leg work, that is, calling or personally going to the person, explaining the problem briefly and asking pertinent questions. Make notes about what you learn or the leads you get. After you're through with the interviews, study notes. Classify and organize them. Focus on the material relative to the problem, and it may give a solution or new insights toward its solution.

Define a problem clearly. Gather all facts and let that material permeate to your subconscious. Engage in some other activity for a while. (Let your boss know what you're doing.) Take a break and take a walk of a few blocks. With new blood in your veins, you'll take a fresh look at the problem. If you get a hunch, think it over, and if it makes sense, try it. If you've not much to lose in trying, and if you can't find any other solution, by all means try, even if the hunch seems illogical! Sometimes the answer comes in an unexpected way. I've gotten solutions to some programming problems in a dream!

How to estimate a maintenance assignment

If you're asked to estimate a maintenance assignment, break down the assignment into different required functions in order to complete it:

1. Review the requirements or specifications of the assignment.
2. Talk with the involved persons, such as an analyst, user, or your boss. This may be a continuous function throughout the assignment.
3. Take an inventory of affected program and documentation.
4. Investigate the affected program.
5. Locate the spots in the program where changes should be made.
6. Check the side-effects of the proposed program changes on the other parts of the program.
7. Code the changes. Get them keypunched and verified.
8. Make the changes and get a clean compile.
9. Walkthrough the changes marked in the program. This can also be done after coding the changes.
10. Create test data, if not available.
11. Set up test JCL, if not available.
12. Test the program.
13. Do the system test if necessary.
14. Review the results.
15. Move program to production.
16. Update the affected documentation.
17. Conduct post-test reviews.

All the above steps may not be necessary for every assignment. Select the functions required and estimate time. Add the estimated time for all functions, add 10% to 15% for contingencies, and you come up with an *approximate* estimate. Review and revise the figures if the total estimate seems unreasonable. The above list can also serve as a checklist, while handling a maintenance/enhancement assignment.

How to make the most of available documentation

1. Get current source listings. Make sure they're the latest and currently in production.
2. Make an inventory of the programs in the system.

3. Get copies of the JCL decks. List them. Get copies of decks useful to set up tests. List them.
4. Get copies of operations documents.
5. Get system and program flowcharts, or other such documentation, if available.
6. Get data formats (layouts) for inputs, outputs, cards, tapes, disks, etc.
7. Get samples of output reports, dumps, etc. If possible, get actual report samples or actual size copy, as it is easier to modify reports from them using a ruler rather than from the reduced copy.
8. Get specifications, change notices, program discrepancies, narratives, etc.
9. Get any other available documentation.
10. Classify and organize the collected documentation for easy reference.
11. Make a comprehensive list of available documentation with cross references.

Always document what you do. Convince your boss to allow you time for this. An assignment is not complete until it is documented. Before going to the next assignment, make it a rule to completely document the assignment just done, while it's fresh in your mind. It never gets done if you or your boss suggest, "We'll do it later when we've more time!" Write with big letters on a card "DOCUMENT *NOW*," and display the card on your desk, NOW.

The following suggestions for program documentation can help a maintenance programmer.

While the maintenance programmer is not directly responsible for building documentation where it does not exist, he must keep available documentation updated. When useful documentation can be produced with reasonable effort while doing an assignment, and time schedule and budget allow it, I think programmers should be encouraged to produce it.

While maintaining an approximately 6,000-line, almost unmaintainable BAL program, whatever segments I studied for a particular maintenance/enhancement assignment, I made notes in semi-pseudocode format; and got the pages typed. For segments of code I didn't understand fully, I put a question mark near the note for it. I believe the notes did save some time of other programmers who had to work on that program.

Try the tips, techniques, and guidelines applicable to your environment before suggesting to include them as guidelines or standards in the standards manual. You may add to the above list, the tips, techniques, guidelines, and short cuts that you have developed or learned during the course of your work.

The Method: A Problem-solving Technique in Program Debugging and Maintenance

A. R. Brown and W. A. Sampson

In this chapter we describe what we have come to call "The Method." The Method has usually been one of the most controversial features of our discussions on debugging, but it was not introduced simply to provide useful discussion: although it is controversial we feel it has a part to play. It is in fact an adaptation of a problem-solving technique developed by Kepner & Tregoe (1965) for use by managers.

The Place of The Method

Figure 1 shows that, out of all possible areas in which The Method could be used, in one only is the use of it (or something akin to it) not required. The exception is usually cause finding while testing a well-planned program, when incorrect processing and its later consequences are relatively easy to find. Verification of such errors is usually straight-forward enough, but nevertheless The Method does have a role to play here, and we will see how when we look at the testing of the case study program.

The Method really comes into its own in situations when one is simply faced with a deviation that has to be put right—commonly in a hurry. The worst example of this is a production fault when, in the middle of a reel of tape, perhaps, and probably in the middle of the night too, the program fails. The operator may or may not notice anything, and the job may or may not get thrown off, but whatever the situation the programmer is faced with a fault, some scanty information about it, and possibly someone important breathing down his neck, waiting for him to come up with the answer—fast.

In this situation the programmer must make the best of a bad job, and that means using all of the information he is given, or can discover, to find and verify the cause of the deviation.

Situation	*Cause Finding*	*Cause Verification*
Well-planned program Normal testing	X	✓
Badly-planned program Normal testing	✓	✓
Unexpected or difficult errors during testing	✓	✓
Production faults Crisis situations	✓	✓

Figure 1. The Place of The Method

What The Method does

In the situation just described the programmer concerned must knowingly or unknowingly, critically examine and evaluate the information he has and then use the results of this examination as a source of inspiration as to which area of the program contains the error. The Method offers him a way of formalizing, and of bringing into the light of day, this process. In a nutshell, it guides his search for information by telling him what to look for, and gives him a powerful means of analyzing this information in order to pinpoint the area of the program in which the error lies. And finally, it makes it easy for him to verify that the cause found is the complete and correct one.

The Method described

Specification of the deviation

The basis of The Method is to define the deviation that has been found, and it is from this definition, or specification, that all else flows. Figure 2 shows the headings that are used.

With these headings in mind, one first gathers information and pigeonholes it into the appropriate slots, and if any particular slot seems sparsely filled then the search for information can be intensified in that area. This structuring and guiding of the search for information is of great help in a task that is usually a very hit-and-miss affair.

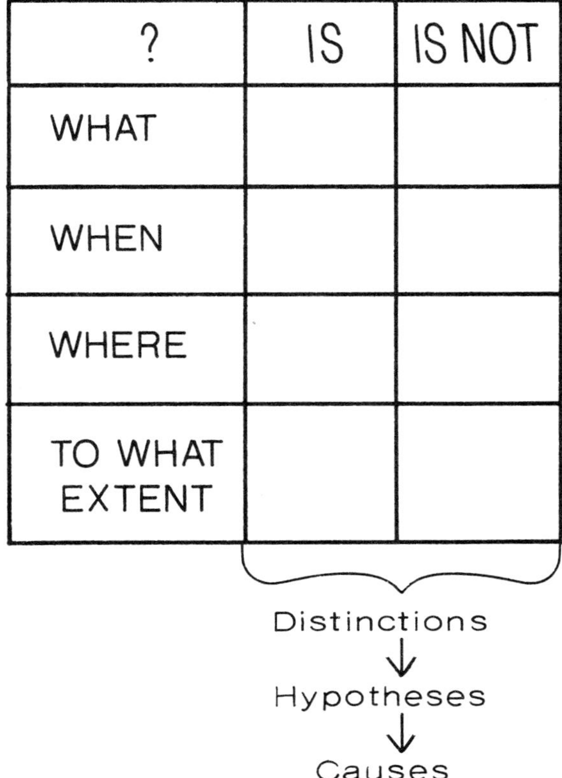

Figure 2. Bug Analysis Grid

The splitting of the specification into IS and IS NOT sides is the unique and vital part of The Method, because it is the presence of clear distinctions between the two sides that provides the clues as to the cause of the deviation. Unfortunately, a beginner finds it rather difficult at first, probably because he is too used to looking for similarities, rather than differences. However, it is something that one gets better at with a little practice, and we shall soon be seeing some examples of the art.

Look for distinctions

Once the information has been pigeonholed, each part of the specification is examined to see if there is any distinction between the IS and IS NOT sides. This is absolutely vital, because if the circumstances or conditions under which a fault does not happen are sharply differentiated from those under which it does happen, then we can pinpoint the most likely areas of the program for the error. For instance, if the fault occurs when processing record type A, but not when processing record type B, then we can say quite definitely that there *must* be something different between the processing of the two record types, and that the error lies in that part of the program that carries out the different processing of record type A.

Obviously, the ideal is to achieve sharp distinctions between the IS and IS NOT sides of each part of the specification, but this is often not possible, and sometimes not necessary.

It is also obvious that if the distinctions are not very sharp then we cannot pinpoint likely areas so closely, and if there are no distinctions at all then the specification as it stands is not much good to us and it must be sharpened up, if possible, before proceeding.

Hypothesize about causes

When the specification is as good as possible, and distinctions can be seen between the IS and IS NOT sides of one or more parts of the specification, then we will have some pointers as to the area in which the error lies; one's experience can now be used to the full by hypothesizing about possible causes of the deviation.

To use another canine analogy, the search for errors without any decent method of directing one's aim is rather like a bloodhound trying to pick up a robber's scent from among a number of different scents without any guidance as to which scent he should follow. In this situation the bloodhound will follow either the freshest or the nicest smell, and similarly the programmer might follow his nose along a path that proved profitable in a similar situation once before. But using The Method is like giving the bloodhound the robber's cap to sniff, after which he knows what he is looking for and can usually pick up and follow the correct scent quite easily.

Follow-up hypothesis

Having come up with a plausible theory, it will next be checked by examination of the program at that point, and hopefully a likely-looking error will be found there.

Verify suspected cause

Finally the erroneous part of the program can be dry run to make certain that the suspected error produces a deviation that *precisely* matches the specification. If it does, then the error has been found—positively. If the specification does not fit, then the cause found may be only part of the cause, or even no part of it at all, and in either case the answer is to try to improve the specification or the hypothesis.

In neither case does one say "That looks like it, I'll try it and see."

Examples of the use of The Method

We now illustrate the use of The Method by two simple examples, one a production problem, and one during poorly planned program testing. They have not been specially chosen, but are simply the first two examples that came to hand when this material was being developed. We use them precisely because they were chosen so randomly and because they would therefore seem to offer the reader the chance of seeing The Method in action in a real situation.

It is doubtful whether in such situations one would actually trouble to write down the specfications as they are here, but at least one would mentally write and analyze the specifications. With more difficult problems, however, where it is more important not to miss anything, and where clues are hard to find, it is a great help to write things down, as one can then pore over them in a much more concentrated fashion.

BROUGHT FORWARD	11/16	0.00	
MOVEMENTS	11/16	15.99	15.99
BROUGHT FORWARD	11/123	19.01	
BROUGHT FORWARD	11/157	47.31	19.01
BROUGHT FORWARD	11/15	63.02	47.31
BROUGHT FORWARD	11/164	23.85	63.02
MOVEMENTS	11/164	23.86	47.71
BROUGHT FORWARD	11/165	183.86	
BROUGHT FORWARD	11/173	0.00	183.86
MOVEMENTS	11/173	34.07	34.07
BROUGHT FORWARD	11/17	8.03	
BROUGHT FORWARD	11/195	1.57	8.03
BROUGHT FORWARD	11/1	0.00	1.57
MOVEMENTS	11/1	16.90	16.90
BROUGHT FORWARD	11/201	17.76	
BROUGHT FORWARD	11/205	145.95	17.76
MOVEMENTS	11/205	10.13	156.08
BROUGHT FORWARD	11/206	34.98	
BROUGHT FORWARD	11/207	10.40	34.98
BROUGHT FORWARD	11/209	36.31	10.40
BROUGHT FORWARD	11/214	28.35	36.31
BROUGHT FORWARD	11/217	95.35	28.35
BROUGHT FORWARD	11/218	8.79	95.35
BROUGHT FORWARD	11/219	0.00	8.79
MOVEMENTS	11/219	42.24	42.24

Figure 3a. The Method—Example 1—Schematic Print Layout

	Account No.	Brought Forward	Carried Forward
BROUGHT FORWARD	nn/nnn	999.99	
MOVEMENTS	nn/nnn	999.99	999.99
BROUGHT FORWARD	nn/nnn	999.99	
MOVEMENTS	nn/nnn	999.99	999.99
etc.			
		Movements	

Figure 3b. The Method—Example 1—Actual Incorrect Printout

Example 1

Program description. The program deals with the updating of a sales ledger and is in two parts. The first part updates the sales ledger file from a transactions tape, and for active accounts prints (amongst other things) b/f balance, movements, and c/f balance. The second part prints the same information in slightly different format, but for all accounts, active this month or now.

Deviation recognition. During a production run it was noticed that the second part of the program was printing wrongly. Figure 3 (a) shows the schematic format expected and part of the actual printout is shown in figure 3 (b). Naturally there was no expected results schedule, but this was not too worrying, as the error would seem to be easy to find.

Deviation specification—1. Information was gathered from the printout and placed in the appropriate category as shown in figure 4, which is a first attempt at a specification of the deviation. Note the large amount of information that has been gathered and categorized.

Analysis for distinctions—1.

WHAT There is no distinction between the IS and IS NOT sides here, so the specification needs sharpening up. What is characteristic of the movements lines omitted (or printed)?

WHERE An immediate distinction is apparent here: there is no fault in the printing of the movements during the first part of the program. Is there anything characteristic about the movements printed in the first part (or second part)?

WHEN Again, a clear distinction is present, but it is not a very helpful one. The characteristic of production running is exhaustive testing, so this particular combination may not have been tested, or the deviation spotted during program or system testing. Also there may have been an amendment since the program has been in production, and the amendment was not thoroughly tested, so the amendments list might possibly be checked.

EXTENT There is no real distinction here, but at least we are reassured that the fault seems consistent. It might be profitable to think a little about the fact that more movements are omitted than are printed; is there any clue there?

?	IS	IS NOT
WHAT	Some movement lines and following underscoring not printed	1. All movement lines and underscoring not printed 2. Only movement lines missing 3. Only underscoring missing
WHERE	Second part of printout	First part of printout
WHEN	During production run	Before line running
TO WHAT EXTENT	1. More movement lines omitted than printed 2. Throughout second part of printout.	1. More printed than omitted 2. Patchy or transient fault

Figure 4. The Method—Example 1—First Error Specification

Deviation specification—2. Let us now see if we can sharpen up on the specification, and particularly to see if we can find out what is characteristic of the movements lines that are not printed.

By comparing the b/f and c/f totals we can find out the value of each movement line that is not printed. Figure 5 is a table of the values of the first few movements, whether or not they have been printed. It is clear from this table that the characteristic of omitted movement lines is that the value of the movement is zero.

We can now sharpen up the WHAT part of the specification to the extent that the IS side says that zero movements and the following underscoring are omitted, and the IS NOT side says that non-zero movements and the following underscoring are omitted. We must not forget that the omission of the underscoring each time must also be explained, but it seems so closely connected with the omission of the movement itself that the same error probably causes both deviations, so we can leave it for now, apart from bearing in mind that we must explain it in full.

Analysis for distinctions—2. There is now a clear distinction in the WHAT of the specification also, so we can move on to hypothesise about causes.

Hypothesize about causes. The cause now seems obvious—this is an error in the printing of zero movements, a conclusion supported by the following points:

a. The error does not occur while printing is taking place during the first part of the program; but active accounts, by definition, have non-zero movements, so the first part of the program never attempts to print any zero movements lines.

b. More movement lines are omitted than printed, and a general characteristic of this business may be that each month there are more inactive customers than active ones.

Look for bug. The first thing to do is to look through the amendments since production running began, but none of the amendments appear relevant.

Upon examination of the program a paragraph called PRINT-ZERO-MOVES is noticed, which obviously looks promising, and in fact, it is found that the zero movement line is set up but is never actually printed.

Value	Omitted	Printed
15.99		✓
0.00	✓	
0.00	✓	
0.00	✓	
23.86		✓
0.00	✓	
34.07		✓
0.00	✓	
0.00	✓	
16.90		✓
0.00	✓	
10.13		✓
0.00	✓	
0.00	✓	
0.00	✓	
0.00	✓	
0.00	✓	
0.00	✓	
42.24		✓

Figure 5. The Method—Example 1—Values of Movements Omitted

Verification of suspected cause. Dry running of this part of the program readily reveals that the error found reproduces the whole of the specified deviation, including the omission of the underscoring. In fact, there are two errors, one of them being the omission of the writing of the movements line, and the other the omission of a separate write to do the underscoring.

Bug elimination. There are no problems here, two PERFORMs only being required. But the amendments must be thoroughly checked before submission of the program for a test of the amendments.

Summary. This may seem an awfully long-winded way to solve a simple problem, and the reader may feel that a complicated problem would be hopelessly difficult to solve in this way. But in fact the reverse is the case.

What the example should have illustrated is how much information is available if one looks for it; if one knows how to classify and represent it well; and if one has a way of looking for further information. How many people, for example, would have assumed that the underscoring would return by correcting the 'obvious' error, and how many would never have spotted that the underscoring was missing in the first place?

It is easy to concentrate on only one aspect of a deviation, but the specification forces one to consider all aspects, and in addition, of course, the specification positively encourages the dry running of the suspected cause, and or the correction, thus avoiding the correction of only half the error.

Example 2

Program description. This program reads a product file until a live product header record is found, and a list of depots stocking this product is then prepared by reference to a table read in from magnetic tape.

Deviation recognition. In this particular example each item is stocked by depots 01 to 08, and the expected printout for two such depots is shown in fig. 6, together with the actual test printout.

Deviation specification. Information was gathered from the printout and placed in the appropriate category as shown in Fig. 7, which is a first attempt at a specification of the deviation. Our first thought from the specification is that it is likely that we are looking for two errors, rather than one, one error being connected with the missing line, and the other with the depot code.

Analysis for distinctions.

WHAT The only distinction between the IS and the IS NOT sides is that all depot codes are wrong and not just some of them, and that they follow a consistent pattern.

We should like to be able to get closer than this; to be able to say, for instance, which line is omitted, so as to find out whether or not it is always the same one and also to discover what is characteristic of this line.

EXPECTED			ACTUAL		
PROD CODE	DEPOT	RECORD TYPE	PROD CODE	DEPOT	RECORD TYPE
0009	01	PRODUCT HEADER	0009		PRODUCT HEADER
0009	02	DEPOT STOCK RECORD	0009	GH	DEPOT STOCK RECORD
0009	03	DEPOT STOCK RECORD	0009		DEPOT STOCK RECORD
0009	04	DEPOT STOCK RECORD	0009	SH	DEPOT STOCK RECORD
0009	05	DEPOT STOCK RECORD	0009	W	DEPOT STOCK RECORD
0009	06	DEPOT STOCK RECORD	0009	L	DEPOT STOCK RECORD
0009	07	DEPOT STOCK RECORD	0009		DEPOT STOCK RECORD
0009	08	DEPOT STOCK RECORD	0010		PRODUCT HEADER
0010	01	PRODUCT HEADER	0010	GH	DEPOT STOCK RECORD
0010	02	DEPOT STOCK RECORD	0010		DEPOT STOCK RECORD
0010	03	DEPOT STOCK RECORD	0010	SH	DEPOT STOCK RECORD
0010	04	DEPOT STOCK RECORD	0010	W	DEPOT STOCK RECORD
0010	05	DEPOT STOCK RECORD	0010	L	DEPOT STOCK RECORD
0010	06	DEPOT STOCK RECORD	0010		DEPOT STOCK RECORD
0010	07	DEPOT STOCK RECORD			
0010	08	DEPOT STOCK RECORD			

Figure 6. The Method—Example 2—Incorrect Printout

WHERE There is no distinction here, except that the depot code is the only field with rubbish in it, which suggests that the error is confined to the processing of this field alone.

WHEN Again there is no distinction here: this is the first test, so there are no previous test results to refer to. Had there been a previous test, it would have been altered by accident when amending the program after the test.

EXTENT Yet again we have no distinction, simply reassurance that it is not a random error.

It is plain that the specification is not sharp enough, and we should particularly like to know which line is missing, but the only way in which we can identify lines is by depot code: and the depot code is rubbish! At this stage we have to admit that the specification cannot be sharpened up, so we simply feel that we have two errors, one to do with the missing line, and one connected with the rubbishy depot code. The depot code error seems slightly easier to deal with, so let us look for that one first.

?	IS	IS NOT
WHAT	1. All depot codes wrong: some blank, some alphabetic: consistent pattern. 2. One line missing for each product header	1. Some codes wrong, some numeric, but wrong: random pattern. 2. More than one line missing
WHERE	Rubbish in depot code column of printout	Any other column
WHEN	On first test	On any other test
TO WHAT EXTENT	Throughout printout for every product printed	Patchy or transient

Figure 7. The Method—Example 2 —First Error Specification

Hypothesise about causes. The consistent rubbish suggests that the program is picking up the wrong field, or that there is a conversion error, or both.

Look for errors—depot code. Since depot code is picked up from the table read in from magnetic tape, it is sensible to check the table layout, and while doing this it is found that the program has described the table incorrectly. In fact the depot code position referred to two characters of an alphabetic field, and these two characters were those printed out, except that the characters for depot 01 were missing.

Look for errors—missing line. It is now entirely reasonable to suppose that the missing line is caused by incorrect depot 01 processing. The logic of the table-processing part of the program is shown in figure 8, from which it can readily be seen that the details of the first depot are being read, but are not being stored for printing, so that line gets missed.

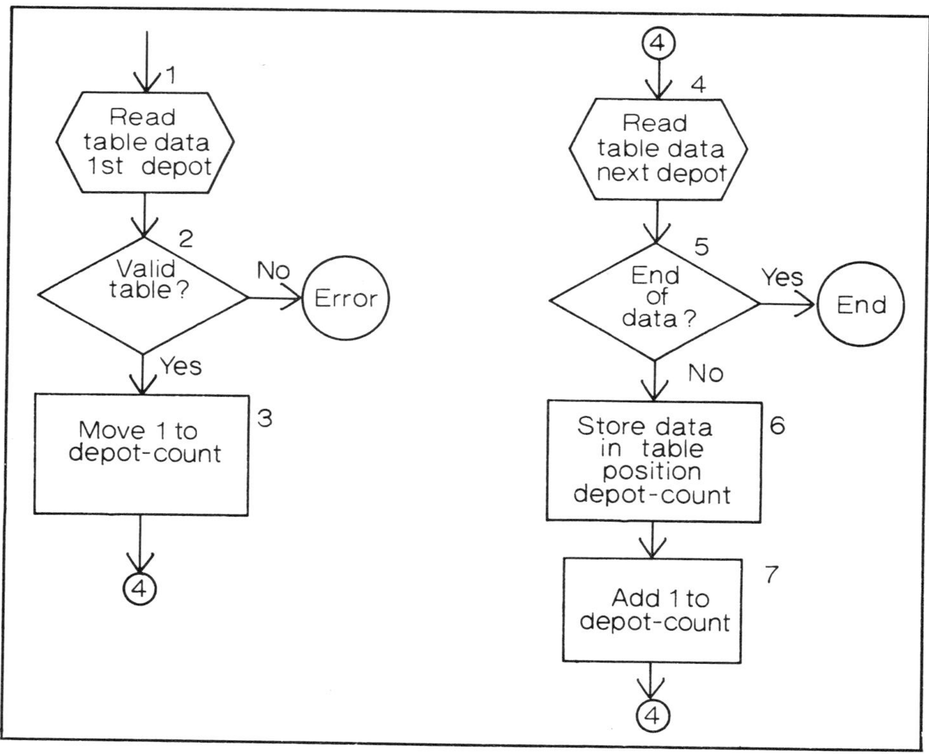

Figure 8. The Method—Example 2—Logic in Error

Verify suspected causes. Once again, dry running of the program as it stands reproduces the precise deviation specified.

Bug elimination. A little more difficult this time, but still trivial, really; simply altering the table layout and the flow of the table processing. We must remember to dry-run the amendments.

Summary. In this case the specification was by no means precise, but it did at least indicate that there were two errors, and it told us that information as to which line was missing would help us quite a lot. Fortunately the depot code error was easily found, and dry-running it also shed a lot of light on the second error. This gradual unveiling is typical of a multierror situation, where one uses information gained from one error to help solve another.

How a COBOL Preprocessor Increases a Maintenance Programmer's Productivity

Girish Parikh

Olin's Fine Paper and Film Group and its Ecusta Paper Division, Pisgah Forest, North Carolina, found most of their COBOL applications already written and in use before today's COBOL standards came into widespread use.

As a result, they found themselves with a large inventory of basically useful but non-standardized software. According to Nick Kaluger, Ecusta's manager, systems development, "It was an almost prohibitive expense to go back and re-do systems that had been running three or four years. But we had to do something about the accumulated problems we faced because of poor programming and lack of standards. So, we bought ADR's MetaCOBOL, mainly as a tool to clean up and standardize programs that were written over the years. These programs were assets, just like our plant building and paper–and cellophane–making machinery. These were assets that we thought could be salvaged. They were. And MetaCOBOL has been a tremendous help in that effort."

Kaluger doesn't believe that any preprocessing system such as Meta-COBOL can correct fundamental logic flaws. "But, what you can do is make the programs more readable so that logic flaws and other errors are readily apparent," he says.

"For example, we had two relatively small non-critical programs with bugs in them that our programmers could not spot for two years. They had spent a lot of time looking but finally just gave up. After we got MetaCOBOL, we ran these two programs through for cleanup and standardization. We found the bugs in both programs the very next day—merely because the programmer could now follow what was going on," Kaluger emphasizes.

"MetaCOBOL helps the programmer get into a program faster. It helps us enforce details like alignment, paragraph numbering, level numbering, common names, etc. Until recently, we had various styles of programs. Each programmer would have his own little pattern. Some would do repeats at the bottom, others would do it in the middle. Some had little loops, others had giant loops. Things like that are still in the programs. But, superficially, they now look the same. We are now able to track down these different styles and get into the problems much more quickly."

Five years ago, thirty people were engaged in programming and maintenance. Today, with more work than ever, fifteen people keep up with the whole operation. "With over one thousand programs in use, we're doing a tremendous amount of maintenance," Kaluger remarks. "We don't have as much time to devote to standardizing our programs as we would like. We have to have automatic tools to help us.

"We do know what our overall data processing budget has done in the last five years. It has stayed the same in spite of inflation and increased wages. We're asking fewer people to accomplish more. And they're doing it," Kaluger enthusiastically comments.[1]

Programmer Productivity and a COBOL Preprocessor

Programmer productivity is becoming important, as the cost of hardware is going down and programming cost is going up. In the next decade, programmer productivity will become one of the key issues in the DP industry.

There are many kinds of productivity. The four important ones are:

1. Program development productivity: increasing the number of debugged program statements produced in a given period.

2. Maintenance and enhancement productivity: reducing the time and effort spent on maintaining and enhancing an application. Here, productivity is a direct function of the quality of the original program when it went into production.

3. Production productivity: decreasing the impact of program errors, inefficient code and heavy utilization of computer resources as related to an operational program.

4. Human interface productivity: ensuring the ease of use and accuracy of all user documentation for those who must work with the operational programs.[2]

A COBOL preprocessor helps increase programmer productivity in new development; maintenance and enhancements; and in optimizing the programs. Improved productivity lends itself to meeting deadline and budgeting constraints.

Programmer productivity may vary widely from programmer to programmer, and from program to program. It may also vary from project to project depending upon management philosophy. In new developments, the total debugged and maintainable output produced in a given period provides the data to measure productivity. In a maintenance environment, it is usually extremely difficult to measure productivity.

I asked several professionals and vendors for specific information on productivity increases. Here are the highlights of their replies:

> The improvement in programmer productivity has not been measured statistically. Most shops do not measure productivity at all—they just have a gut feeling about it. The gut feeling of the precompiler users has been that, it (precompiler) is helping them.
>
> Programmer productivity increases vary greatly depending on circumstances and are very hard to measure.
>
> On the whole a good "reformat" program will improve productivity among maintenance programmers from 10% to 50%, and developmental programmers about 5%. There is, of course, a diminishing return on the maintenance programmer; after every program in the shop has been processed through the reformat program, productivity will not continue to improve, but remain at a constant level in comparison to the previous level.

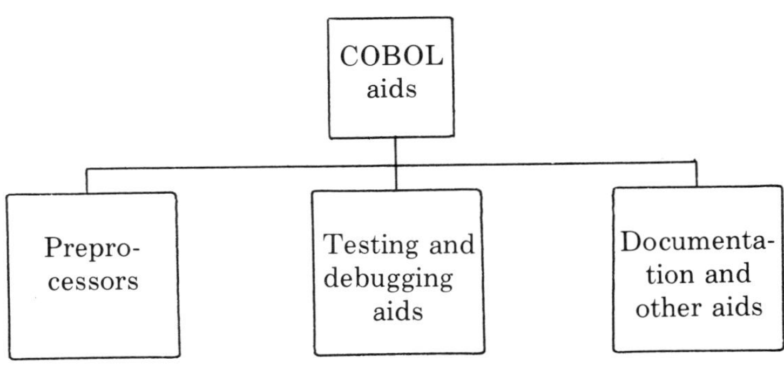

1. Shorthands
2. Macro preprocessors
3. Reformatters
4. Restructuring programs
5. Data Management Systems (DMS)
6. Decision Table Preprocessors
7. Program analyzers
8. Conversion packages

1. Test data generators (TDG)
2. Debug packages
3. Cross reference listers
4. Executive monitors

1. Flowcharters
2. Librarians
3. Standards enforcers
4. Optimizers

Figure 1: An Overview of COBOL Aids

COBOL preprocessor functions which increase maintenance programmer's productivity

A preprocessor package may be named after its major or only feature. Let's take a closer look at some preprocessor functions and how each can increase maintenance programmer's productivity.

A "shorthand" provides abbreviations for commonly-used COBOL reserved words and phrases to reduce the physical coding effort. Some shorthands have the capability of accepting user-defined abbreviations for expansion. While using user-defined abbreviations (if this feature is supported), documentation is improved, as shorthand abbreviations expand into standardized data names. For example, PMR becomes PAYROLL-MASTER-RECORD. Thus, meaningful names can be introduced in the program any time. For on-line application development and maintenance, shorthand reduces the size of messages and/or increases effective screen capacity, and improves the network throughout.

Reformatter

The reformatter, by reformatting a program, improves the readability of the program. The effect of better readability may sometimes be dramatic, as we saw in the case of Olin Company in the beginning of this report. The programmers in an installation may have different coding styles. It may be difficult and unpleasant to enforce the installation standards. A reformatter will provide readable versions of programs according to the standards, depending on the capabilities of the reformatter. Some reformatters have built-in standards (with a few options), while others have more flexibility and allow the user to tailor them to his own standards.

With the advent of structured programming the indentation and formatting of the code, such as nested IF's, 55-lines per page convention, and PERFORM statements, etc., have become increasingly important. A reformatter makes this formatting (and following conventions) painless. A missing or misplaced period in nested IF's can create a disastrous situation; such a situation becomes readily apparent when code is reformatted. The reformatter can also indent the new code according to the actual logic structure. The automatic indentation leaves no chance for indentation to be out of phase with the actual structure.

Another important feature of a reformatter is (if supported) paragraph numbering/renumbering. (Although it's sometimes called prefixing, prefixing has a different meaning.) The numbered paragraphs make it easier and faster for the programmer to find his way. The reformatter is equally effective on new and existing programs. It eliminates the need for the maintenance programmer to make cosmetic changes in the vicinity of changed code. Prefixing (if supported) works this way: when the same record format is to be used for input and output from a library, by prefixing input and output formats, a preprocessor eliminates the need for qualifying data names. For example, input record may be prefixed by IN-MSTR, and output record by OUT-MSTR.

Restructuring Program or "Structuring Engine"

Restructuring of the programs goes beyond reformatting, so that the programs conform to the structured programming standards.

Program Analyzer

A program analyzer analyzes source code for inefficiencies and produces analysis reports to help optimize the original program. The analysis reports can help in program testing and debugging also. The detailed discussion of a program analyzer is beyond the scope of this report, but in general a program analyzer helps programmers to locate inefficient code, incorrect looping, etc., and helps increase productivity. A program analyzer, by flagging areas that are inefficient (if this feature is supported), alerts the programmer where he can spend his time most profitably.

Conversion Package

A conversion package helps convert a COBOL program from one dialect to another. Conversion software, to translate programs from another language to COBOL, such as RPG/RPG II to COBOL, BAL to COBOL, etc. are also available.

[1]The Olin story is extracted from "Non-Standard COBOL programs Get Treatment (Users Report), *Infosystems,* (July, 1977), pp. 82–83, with permission.

[2]Martin A. Goetz, "New Software Tools Increase Productivity," *Infosystems,* (February, 1977), p. 66.

Abend Debugging and the COBOL Programmer

Bernard H. Boar

Program testing and debugging are the greatest problems confronting the Cobol programmer. Although the testing and debugging of a program are both more difficult and time-consuming than the job of coding it, relatively little time, energy and interest is spent in analyzing how best to perform these complementary tasks.

Common industry practice indicates that testing and debugging (module, program, subsystem, system, acceptance, parallel, release, update, etc.) will consume 33% to 70% of a project's time. While these tasks represent the major cost component of the development or maintenance budget, they are addressed only minimally in both Cobol courses and the professional literature.

A typical training session might consist of eight weeks of instruction on Cobol, JCL, utilities and linkage-editors, with little or no time spent on testing and debugging—which can comprise 70% of the student's job. Similarly, *Computing Newsletter,* a yearly bibliography of DP books for academic instructors, offers more than 50 selections which instruct the reader in "Essentials," "Basics," "Elements of" and "Functions of" Cobol; only four books use the words "Testing" or "Debugging" in their titles.

Program debugging remains a largely ignored area, without the analysis and investigation commensurate with its importance.

Because little formal guidance exists in how to approach, structure and control testing and debugging in general, the situation becomes acute when a programmer is confronted with an Abend dump (IBM OS and OS/VS operating systems). The selection, format and presentation of the dump, a raw machine-level hexadecimal dump of core storage at the time of the program or system logic error, is completely unrelated to the source Cobol program.

This presents both a dilemma and paradox to the programmer. A primary objective of Cobol was to provide a machine-independent and English-like language. High-level programmers would not need to know the intricacies and dynamics of either the operating system or hardware.

Unfortunately, this objective, when implemented, was confined to the input side only. As illustrated in figure 1, the compiler and linkage-editor convert the familiar

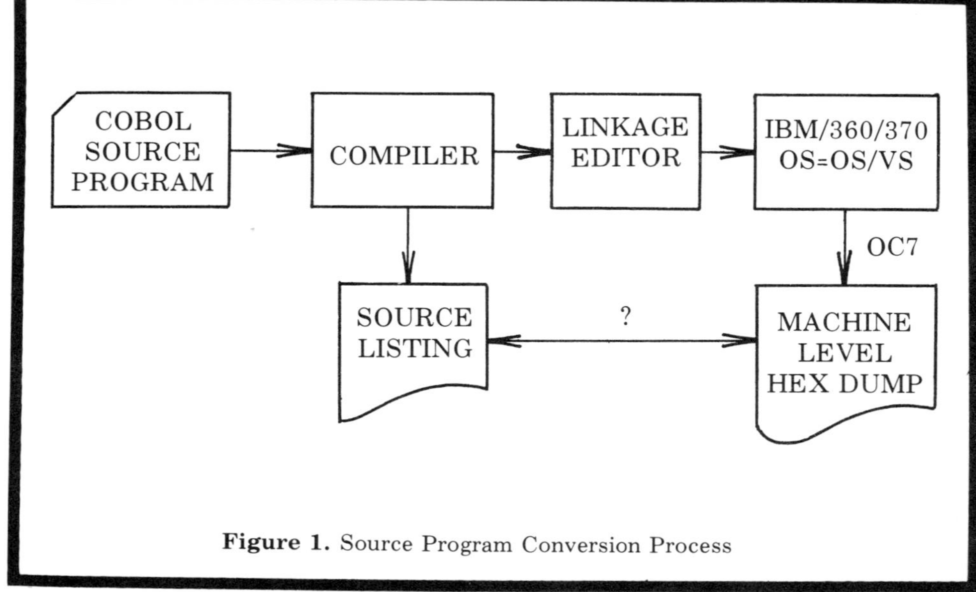

Figure 1. Source Program Conversion Process

Cobol source code into a machine-executable format. If an Abend should occur, however, no reverse (machine-level to source-level) conversion occurs on the output side.

Ill-prepared, the programmer is papered under by pages of hex and storage and system-level control blocks that are all irrelevant to Cobol. Since Cobol is a high-level language, most programmers are not formally trained in how to relate the raw core dump back to the source code and/or JCL.

Yet, the standard debugging aid provided to the programmer when a test or production system fails is a machine-level dump. What, then, is the programmer to do to solve this dilemma?

A general approach to solving this problem is to avoid the need to debug at the dump level by either writing bug-free programs or by using source-level debugging tools when available. As J. D. Aron of IBM has said, "The best way to write a correct program is to leave out the bugs."

This might seem a bit obvious, but it sums up the thrust of a great deal of current literature related to program design, testing, debugging and development. The goal is to build systems which by their inherent construction will be bug-free. The strategems used—from system conception through implementation to maintenance—will prevent bugs from entering the program code or, at minimum, catch them early in the development cycle.

This philosophy is often summarized under the broad categories of software engineering and programmer productivity techniques (figure 2). These techniques represent an evolutionary approach to program and system development which will minimize bugs and, consequently, Abends.

- Structured Design
- Top-Down Design
- Functional Design
- Composite Design
- Top-Down Development
- Hipo
- Structured Programming
- Chief (Super) Programmer Teams
- Development Libraries/-Librarians
- Structured Walkthroughs
- Modular Programs
- Defensive Programming
- Antidebugging coding

Figure 2. Programmer Productivity Techniques

Of particular value to the debugging analyst are defensive programming and antidebugging coding. They acknowledge the error-prone nature of program development and provide guidelines for minimizing it.

In spite of the considerable success that comes from using these techniques, programs still Abend. A correctness proof does not yet exist; in the foreseeable future, programmers will still:

1. Fail to initialize fields.
2. Miss validation checks.
3. Subscript (index) incorrectly.
4. Invert CALL/ENTRY linkage.
5. Leave out or incorrectly insert periods.

Bug-free programs remain an unrealized goal.

Since Abend debugging cannot be totally eliminated, the programmer requires an effective set of methods and techniques to deal with it. Toward this end, he needs to know how to use the available debugging tools and, of primary concern, he must have a clear understanding of what type of information is required to isolate the cause and solve each occurrence.

The common types of Abends confronting the Cobol programmer can be divided into three classifications:

1. Problem program.
2. Data management.
3. Supervisor.

Problem program Abends are the most prevalent. They signify errors which represent the improper use of data and/or instructions by the program. OC7, OCB and OC4 error messages are frequent in this group.

When confronted with an OCX series Abend, the analyst needs to know the information itemized in figure 3.

- Module in Error
- Instruction in Error
- Contents of Data Fields Being Operated on by Erroneous Instruction
- Contents of Other Data Fields
- Intramodule Flow
- Intermodule Flow

Figure 3. Problem Program Abends

The first three items establish the immediate technical cause of the Abend (e.g., a subscript value exceeds the size of a table). The last three are used to establish the logic failure. They address the flow reconstruction question of "What was the series of events which precipitated the error?"

Data management Abends are the second most prevalent type of Abends confronting the Cobol programmer. They signal an incorrect interface between the program and an Open-Close-End-of-Volume (O/C/EOQ) function.

A common example of this family is a B37, which denotes that space became unavailable while writing to a direct access storage device (DASD). In these cases, the analyst needs to know both the file in error and a clue to the interface malfunction. A B37 could be caused by a variety of events:

1. A write-loop which has exceeded the permissible number of extents.
2. An excessive output file size, one which has exceeded the permissible number of extents.
3. A secondary requested space allocation too large for the available space.
4. A lack of secondary space.

The corrective action would be different in each case.

Supervisor Abends encompass all other Abends resulting from an interface error between the program and the operating system. A typical example is an 804, which signifies that insufficient core was requested by the JCL REGION parameter.

The programmer needs to know the actual needed core. With this data, a corrected REGION value can be calculated.

Independent of the Abend category, the data provided to assist in analyzing the error should be in high-level format. Since the programmer's training and experience are in Cobol, any alien format requires new skills to be mastered, many of which would require hardware and operating system knowledge beyond what is customarily expected of an application programmer.

There are five categories of debugging tools (figure 4). Cobol Debugging verbs are part of the Cobol language and as such are immediately understandable to the programmer. As an Abend debugging aid, they have mixed value, as figure 5 illustrates.

- Cobol Debugging Verbs
- Vendor Software Monitors
- Time-Sharing Interactive Debuggers
- Cobol Version 4 Symbolic Debugging Options (State Flow, Symdmp)
- Core Dump Debugging

Figure 4. Abend Debugging Tools

VERBS
Ready/Reset Trace
Exhibit
On
Debug

DEBUGGING VALUE

POSITIVE	NEGATIVE
● Cobol source level	● Clumsy and time-consuming
● Output Cobol format	● All trial and error
● Tracing capability	● Always requires additional runs after the fact

Figure 5. COBOL Debugging Verbs

Consider a modular program consisting of 10 modules. If the program were to Abend with an OC7, perhaps nine trial-and-error recompiles and link-edits would be required to isolate the erroneous module, instruction and core data values.

Although this is a possible approach in a test environment, it is not feasible with production Abends.

The impact of these Abends on both operations and the user requires them to be fixed as quickly and efficiently as possible. A trial-and-error debugging verb approach would provide neither a satisfactory support level nor a satisfactory response level.

Abends monitors, developed by numerous software vendors, provide various debugging aids. In general, when a problem program Abend occurs, the monitor intercepts the Abend, prints an edited dump which highlights certain key debugging control data and resumes program execution by reinitializing the erroneous field with a valid numeric value.

The number of Abends so "trapped" per run is usually user-determined. The manner of using them is product-determined. In some instances, source code must be altered, while in other instances only additional DD files must be defined.

Monitors provide a number of benefits to the programmer:

1. Dumps are small (one to five pages instead of 50 to 250 pages).
2. In a test mode, automatic patching of data by a 0 or 1 is often OK and the overall run is not wasted because of a minor mistake.
3. Important debugging data (control blocks and core storage) is selected, highlighted and formatted.
4. A partial analysis of the error's cause is often mechanically performed.

Unfortunately, the user must also be aware of some negative considerations. First, although highlighted and edited, the data is still most often presented at the machine level. An intelligent analysis must still be performed to relate the monitor data to the source code.

Secondly, automatic patching by rote insertion of a 0 or 1 may correct the immediate problem, but cause further logical failures. If, for example, the Abend was caused by a bad subscript, substituting 0 for the subscript will merely cause further errors. The simple "numerization" of fields leaves the logical failure intact.

Third, little is provided to help analyze the actual logic error. The selective dumps provide sufficient data to isolate the immediate technical failure, but the data needed for flow reconstruction is often not available.

Last, monitors cannot be used in a production environment. The actual logic failure must be isolated and corrected to ensure the system's integrity. Nonintelligent artificial patching can cause subtle—if not disastrous—damage to the overall utility of a system.

Software monitors can be used as a valuable aid, but with proper respect for their drawbacks.

Time-sharing interactive debuggers provide a facility from which the programmer can interactively control, modify and examine program execution in a real-time environment. While the program is executing, via terminal commands, the programmer can dynamically trace instruction flow, display field values and modify the execution sequence, among other things. TESTCOB and SYMDMP are two widely used examples of the interactive debuggers.

What is particularly valuable is that when a program under its control Abends, the program can be debugged at the source code level. When an Abend occurs, the debugger automatically displays the module name, source line number and relative verb number causing the Abend. Field values may be requested by source data name. If necessary, dynamic traces and field displays may be requested.

The programmer does not see or need to analyze a core-level dump. The debugging process is handled at the desired source level.

Unfortunately, interactive debuggers are confined to the time-sharing environment. After the system is transferred to a batch production environment, this excellent tool is not available.

The primary benefit of interactive debuggers is that they provide the necessary data at the source level. To a lesser extent, this source code presentation is provided in a batch mode by the Cobol version 4 compile time options of STATE, FLOW and SYMDMP. When used in combination, they often eliminate the need for a core dump analysis.

The STATE option is illustrated in figure 6. It is invoked by the compile time parm option of STATE and requires minor execution JCL changes.

```
//A EXEC COBUCLG,PARM.COB=STATE
//COB.SYSIN DD *

      source program

/*
//GO.SYSDBOUT DD SYSOUT=A
//GO.STEPLIB  DD DSN=SYS1.COBLIB,DISP=OLD

PROGRAM TESTTAPE
LAST PSW BEFORE ABEND=
SYSTEM COMPLETION CODE=0C7
LAST CARD NUMBER/VERB NUMBER EXECUTED
     CARD NUMBER 000796/VERB NUMBER 02
END OF COBOL DIAGNOSTIC AIDS
```

Figure 6. State Option

The primary benefits of STATE are:

1. It identifies at source level the module, source line and verb causing the Abend. This is especially beneficial in highly modularized or overlay programs.
2. It is easily used.
3. It requires minimal increased overhead for the incurred benefit.

STATE, however, also has several drawbacks: It must be specified for each and every module of an executable program; it is not available on all current popular compilers; and it doesn't provide assistance in locating data field value or tracing inter- or intramodule flow.

The FLOW option is illustrated in figure 7. Like STATE, it is invoked as a compile time option and requires minor JCL changes. FLOW has the benefits of being easy to use as a compile option and addresses the problem of tracing intramodule flow.

```
//A EXEC COBUCLG,PARM.COB='FLOW=10'
//COB.SYSIN DD *

      source program

/*
//GO.SYSDBOUT DD SYSOUT=A
//GO.STEPLIB  DD DSN=SYS1.COBLIB,DISP=OLD

PROGRAM TESTTAPE
LAST PSW BEFORE ABEND=
SYSTEM COMPLETION CODE=0C7

FLOW TRACE
TESTTAPE 000796,000799,000802
END OF COBOL DIAGNOSTIC AIDS
```

Figure 7. Flow Option

However, it doesn't do what STATE does. It has a high execution overhead and it must be specified in each and every module if an intermodule flow is to be obtained.

The SYMDMP option (not illustrated) provides what STATE does but, in addition, provides a source-level core dump. When combined with the FLOW option, it essentially provides a full source-level debugging tool and minimizes the need for core-level debugging.

SYMDMP will identify the module, source line and source verb in error and provide a source-level presentation of all data fields. It is also easy to use on stand-alone or small modular systems.

Its drawbacks? The SYMDMP option requires a high overhead utilization of resources; it is not geared for use in highly modular programs; it can be clumsy and difficult to use because of the additional file allocations needed; and it is not appropriate for a production environment.

Core dump debugging is the historical means of addressing the Abend problem. Depending on whether a SYSUDUMP or SYSABEND option was selected at execution time, either a huge or horrendously huge raw hexadecimal core image of the state of the system is provided.

Nevertheless the dump remains a vital debugging aid because:

- It is the only standard aid provided. All other tools are superimposed on the operating environment and may or may not be available in a critical situation.
- Once mastered, the dump provides a complete picture of the system at the point of error and a virtually unlimited reservoir of information to analyze.
- Core-level debugging is the bottom line in a production environment.

Figure 8 highlights the critical importance of core dump debugging. While the other tools are available and valuable (especially in a test mode), the core dump remains the only assured aid in the production mode.

TOOL	ENVIRONMENT TEST	 PRODUCTION
Cobol Debugging Verbs	Adequate But Time-Consuming	Inappropriate
Vendor Software Monitors	Usable	Inappropriate to Dangerous
Time-Sharing Interactive Debuggers	Excellent	Not Available
Cobol Version 4 Symbolic Options	Good	Good, But High Overhead
Core Dump	Difficult to Use Unless Staff Properly Trained	Bottom Line Standard Error Report

Figure 8. Debugging Tool Summary

In spite of the many advances made in system and program design by the advent of software engineering techniques, programming remains a very error-prone activity performed by error-prone people. The available dump debugging aids provide substantial help in analyzing and correcting errors.

Unfortunately, the core dump still remains the necessary pillar of debugging activity. Hopefully, in the future, a source-level debugging report will become the standard aid and alleviate the problems of dump debugging.

Programming for Maintenance

Mick Punter

Once the world was young, summers were always sunny, Christmas was always white, you could get a room in a Spanish hotel, and computers were always spelt with a capital C—which meant that simply having a computer was more important than actually using it.

But now it rains through most of the summer and all through Christmas too; and you share your breakfast paella with a dozen other people. And computing has at last joined the other money-guzzlers as fair game for the accountants.

"Soon we'll be giving a computer away with every bit of software," said a man from one of the major hardware companies a few months ago. And there's the rub: software is crucial in any system; it's what makes the difference between having a computer and using it. Programming costs are people costs, people costs are rocketing, and software is representing an ever-increasing proportion of computer systems and what's more, software is never stable. Very few programs work immediately: they need testing and debugging. They are also expected to have a fairly long working life, which means modifications in the future—modifications to fit altered user requirements or a different hardware environment or merely to get improved performance out of the programs.

Software modifications are the hidden part of the software cost iceberg. It's impossible to forecast precisely what maintenance will be required, and so it is impossible to assess exactly how much a program will have cost by the time it has "passed on."

The designer must therefore cater for the likelihood of change, and the programmer must bear change in mind when he is writing the original code. So here are a few aphorisms for the office wall:

What can go wrong, will *go wrong.*

All programs will have to be changed some day.

Sooner or later someone else is going to have to understand the programs you write.

Programs must be written for people as well as for computers.

Knowing that a program can be understood and amended by someone else ought to be one of the programmer's criteria for success.

Programmers who write non-communicative programs should be drummed out of the profession.

Programming for maintenance should begin as soon as possible. The design team should be in a position to assess the consequences of changes during and after a project's life; and most of the considerations in programming for the likelihood of future maintenance are in any case desirable elements of programming practice.

Systems diagrams showing program and data flow are of course crucial at the design stage. They make for instant compatibility: everyone has the same framework to work in.

Glossaries are less usual but equally important. The design team should create—and keep up-to-date—glossaries of program names and data names. The program glossary will include a brief description of the system's software, which programs call others, which data they use, and the like. The data name glossary serves a similar function, describing data types and cross-referencing them to programs. Full data dictionaries indicating who is responsible for overseeing which data items may be required later and would be a development from the data glossary; as would a dictionary of buzz words, and abbreviations peculiar to the project.

The program listing is the maintenance programmer's main tool; bear him in mind. Layout is particularly important and you ought to take full advantage of the facilities in your compiler which give you the layout you want: blank lines, asterisks, indentation, and so on. Do that from the start, because you won't have the time or the inclination to improve the listing later— and when the thing is working, you won't dare alter it.

Comments on the code are the other important feature of the listing. Comments should never be written in afterwards as a translation into English of the code. They should give an account of your intentions, not of your actions: they should refer to the problem, not the code you used to solve it. The point is that comment should be an integral part of the program, saying *why* you do something and allowing the code itself to say *how*.

To illustrate this, consider a three-instruction code sequence:

```
LD   A, DEVSTAT   ;LOAD DEVSTAT
OR   A, X'08'     ;OR IN X'08'
ST   A, DEVSTAT   ;STORE DEVSTAT
```

A simple enough sequence—but the comments are devastatingly unhelpful, being merely a line-by-line repetition of the instructions.

```
LD   A,DEVSTAT   ;SET BIT X'08'
OR   A,X'08'     ;IN DEVSTAT
ST   A, DEVSTAT
```

Marginally better comments: at least they relate to what the sequence does. But still they give no indication of why the programmer did this.

```
LD   A, DEVSTAT   ;SET 'READER INOPERABLE'
OR   A, X'08'     ;CONDITION FLAG IN
ST   A, DEVSTAT   ;DEVICE STATUS WORD
```

And that tells us everything we need to know, why this code exists and what it does.

Glossaries are complementary to flowcharts: no confusing synonyms, no chance to overlook inter-program interactions.

Both must be maintained at all levels as the design work progresses into implementation. Also, compatibility must be maintained so that everyone involved is talking the same language—that means using the same specified flowcharting conventions.

Good coding means more than an elegant solution to the specified problem: it also means clarity. A program should be *seen* to work.

For instance, design open-endedly if you can. If your program is at all useful someone will want to expand it to do more than you originally intended. Design your modules and data areas so that they will fit anywhere in store: in this connection it might be worth using a good deal of indirect addressing.

Use equivalences where you can. If your present line printer prints 120 characters to a line, don't call the printer buffer area "120": next month the installation might get a 160 cpl printer—or worse, they might acquire one with 80 characters per line. Call the buffer "PWIDTH" or something, and equate it to 120 characters length for now.

Another example: if your program branches to a numeric offset relative to the current location, anyone amending or expanding the non-branch code is likely to overlook your statement. Thus JMP $+6 could easily be followed by more than five lines of code when someone has expanded it. Use symbolic names wherever possible—and make sure the same names appear in the flowcharts!

On the other hand, beware of duplications in names. The data and program name glossaries could be expanded to keep a running dictionary of what names have been used where, but the programmer can contribute by exercising some discipline over his naming. One solution is to prefix or suffix all names with a unique identifier—these base labels could be allocated by the project leader on a large job, but the same technique can usefully be applied within a program or a module by the single programmer.

But don't try too hard to make labels necessarily meaningful; you can't get much unambiguous meaning into a few characters, and you do have the facility for lengthy commenting to expand on what the label does mean.

Clarity should not suffer from your desire to save time or space. Where possible, programmers should avoid using the same variable for a variety of different purposes; and don't use a register to hold an intermediate result when doing so saves you a couple of code lines in storing it and fetching it back when you need it (after all, when your program crashes half-way through its run, you may want to be able to look at that value).

"Avoid unnecessary complexity" is probably the best advice any programmer can receive. Programmers often allow themselves to be seduced by the variety of constructions the language makes available to them. The result is code that is more opaque than necessary in order to achieve insignificant savings on run time or memory occupancy: if in the future someone else has to work through your code trying to understand it before amending some other part of the system, any such savings will be more than wiped out.

Always code in the simplest possible way. That might mean separating your program into paragraphs—sections that are not necessarily functionally separate modules. Break up long stretches of code with labels and/or comment: the reader who avoids mental indigestion may be you.

The programmer should take care to avoid conspiracies with other programs—in particular, he should be wary of using values generated by other programs in his own. One day someone will alter that program without realizing your reliance on it. The same applies to using idiosyncrasies of the operating system software: the next release of the machine's executive may have the bugs removed.

Comments may be tedious to write, but they don't add to the run time. So comment freely; not only on code lines, but also with introductory prose at the start of a program or subroutine to explain and identify what the code following will do. Header comments like this need be no more than two or three lines.

Interfaces to other programs or other modules should always be fully commented, particularly when there is a choice of exits from a subroutine.

If the flowchart method of pictorial representation is to be used as opposed to structured tables and similar alternatives then these should form the nucleus of the documentation handed over on completion. Flowchart diagrams must be tied layout-wise and label-wise to listings in such a way that following logic paths on both is a simple matter in the maintenance environment. Often complex logical or timing bugs cannot be found from listings alone and it will take flowcharts to show the true nature of erroneous actions of the programs. Furthermore, a professional standard of documentation must be given, especially where a client is paying for a system. Anything which does not fit into a properly indexed manual is a poor advertisement for your services.

Anyone receiving software should expect the majority of the following items in the total package: up-to-date systems specifications, program functional specifications, program implementation descriptions and instructions, the glossary of programs together with the cross-reference, the glossary of system data names which includes the programs which use them, an overall data flowchart, individual program flowcharts and data flowcharts, up-to-date source code listings showing how they were compiled and linked into the system, detailed instructions on how to create the system, operate it and use it, and a detailed list of all error reports and their meaning and an indication as to which part of the system generated them. Let the proverbial cigarette packet programmer try handing his system over to the well informed.

Programs do need maintaining, and everyone knows it. But maintenance is usually ignored completely in the development stage: at best it may be treated as a necessary evil for which no one wants responsibility.

Programming for maintenance is not difficult, and writing software to facilitate maintenance inevitably means better programming practice generally. In the end, everyone benefits.

AN ODE TO AN INDISPENSABLE MAN

Sometime, when you're feeling important,
Sometime, when your ego's in bloom,
Sometime, when you take it for granted
You're the best qualified in the room;
Sometime when you feel that your going
Would leave an unfillable hole,
Just follow this simple instruction
And see how it humbles your soul.
Take a bucket and fill it with water;
Put your hand in it, up to the wrist.
Pull it out and the hole that's remaining
Is the measure of how you'll be missed.
You may splash all you please when you enter,
You can stir up the water galore,
But stop, and you'll find in a minute
That it looks quite the same as before.
The moral in this quaint example
Is to do the best that you can.
Be proud of yourself, but remember—
There is no indispensable man.

—Anonymous

Found in *Towers Club, USA Newsletter,* September 1978. A publication for freelance writers, edited and published by Jerry Buchanan, Vancouver, Washington.

The Perfect Programmer

"No program is that perfect."
They said with a shrug.
"The client is happy—
What's one little bug?"

But he was determined.
The others went home.
He dug out the flow chart
Deserted, alone.

Night passed into morning.
The room was cluttered
With memory dumps, microfiche,
"I'm close," he muttered.

Chain smoking, cold coffee,
Logic, deduction.
I've got it," he cried, "Just
Change one instruction."

Then change two, then three more
As year followed year.
And strangers would comment.
"Is that guy still here?"

He died at the console
Of hunger and thirst.
Next day he was buried
Face down, nine edge first.

And his wife through her tears.
Accepted his fate.
Said, "He's not really gone,
He's just working late."

From *The Big Byte,* September 1976. A Pansophic Systems Inc. publication.

Section III

Management Considerations and Techniques

. . . I firmly believe that the maintainability of a system is a direct function of how well it was developed initially; the success of any maintenance effort is directly related to the management attitudes surrounding it. There really cannot be any useful prescription for maintaining inherently unmaintainable software in an environment which regards maintenance as a low-prestige, "dirty" activity.

Lois A. Rose
November 14, 1978

Maintenance Reviews and Management

Daniel P. Freedman and Gerald M. Weinberg

Our problem is that our old code is so bad that it wouldn't pass a maintenance review. If we start reviewing it, won't our maintenance programmers become aware of how bad it really is, thus leading to a revolt?

Although management may not be aware of the sorry state of existing code, it's doubtful whether the maintenance programmers are unaware. If a revolt comes, it won't be the introduction of reviews that causes it. What the review can do is make *management* more aware of the pitiful state of code under maintenance. With this information documented in the review reports, it will be harder for the ostrich-type manager's head to stay under the sand.

Suppose management becomes aware of the situation and wants to do something. In what ways can reviews help correct the poor situation we've gotten into over many years of non-reviewed maintenance?

There are 3 types of review that can help alleviate the situation of poor code from the past:

a. SIMPLE REVIEW OF NEW CHANGES. This review at least keeps the situation from getting worse—i.e., stops the polluting.

b. FIX-AND-IMPROVE REVIEW OF NEW CHANGES. This type of review provides a gradual improvement in old, bad code—i.e., removes the pollution.

c. SEPARATE PRODUCTION AND MAINTENANCE ACCEPTANCE REVIEWS. This separation of function stems the tide of nonmaintainable new work coming into maintenance.

What's a fix-and-improve review?

Instead of limiting the maintenance work to externally originated changes, the maintenance group undertakes to apply an old Boy Scout principle: Leave the product a bit better than you found it. In a fix-and-improve review, we add one question to the list of CORRECT, CONSOLIDATED, and CLEAN:

'd.' Does the proposed change leave the product easier to maintain in the future? In the words of the farmer, is it CULTIVATED? Successful farmers thoroughly understand the principle of cultivation. It's not enough to take crop after crop out of the ground. If you don't actively improve the soil, it inevitably grows worse. Programs may be exactly the same as soil, in which case passive correction will lead to depletion of maintainability. Since we can't be sure that a correction is entirely CLEAN, why not ensure cleanliness by leaving the product obviously CLEANER, more CULTIVATED, than it was before?

Each of these improvements must, of course, satisfy the other review criteria. The review committee must ask:

a. Does this change cultivate the program, leaving it better than before?

b. Does the attempt at cultivation create other problems?

If the answer to the first question is NO, then the product fails the IMPROVE criterion of the review. But if the second answer is YES, then the FIX requirement fails. We want positive side-effects, not negative ones.

One interesting side-effect of fix-and-improve reviews is the effect on the morale of the maintenance programmers. When some improvement is demanded along with the fix, the programmer can employ and demonstrate creative talents—talents which may have been long suppressed in the highly constrained maintenance environment. Thus, the fix-and-improve review not only improves a deteriorating product, it also improves a deteriorating staff.

Doesn't it cost a lot of time and effort to make these improvements? We can see that the fix-and-improve strategy might eventually pay off, but we really can't afford to increase present maintenance costs.

It's been our experience that it costs no more to make an improvement than not to make an improvement, as long as you keep the improvement under control by reviewing it. What you may lose in extra material to review, you gain in a cleaner product to review. Just be sure that the improvers realize that the improvement should be no bigger than the requested change. It may not seem like much, but the additive effect is tremendous.

What is meant by a separation of production and maintenance acceptance reviews?

As part of a program to ameliorate the maintenance situation, an obvious step is to put some maintenance programmers on reviews of new developments. (A not so obvious, but perhaps even more effective step is to put some development programmers on maintenance reviews, so they'll better understand what's going to happen to their products.) The people currently working on previously developed systems will undoubtedly have worthwhile contributions to make from the point of view of maintainability of the product.

If you do add maintenance programmers to a production review, you may find that a program is rejected by the committee on grounds of non-maintainability. If management didn't consider this a valid or important criticism in the past, the rejection may be disregarded in an effort to get a crucial job into production. But if management decides to accept a product which the review committee has judged unacceptable, the review process will soon become totally meaningless. Thus a conflict arises between timely production and proper maintainability.

Before reviews, the conflict existed but was hidden. Because it was hidden, it was always resolved in favor of early production and against maintainability, which is one reason maintenance is such a morass today. For a long time, we pleaded with managers to give more weight to maintainability in this argument, but we always lost to hard-nosed short-term practicality. Then, while sitting in yet another review where the production-maintenance conflict arose, we suddenly saw the resolution in a flash.

Whenever a piece of work changes hands, there should be some kind of review, though of course there may be other reviews when the work is not changing hands but only changing from one point in its life-cycle to another. What we had overlooked was that when a piece of work goes into production, there are, in certain installations, TWO changes of hands:

a. from development to operations
b. from development to maintenance

Just because those two changes happen at about the same time, there is no reason why they have to be tied together! If they are tied together, it will always be maintenance that drowns! Therefore, if we want to improve the situation in maintenance, we must institute two separate reviews, with two separate decisions.

One review assures the correctness of the code or other product, from the point of view of readiness to ship or put into production. The other review is conducted largely by maintenance people. At the end of the review, if the product is accepted, the maintenance people have assumed responsibility for keeping it up and running properly forevermore. If they don't accept it, however, the development team retains responsibility, until such time as they have managed to get it into acceptable shape, as certified by another review.

That won't work because our maintenance people will reject all work, just to make their jobs easier.

In practice, this prediction doesn't come true. To begin with, the maintenance people must have reasons for their conclusions. When they state explicitly what they find unacceptable about the product, the development people have the opportunity to improve the quality in these specific areas. Secondly, the review committee, properly constituted, will also contain non-maintenance people who can be expected to provide an unbiased view.

If a conflict does arise that can't be resolved by the technical people, then there is indeed an inherent conflict between the needs of development and maintenance. Such a contradiction cannot be resolved by technical people acting alone, but requires management decision. To take an analogous case, consider the purchase of any piece of capital equipment—a truck, say. If there is a choice between two trucks, the decision will rest on the relative costs of purchasing and operating the trucks. If truck A is both cheaper to buy and cheaper to maintain, then the decision over truck B is obvious. But if A is cheaper initially but costs more to keep running, then only management can decide how much present cost can be traded for how much future cost. It is not a technical decision. The role of the technical people is merely to supply accurate information on what the costs actually are, after which management must make a decision.

How can we tell management what the costs of maintenance are going to be?

Naturally, any statement about future maintenance costs will be statistical, but so will statements about additional development costs. Here are some questions we've found useful to ask in a maintenance review if there is some doubt about management's acceptance of a negative decision:

a. What is the probability that this code contains an error that will cost more than

1. $1,000	1. 1 person-week
2. $10,000	2. 10 person-weeks
3. $100,000	3. 100 person-weeks

to fix during its first three months of production running?

b. If a "typical" change in your installation takes 100 units of maintenance work (cost), how many units would such a typical change take in the code being reviewed? How much would a one-line change cost?

c. If a "typical" program in your installation has to be changed 100 times in a certain time period, how many times will this program have to be changed in that time period?

From these figures, management should be able to estimate what kind of costs they are committing to by sending the work into maintenance as is.

Those questions seem awfully subjective to me. How much faith can be placed in the answers the review committee comes up with?

It's true that the whole question of maintainability is harder to quantify, in advance, than some other review questions. When there is an error, there's not much controversy about its existence, but when someone says "a typical change to this program might cost 175 units" we are left with a wide margin for doubt.

Yet if you examine the statement about an error, you'll see that there's a lot of doubt there, too. Some errors cost millions if undetected, while others cost pennies or nothing at all. Consequently, a simple listing of errors contains an implicit statement that all are of equal importance, a statement which obviously isn't true. If we try to quantify the costs associated with the errors, we become just as subjective as when we try to quantify the costs associated with poorly maintainable code.

Once again, part of the problem comes from not having kept good records in the past. If we keep track of true maintenance costs in the future, we'll be able to compare them with what the reviewers predicted. Eventually, as this information feeds back into the review process, we'll find that we can make reliable estimates of code maintainability.

Should operations people be involved in maintenance reviews?

Several questions about maintainability impinge directly on operations, so if there are qualified technical people in operations, they should be invited to the maintenance reviews. And, of course, they should participate in the review that transfers development work into operations.

Worst First Maintenance

Gerald M. Weinberg

We work with computers. We are influenced by computers the way a pickle is influenced by brine. Sometimes we forget that a simple idea can be more powerful than a complicated one. If there were too many simple ideas, we might not need computers at all.

Take the greatest problem most installations face today. Ask anyone, "What is your greatest problem?" Seven out of ten will say "maintenance of old programs." The problem just keeps building, with all the force and inevitability of silt on the bottom of a glacial lake. Isn't there some way to dig ourselves out?

I contend there is. Using one simple idea, a dozen of our clients have found a way to halt, then reverse, the accumulation of maintenance problems. The idea is based on the observation that not all parts of a system, and not all systems, require the same amount of maintenance effort. There may be an 80/20 rule operating here, or a 90/10 rule. That is, 80% of your maintenance efforts may be directed at only 20% of your code. Or 90% to 10%. It does vary from place to place, but on one very large system we studied, the rule was 80/2—80% of the maintenance effort was devoted to just two percent of the system!

When we discovered this 80/2 figure, we saw an escape from the maintenance morass. A small redesign, redevelopment effort was mounted against that 2% of code. With an expenditure of a tiny fraction of the annual maintenance budget, we brought the ill-behaved 2% down to the level of the other code. After this improvement, 80% of the problems came from about 20% of the code, which was more reasonable. There was still room for improvement, but we had reduced the overall maintenance effort on this system by a factor of about 3.5 in less than one year.

Of course, it required a bit of an investment. And there was the risk that the new 2% wouldn't be any better than the old. It took some convincing to get authorization, because the general feeling was, as usual, "My God, don't touch the code! Especially not that code!" But when the first piece of the 2% was finished—one module of about 800 lines which accounted for almost 30% of the maintenance in the entire system—the rest of the work could be done with the initial savings.

For this "worst-first" approach to work, there are several factors that must be right:

1. You must have a way of accurately identifying the cost involved in maintaining each segment of the systems under maintenance.

2. You must be willing to invest some amount of effort to get the savings.

3. You must be able to produce better code now, with some reliability, than was produced in the worst few percent of your system at some time in the past.

The first step is crucial. Very few installations seem to know exactly what part is costing how much in maintenance. They seem afraid to find out. A smidgin of record-keeping is required, but it doesn't even have to be precise. Lacking this minimal information, it's not possible to make sensible management decisions about maintenance. With this information, the proper choice becomes obvious.

It should be easy enough to associate each piece of maintenance effort with a particular system or subsystem. If people don't want to record their time, try capturing the amount of recompilation time. This figure may give a pretty accurate first approximation with little or no burden on anyone. You may already have this information lying about in your accounting data, or it may be there on tape simply lacking an RPG program to extract it. The "worst" systems are usually so gross that it doesn't take a microscope to find them. In fact, you can probably do just as well by asking people, "What's your worst problem in maintenance?"

But merely asking isn't a very reliable basis for our second requirement—investing a little money. Management has a right to ask for hard figures—or at least plausible figures—to justify the expenditure of rebuilding the bad factors. This kind of justification will be especially necessary if it happens that the worst module was written by the present department manager, several years ago when he was one of the programmers. It can be hard to overcome this feeling of paternity, so get yourself well armed with facts and figures. Many of our clients, once they have the necessary figures in hand, are afraid to present them to management. Why? Because they aren't sure they can reliably do any better than the old system.

The other extreme also creates a problem—the programmers who haven't the least shadow of a doubt that they can do better than the old timers did. This kind of optimism, or arrogance, tends to irritate experienced managers. They've seen this attitude far too often in the past. And they've seen the resulting programs, which were worse than anyone ever imagined they could be. If you let the blind optimists have their way, you might come to appreciate that the old program isn't so bad after all. But most of those optimistic disasters arose from situations without hard data on how bad programs really were. If you really and truly identify the most costly programs, it's likely that you'll be able to improve them with a concentrated reconstruction effort.

Don't you believe this claim? You don't have to. The idea is valuable *even if you can't improve the worst program you have.* If your programming is that bad, your problem isn't maintenance, as you believed. Your problem goes much deeper, and that information alone should be worth the cost of one program.

But the claim is plausible. In the first place, it's always easier to write a program a second time, if only because you have so much test data and results to work toward. And, in our experience, when you rewrite your worst program from scratch, the errors you uncover will pay for the job, even if you throw the new version away.

The whole idea, then, turns on the concept of finding the worst program. To be more accurate, you must find the program with the most costly maintenance. It could be a fine, upstanding program, well designed and well coded. Because we lump so many activities under the single term, "maintenance," the source of the problem could be outside the program itself. The important principle is merely that if you attack your most costly problem, you're most likely to receive worthwhile savings.

In one instance, the most costly program turned out to be nicely structured and relatively easy to change. The user environment, however, was not what the program designer had anticipated. Most of the program's "constants" were, in fact, variables. Because they were coded into the program as constants, each change required a recompilation. And, because of the installation's standards, each recompilation required an extensive rerun of a library of test data.

Once the costly behavior was identified, the program was redesigned—not because the design was awful, but because the underlying assumptions had changed. The "constants" were made into tables, with a separate program ahead of each production run to update the tables used that day. The input to the table-builder was humanized to the point that the user himself could reliably create each day's changes and check their acceptance by the program. What had previously represented weekly maintenance now became no maintenance at all. The job that had previously accounted for some 16% of the maintenance budget now accounted for 0%!

To summarize: find out where you're spending your maintenance money. And don't put it off by complicating the idea. You don't need a computer program to tabulate the costs before you can start—that's just a delaying tactic. See what you can do with one good day's manual data gathering. If you like what you see, start a computer system in parallel. Or if you wish, wait until you've reduced the maintenance load and pay for the tabulation out of the savings. And don't stop at one. Once you get going, that's the time to set up a routine computer system to track maintenance costs. In the future, there will be no reason for you to get as far out of touch with maintenance realities as you are at present—unless you fail to maintain the maintenance report writer.

Managerial Tips, Techniques, and Guidelines for Program and System Maintenance

Girish Parikh

This chapter presents some managerial techniques of maintenance, since managerial functions are important to software maintenance.

Get familiar with the system and programs and maintenance problems. Probe the system to find out *what* it does. Study operations documents. Find out *what* each program in the system does. Summarize the findings for an overall *picture* of the system and programs, if not already done. Let the programmer solve *how,* but you, the manager, should generally know *what* and be able to communicate it.

A first-line manager can get a feeling of maintenance problems by working on a typical maintenance assignment occasionally. If this is not possible, he should work once in a while with one of the maintenance programmers. This does not show distrust of the programmer, but allows the manager to get the feeling of problems. It also familiarizes him with the process of maintenance, and the special problems associated with a particular system or program.

Keep a "program maintenance log"

Keep a "Program Maintenance Log" for each program. It should include for each change such information: program name, name of programmer who worked on it, date change made, short description of change, estimated and actual time spent on it, reason for the change, who requested it, when the change was made effective, any after-effects, approximate lines of code added/changed/deleted, other programs affected, and any other comments. An accurate log analyzed periodically gives valuable information about the maintenance activity. It also reveals where most of the maintenance effort is going, and thus indicates where redesign and recoding is needed in the system.[1]

Develop forms to record maintenance activities

The following forms can be developed to record different aspects of maintenance activities, depending on your requirements. The list is not complete.

1. Program change/enhancements request form
2. Program change/enhancements estimating form
3. Programmer performance sheet
4. Program/system discrepancy notice
5. Program maintenance log
6. Progress report form
7. Maintenance review (walkthrough) form
8. Documentation update checklist form

A few of the above forms may not be formally designed. The information is recorded on plain paper in free format in such cases. Include some specimens showing the typical information included and its format. Include sample, filled forms with description of each in the standards manual.

Managerial tips

1. Have an informal walkthrough with the programmer. Even if you're not technically oriented, you may find something that the programmer missed.
2. Enforce documentation standards and proper work methods. Systematic methods pay off in the long run. But "proper work methods" is a relative term. Discuss it with programmers.
3. Motivate and appreciate your programmers. Incentives could be pay raises, rewards, time off, bonus, education, conferences and seminars, etc.
4. Occasionally, give a new program (if there is one) to the maintenance programmer.
5. Remember: Problems in maintenance may be due to the past sins of management, possibly yours!

The topics in this chapter should set you thinking about possible improvements in your maintenance department. Thus you can make the burden of software maintenance a little lighter and increase maintenance programming productivity.

Notes

1 I'm grateful to Gerald M. Weinberg for pointing out this use of the log. He calls it "one of the most important maintenance ideas."

Selections from *Managing the Structured Techniques*

Edward Yourdon

Programmers are not very good at fixing bugs

Interestingly, if the programmer modifies *fewer* than five to ten lines of code in his attempt to correct the bug, his chances of success also drop—though only slightly. Although this might seem surprising at first, it probably can be explained by human psychology: One tends to be overconfident when changing a single line of code to correct a trivial bug. If the bug is serious enough to require several lines of code to be changed, one tends to be more careful.

Obviously, some of the problems associated with correcting bugs are *human* problems: keypunching errors, coding mistakes, psychological errors, and so forth. However, we are beginning to recognize that many problems are of a different sort: We may successfully fix a bug in subroutine X, only to find later (sometimes several *months* later) that the supposed fix has introduced a new bug in subroutine Y. This phenomenon is becoming more and more troublesome, particularly in regard to larger systems having many modules with which the programmer is unfamiliar. It is even more impossible for him to be aware of the subtle interactions between the modules.

Largely because of this problem, interest has grown in the techniques of structured design, which attempt to minimize the interdependencies between modules.

(P. 30)

Maintenance is becoming too expensive

A survey in the October 1972 issue of *EDP Analyzer* (Canning, 1972) indicated perhaps for the first time that most EDP organizations were spending about 50% of their budgets on maintenance. Since then, occasional articles in the literature and my own informal surveys have confirmed this rule of thumb. Indeed many large organizations spend 75% or even perhaps as much as 80% of their data processing budgets on maintaining existing systems.

Nobody is suggesting that maintenance could be eliminated altogether—but we *are* stating that 80%, or 75%, or even 50% is too much to be spending on existing programs. Why? Well, consider how we currently are spending our maintenance money:

1. ongoing debugging
2. changes required by new hardware, new versions of vendor operating systems, new compilers, and so on
3. expansions, changes, and new features requested by users

The first two points are possible to control. As suggested earlier, *any* money spent on debugging is too much. We should be able to code programs with virtually no bugs. Similarly, we should be able to write programs that can run essentially unchanged whenever the vendor upgrades his operating system or compiler. The fact that we spend a great deal of money in these two areas suggests there is a problem.

The third category in our maintenance list—new features for the user—never can be eliminated. (However, the cost for these changes could be minimized if our computer systems were easier to change.) A rule of thumb to follow in this case (but one that probably would be considered heresy by most programmers) is, if a modification or a new feature to a system can be explained easily by a user, then it *should* be easy to introduce into the computer system. If it is *not* easy, then the system probably was designed inadequately.

(Pp. 30–31)

Difficulty using structured programming in a maintenance environment

We observe that 50% (or more) of the data processing effort in many organizations today is maintenance—patching, correcting, and improving existing programs. Most, if not all, of these programs were written in an unstructured fashion. So what relevance does structured programming have in an environment like this?

Unfortunately, there are no magic answers to this problem. One can make a few common-sense suggestions: For example, the advantages of structured programming may influence an organization to rewrite an old application sooner than would have been politically possible otherwise. Also, if large chunks of code are to be changed or inserted into an existing program, it should be possible to do such work in a structured fashion.

A few organizations have toyed with the idea of a "structuring engine," a package that automatically converts an unstructured program into an equivalent structured program. Such an engine is theoretically possible (indeed, the original Böhm and Jacopini paper suggested the outlines of such an engine), and at least one software firm actually has developed such a package (de Balbine 1975). However, keep in mind that there are problems that arise in connection with this kind of package:

1. After five or ten years of maintaining a rotten old program, your maintenance programmers finally may *understand* it. A structuring engine would rearrange the code so that they probably wouldn't understand it any more.

2. A structuring engine usually is based on the assumption that the program obeys the legal syntax of the language. This is not always true, and is particularly invalid for those programs written in COBOL. Programmers have a way of using undocumented, illegal features of the language that shouldn't work, but *do.* A structuring engine would upset this delicate balance.

3. A structuring engine cannot transmute lead into gold. It cannot convert a truly bad program into a truly good program. It *can* eliminate the GOTO statements, and it may improve the organization of the procedural logic . . . but there always is the chance that it will do nothing more than transform a bad unstructured program into an equally bad structured program.

There also is another problem that you should anticipate: If you teach your maintenance programmers all about structured programming, they will become very frustrated if they are sent back to their department to continue patching unstructured rat's-nest code. It might be safer to leave your maintenance programmers in the dark. However, failing to teach maintenance programmers anything about structured programming leads to another problem: The first time they are given a *structured* program to maintain, they'll probably have a nervous fit. "What's this?" they'll ask. "Nested IF statements? And subroutine calls? My God! I can't read any of this!" Perhaps, you should teach them structured programming after all.

Keep one other thing in mind: The *first few* structured programs written by your development programmers actually may be a little difficult to maintain. As we suggested earlier, a structured GOTO-less program is not necessarily a *good* program; and until your programmers fully understand what they're doing, they actually may write some *bad* structured code. Your maintenance programmers certainly will let you know if that's the case, and you should listen to them.

(Pp. 131–133)

Maintenance problems

The final problem has been mentioned several times in the book: Even with all the new structured techniques, you still have to maintain the programming garbage accumulated over ten or twenty years.

I don't have to tell you how much fun it is to maintain an IBM 1401 AUTOCODER program on a 370/168, especially when the listing and the source program for the 1401 program were lost long ago, and all you have is a patched object module. Some organizations have *hundreds* of such rotten, old programs.

If you're one of those unlucky managers who is stuck with the maintenance of 1,000 man-years of unstructured code, there's not much I can do for you, other than offer you a lot of sympathy—and one last little bit of advice: If you don't start *now* to write your new systems in a structured fashion, you'll be in the same position ten years from now.

(P. 235)

Organized Program Maintenance

John W. Mooney

Planning, staffing, and organizing a completely new approach to program maintenance made 1973 a turnaround year in data processing for Spring Mills, Inc., a major Fort Mill, South Carolina, based textile manufacturer. Now, two years later, we have collected enough information to know that the approach we adopted was the right one.

Spring's Computer Information Services (CIS), based at the Company's Customer Service Center in Lancaster, South Carolina, was at that time operating 24 hours per day, 6 days per week, with an IBM MP/65 and over 3,000 productive programs written in COBOL, RPG, and BAL. Two 1401s and two 7070s were supported with an additional 800 productive programs each. In addition, thousands of frames of microfilm and microfiche were produced daily. And approximately 700 new programs were being placed into production each year. (No new programs were being written for the second generation equipment, and attrition was diminishing the number of old ones.)

No records were kept before 1972 to provide statistics relating to cost and effort, although deficiencies in new development were evident. New systems were implemented behind schedule and over budget. One or more programmers remained on the projects, often as long as six months, correcting and enhancing the systems to make them operational and acceptable to the users. This, then, affected manpower scheduling for systems waiting to be staffed and taxed the users' patience and confidence in data processing in general.

Records were compiled during 1972 showing where all efforts were expended, to determine what percentage of time was actually being devoted to new development and what was happening to the rest of the time. Efforts were categorized as: new development, maintenance, special projects, and administrative overhead.

Prior to 1973, CIS had no particular staff members assigned to maintenance. Instead, it was performed in conjunction with new development. No plans were made for servicing requests and no personnel were budgeted for performing this necessary and sometimes critical function. Therefore, in 1972, 30.1% of total programmer effort was spent in maintenance while only 45.2% went to new development. The remaining time went to special projects (10.5%) and administrative overhead (14.2%).

A few words of explanation are needed to clarify terminology. "Special projects," as defined by CIS means: "one time" programs, conversions from one language to another, and special reporting necessitated by wage and price controls. Maintenance falls into one of three categories:

1. Repair—correcting program deficiencies
2. Revisions—business or government oriented changes such as payroll changes, and changes to improve job or program efficiency
3. Enhancements—different reporting from or additions to existing systems

Repairs and revisions are performed on an "as needed" basis without regard to cost justification. The user submits a written request for an enhancement cost estimate. When he receives the estimate, he evaluates the cost versus the payback and benefits he expects to receive. If his findings are favorable he then submits a request to have the task performed.

Administrative overhead is defined as non-project oriented activities such as supervision, education, vacations, holidays, sick leave and other time off.

The 45.2% effort applied to new development sounded great, but we knew it could stand a lot of improvement. Not only were new and needed systems going undone, the 45.2% being developed was full of errors due to constant interruptions created by maintenance, thus compounding the maintenance problems. Maintained programs often required re-maintaining because programmers, in their haste to be rid of the burden, would neglect to upgrade documentation or ensure that only the correct version of the program remained in the libraries. With a staff of 40 programmers servicing between 70 and 80 requests each month, any type of control using this method of handling maintenance was impossible. At one point the test libraries contained more modules than the production libraries.

At the beginning of 1973, we created a maintenance team made up of a selected group of senior and junior programmers. A project manager was assigned to organize the team and operate as follows:

1. Prepare a log and record all requests in and out, by date, for control.
2. Evaluate each request for its severity and assign priorities.
3. Assign tasks to the programmers in the group.
4. Ensure standards were met and documentation upgraded.
5. Ensure that maintained programs were thoroughly tested before being placed in production.
6. Get programs back into production as expeditiously as possible.

Since maintenance has traditionally been regarded as distasteful and unrewarding, we braced ourselves for a mutiny or, at best, a slump in morale. To help ease the situation, certain promises were made to the personnel selected to serve in this area. They were assured that while serving on this team they would always receive the largest merit increase allowed by company policy. They were also assured that if they wished, they would be rotated out of maintenance after serving six months, without forfeiting the promised increase earned during their stay. It was also explained to them that this task was more important to the company than any other programming function. When the maintenance backlog permitted, members of the team were assigned one time special programs to write so they would be prepared to work on new development when they desired the change. (At this writing, I have received no request for rotation.)

Instead of the anticipated low morale problem, maintenance personnel accepted their new responsibilities as a challenge and a way of learning how *not* to write programs. Their morale has remained high; they offer suggestions of what not to do to new development personnel; and, they voluntarily arranged Saturday staffing among themselves which was not then one of their required duties. The team developed into multilingual experts capable of handling any program change or any abend. They take pride in their work and are respected by others and praised by management. They have offered many suggestions causing standards and documentation changes affecting program maintenance.

In 1973, this team serviced nearly 1,000 requests for revisions, enhancements, repairs, etc., while reducing the total maintenance percentage to 20.1%, allowing new development to reach an all time Springs Mills high of 57.9%. This amounted to a 10% decrease in maintenance effort and a 12.7% increase in new development. (The additional 2.7% difference occurred in administrative overhead and special projects.)

The fact that new development personnel were concerned with only new development and the maintenance staff concerned only with maintenance seemed to have a positive affect on morale within the programming department. The newly developed systems went in on time, under budget, and operational. Programmer turnover for 1973 averaged 9.3%.

In 1973, we were staffed with 40 programmers, of which 10 were assigned to the maintenance team. New projects made it necessary to increase the staff to 44 early in 1974, but none were added to the maintenance group. The turnover rate for 1974 settled out at about 11.3%. Five programmers left the company; but none left from the team. So far, no one on the team has even asked to be reassigned.

In 1974, maintenance ran 20.2% of total effort, a marginal increase of 0.1% over 1973. There are now eight programmers in maintenance; two were placed on new development projects in July (and *objected* to the move).

The computer department is replacing its old configuration of hardware with two 370/158s. Springs Mills Management is pleased that more effort is now going into new development, and we are constantly looking for ways to improve what we already have. For example, a programmer implementing a program change rarely knows the effect the change could have in succeeding jobs or systems. Consequently, one systems analyst has been assigned to the team to research changes when dependencies are not known.

Now all new programs are implemented with the possibilities of future maintenance in mind. New systems undergo a rigid review prior to the detail design stage. Reviews, presented by the senior systems analyst, are attended by the CIS Director, a data processing auditor, the managers of Program Development,

Systems Development. Technical Support, and Operations, and the senior programmer that will be assigned to the project. An attempt is made, by all persons involved, to pick holes in the system or discover loose ends or uncertainties. Once the system appears sound, the analyst reviews the system with the user. At that time the user accepts or rejects the system.

When a system design is accepted by the user, program estimating is done, schedules established and program specifications are begun. All program specifications are edited and reviewed by a senior analyst or project manager before being accepted by the programming staff. Edit program specifications are further reviewed by a programming project manager for completeness and clarity.

At implementation, all programs are thoroughly examined for adherence to standards before being approved for production. All programs must be modularly constructed with clear and meaningful notes explaining the purpose of each module. Program options, constants, tables, etc. must be external to a program to reduce future program changes. Programs, particularly edits, must produce a program control summary accounting for records in, records out, number and type of errors produced on error lists, money and/or quantity amounts.

If all programs meet standards the system is given a shakedown run by the development team and an operations analyst where operator instructions and other such considerations are reviewed. If the system passes these rigid examinations it is then classified as productive; however, all new programs must run productively and trouble free for a 90 day period before they become the responsibility of the maintenance team.

In addition to all previously mentioned checks and examinations systems that programs must pass, our data processing auditors periodically pull documentation folders from the library and audit either an individual program or an entire system. Their role is to ensure that the system complies with the user's accepted goals, that users get what they need, and that what they get is accurate. Often the auditors recommend certain changes that can further benefit the user or make maintenance easier.

Springs places a lot of emphasis on reducing future maintenance. With the number of new producing programs being implemented yearly, surely the percentage of total effort spent on maintenance must grow accordingly. We realize of course that certain kinds of maintenance must always be performed—our objective is to minimize the effort. Consequently, it is evident that no matter what we do nor how sophisticated our systems or installations become, maintenance is a fact of everyday life, it is expensive, and it is here to stay. Therefore, it is something that must be planned, staffed, and above all "organized."

Scheduled Program Maintenance

W. Mike Lindhorst

Last year The Boatmen's National Bank embarked on several courses of action designed to directly or indirectly help control the rising costs of programming. Among the steps taken were the establishment of: a workable, meaningful project control system; a systems and programming control function to set and enforce systems and programming standards; and a scheduled maintenance policy.

It is this last concept, that of scheduled maintenance, that I would like to discuss in this article.

Scheduled maintenance is the policy whereby maintenance for each installed application, instead of being performed continually as each maintenance request is received, is deferred until a predetermined month or months when all maintenance changes for that application are performed. For example, our Demand Deposit Accounting (DDA) system is scheduled for maintenance in February and August.

All maintenance requests for DDA received from February through July, whether they be for a simple report heading change or for an entire new report, are held until July before being considered for implementation. In July a consolidated list of all requests received for the application is sent to the head of the user department responsible for the application. Additions, deletions, and or changes to the list may be suggested at this time by the user department. The adjusted list is then reviewed jointly by the user department and the data processing department, and a final change request list is prepared.

A feasibility study is then performed for each item or group of items on the list to determine the cost of the changes. These feasibility studies are presented to the user department. If the user department agrees to pay for the changes, and the data processing department concurs in the advisability of the changes, they are implemented. The cycle then repeats for the next six-month period.

The benefits of this scheduled maintenance policy are as follows:

1. *Consolidation of requests.* Under scheduled maintenance it is possible to consolidate requests for changes that pertain to a single program or a series of programs. Over a six-month period it is quite possible that more than one request for change to a particular program may be received. By consolidating changes, a source deck must be retrieved only once (rather than multiple times), the program

can be tested only once, cataloging must take place only once, and documentation updated only once.

A basic efficiency results also because the cost of the general familiarization required of a maintenance programmer before he makes a change is spread over all the changes in a given batch. As a result of these consolidations, the cost per change goes down. This can enable justification of changes that, looked at individually, may not be justified. For instance, if you have to go into a program and add, say, a total figure, it takes little additional effort to interject a desired heading change.

2. *Programmer job enrichment.* A particular programmer will no longer need to be dedicated almost full time to a particular application. Since changes to any application occur at most once every six months, during an application's off months a programmer will become involved in other applications. This enriches the programmer's job and broadens his experience.

3. *Forces user department to think more about the changes they are requesting.* The individual who requested the change, when given a period of time to consider his request, may feel that it is not really as necessary as he first believed. This is especially true when he sees the cost of the change. Also, a change in circumstance in the user department may negate the need for what was a short time ago a legitimate request.

4. *Periodic application evaluation.* Under scheduled maintenance, the data processing department and the user department are forced to periodically step back and look at the maintenance cost of each application. These figures are helpful in determining where an application is in its life cycle and when a replacement system should be considered.

5. *Elimination of the "squeaky wheel syndrome."* Under scheduled maintenance, all applications are given the same degree of emphasis. For example, maintenance of the Certificate of Deposit system is not held up because someone feels DDA maintenance is more important. There are no "pet" applications within the department. All systems are handled in their preassigned months regardless of how much pressure is brought to bear by one user department.

6. *Programmer back-up.* With scheduled maintenance, in-house back-up programming knowledge will develop automatically for each application. It has been our experience that during an application's maintenance month the number of changes will often exceed the number that can be handled by a single programmer. Hence more than one programmer will become involved in each application.

7. *Better planning.* Scheduled maintenance allows data processing management to plan more effectively. We now know what applications will be maintained in which months and we can plan vacations, education, and other projects around this schedule. We hope, in the near future, to establish a "standard" maintenance manpower load by month. This will enable us to determine what staffing level would be needed to make available any given number of man-hours for new projects. Also, the planning burden on the data processing department is eased because it is no longer necessary to prioritize maintenance projects. They are automatically prioritized by the maintenance schedule.

8. *Data Processing change requests are regarded as being as important as user requests.* Data processing department requests pertaining to an application (such as adding date checking of files within an application, or reblocking application files for processing efficiency) are handled right along with the user requests during an application's maintenance month. They do not sit undone for an extended period of time because of the crush of user requests.

Another portion of the scheduled maintenance policy pertains to the installation of new applications. It states simply that new applications or newly developed subsystems of an existing application will not be modified until six months after installation. This forces the user department to work with a new system for a period of time rather than rush into an immediate flurry of change requests. It also prevents the acquisition of a package that only approximates what is really needed. The user department knows that if they buy a package, they will have to live with it as is for at least six months.

We have identified the need for certain exceptions to our scheduled maintenance policy. Changes are made to an application out of its regularly scheduled maintenance months in the case of: problems which prohibit running the particular system; requests which are approved by the president and chief operating officer of the bank; requests which are required by regulatory authorities; requests from paying customers agreed upon by the senior vice president in charge of banking service and the head of the data processing department.

Scheduled maintenance is a concept that must first be sold to upper management, and then presented to the user departments by upper management. Without this involvement from above, the data processing department would be incapable of enforcing such a policy. In our case, the concept of scheduled maintenance, and the strict adherence to it that was expected, was presented by our bank president to the assembled heads of our user departments in April of 1972. We have been on scheduled maintenance ever since.

Our experience with scheduled maintenance has, overall, been very rewarding. We feel that we have achieved much along the lines of the eight benefits previously mentioned.

There were, however, several problems that we ran into in implementing the policy. We did not notice, for instance, that at the time the application schedule was prepared we had placed too many assembler language applications in certain months. Not all of our programmers know assembler language, and we found ourselves in a position of not being able to assign the necessary work because of the language requirement even though programmers were available. We remedied the problem with assembler language education for certain of our programmers.

We also had a problem initially in phasing into scheduled maintenance because of all the projects that were active in April that we could not simply abandon. The scheduled maintenance pattern became more and more apparent only after a month passed and the residue of pre-"scheduled maintenance" projects disappeared.

Another problem revolved around the non-application related data processing projects (for example, the running of certain benchmark tests). We were so intent on making scheduled maintenance work, and we put such an emphasis on it, that data processing projects not relating to a particular application were, for a time, overlooked. All of these problems have now been resolved.

We have found that in the great majority of cases maintenance changes *can indeed* wait until the scheduled month. Our biggest problem in this regard has been the payroll application. We perform payroll processing for numerous corporations and banks, and as a result necessary modification and or addition of state tax routines has been rather frequent.

One of the questions we asked ourselves when we were beginning scheduled maintenance was: "Would the number of maintenance requests drop as we entered the second cycle of maintenance for each application?" Based on the first five applications that have entered their second cycle of maintenance, the total number of projects dropped from 45 requests (first cycle) to 21 requests (second cycle). In fairness it should be mentioned that we entered scheduled maintenance with a huge backlog of requests, so not all of this reduction can be attributed to scheduled maintenance.

In conclusion, I would recommend that you consider whether or not a scheduled maintenance policy would be applicable and beneficial to your organization. I sincerely believe that the potential benefits of consolidation of requests, programmer job enrichment, forcing the user department to think more about requested changes, periodic application evaluation, equal consideration to requests of all user departments, development of programmer back-up, better planning, and the assurance that data processing change requests will be handled at the same time as user requests warrant giving scheduled maintenance serious consideration. We at Boatmen's feel that it has been a significant step in our efforts to control the rising costs of programming.

Computer Systems Maintenance

Robert Riggs

In an era of exciting new developments in computer systems, data communications, and sophisticated new hardware and software, it isn't surprising that very little is said or written concerning the maintenance of 2-to-10-year-old conventional batch sequential systems that have been paying the data processing bill for these many years. These are the systems that grind through the day-to-day transactions of the business such as payroll, accounts payable, accounts receivable, billing, cost distribution, etc. In the process of being "liberated," "converted," or "recorded" several times in the past few years as we have shuffled them from one computer to another, the programs have been changed, improved, and extended to the point that they are as sensitive to the touch as a defective bomb fuse—one false move and the whole system blows. Systems analysts, programmers, and particularly the manager of systems and programming are rightfully concerned when approaching these systems. They are usually of first generation design running in emulation mode, or some equally unsatisfactory approach on third generation computers. The manager of the computer operations is even more concerned over the condition of these systems because he never knows whether or not he can meet the production schedule.

This paper will discuss what can or should be done to control and improve the maintenance of these systems.

Before proceeding it may be well to describe systems maintenance in the context used here. Systems maintenance, as I use the term, is the activity associated with keeping operational computer systems continuously in time with the requirements of users, data processing operations, associated clerical functions, and external demands from governmental and other agencies.

Usually, systems that have been around for a while constitute a fairly large segment of computer room production. Maintenance of these systems represents a very significant demand on the systems and programming resources—possibly as high as 40% to 60% for most companies who have had a computer systems effort for a number of years. Why, under these circumstances, do we hear so little about systems maintenance? One reason is that few companies recognize the existence of systems maintenance through formal organization. Organization planners for data processing, systems design, and programming will go to any lengths to avoid the grim truth. The usual argument heard whispered at professional associations and other gatherings is that systems and programming personnel would quit or otherwise refuse to work in "maintenance." This attitude casts a second class citizen connotation over the systems maintenance function. So management drives maintenance underground. They will call it by many names but never identify the work for what it really is. They will organize their systems and programming groups functionally, or by product line, or by division or group, but rarely establish an organization component designated "systems maintenance." Yet any systems analyst or programmer knows whether he is working in maintenance or new systems development. No one who knows the business is fooled by calling maintenance by another name. I subscribe to the thesis that it is far better to delineate the systems maintenance function and properly staff it than to drive it underground by acting as though it doesn't exist. Not all systems analysts and programmers insist on working on the sophisticated new systems, though admittedly a great many do. The answer is to sort out the personnel between those who do and those who don't. Often the best approach is direct—ask a programmer which type of work he prefers. Careful observation of the programmer at work will sometimes provide a clue to who will gain more job satisfaction in maintenance versus original programming.

The systems and programming activities associated with maintenance can be exciting and challenging. Certainly these computer systems are dynamic. They change and they are constantly evolving. A good maintenance programmer is a highly skilled professional. He is a brilliant diagnostician and responds enthusiastically to the "factory floor" crisis in the computer room 24 hours a day, seven days a week. The payroll is due out tomorrow and the system hangs on the seventeenth program in a 20-program string. The problem may or may not be in program 17. But it is the maintenance programmer's job to find out exactly what the problem is, often among a maze of thousands of computer instructions. It may be a unique condition of input, which suddenly appears after five years of daily operation. Or it may be a hardware failure or a combination of both. Nearly all major industrial corporations are dependent upon their computers for support of the main stream of corporate record keeping. In these circumstances, good maintenance programming support is indispensable—a vital link between the computer and the customer or user or management or all three.

Maintenance programming can be more varied, more professionally demanding, and more important than any other programming assignment. Also, the relatively short time for any given assignment provides a fast turnaround to begin a new task, so the satisfaction and recognition of finishing a job and doing it well comes often.

There are three major steps required to establish a systems maintenance function: 1) completely document all systems and programs currently in production, 2) establish a log of maintenance activity, and 3) organize. I mention good documentation as the first requirement because of its overriding importance. If you run a sloppy systems and programming shop, you might as well forget the organization and management of a systems maintenance group and just hope that the authors stay around. In fact, a very high percentage of production programs must be maintained by a programmer other than the original author. Failure to complete good documentation puts you in a vicious, never ending circle of crises.

The next step which can be taken concurrently with cleaning up the documentation is to establish a maintenance log. The requirements for system maintenance support are directly related to the number of requests for changes received by the system and programming group. The number of requests and the time required to service each is closely related to the types of systems in production, the number of programs in the library, the condition of documentation, and the quality of the programming staff. The maintenance log is the only really effective means of finding out what is happening. Each request for maintenance work should be logged in and show who requested the work; a definitive statement of the problem; an estimate of the number of man-hours or days required to make the change; the name of the programmer assigned; date the request was received; date of completion; and, actual man-hours or days spent on the job. Gathering this type of information over a representative period of time will begin to show what is happening to the resources of the systems and programming group. This log of systems maintenance activity can be the basis for organization planning, allocation of manpower, and day-to-day control of computer systems maintenance work. Since maintenance of existing computer systems is a vitally important responsibility of the computer systems group, an understanding of what is really happening is essential to the effective management of the function. When the basis for analysis has been established and the systems group organized to effectively handle maintenance, the systems and programming manager will have at least part of the answer to the perennial question from his management of what all those analysts and programmers are doing.

The organization alignment of the systems maintenance group could fit into the over-all edp organization with the manager of systems maintenance as one of four key managers in the total edp function.

A brief review of the functions of the three maintenance groups may be of interest. Contrary to popular opinion there is a good deal of systems analysis and evaluation work required of a well-managed maintenance group. The customer or client does not always know exactly what he wants, and would not know how to go about getting it if he did. The systems and evaluation group, within systems maintenance, should work with the user to determine exactly what is wanted, and, based on a knowledge of computer systems in general and the application involved in particular, devise the most economical and practical approach to satisfy the request. There is also a need to do some limited economic evaluation of requests for system changes. In some cases it would be far more economical and sensible to obtain the information manually or by some other means. The systems maintenance group must be constantly on guard against the tendency to dissipate systems and programming resources by frittering away manpower and computer time doing things by computer that should be done some other way. Thus the systems analysis and evaluation group plays an important role in the effective utilization of system resources. Also, this group would formalize specifications for systems maintenance requests. Failure to insist on good specifications covering systems maintenance requests has cost many companies significant amounts of money as well as wasted manpower. Without good specifications agreed to by the user, the job will take much more time to complete, because the programmer will start over or patch what he has already done as the specifications "evolve." Specifications should not be allowed to evolve. They should be established precisely and formally, and then, and only then, should work begin to program the change.

In order to control the flow of work, meet commitments, and provide excellent service to all clients or users of edp systems, the manager of systems maintenance must have good statistics and good library control. He needs statistics to measure work loads and allocate manpower. He needs library control procedures to assure the quality of the systems and programming documentation, both at time of entry into the library and as systems changes are implemented. The statistics required by the statistics and library control group come from the maintenance log referred to above and from data describing the program library, such as the number of programs in production, language used, and core requirements (an indication of complexity). These kinds of data should be kept current at all times.

Library control procedures include: 1) a set of standards for both systems and programming documentation; 2) a procedure for securing approval from data processing operations, client user, and the maintenance manager, before a new system is transferred from new systems development to a production and maintenance status. Data processing operations should "sign off" with respect to the operational documentation and day-to-day performance of the system. The client or user should sign off that he is satisfied with the over-all effectiveness of the system and that it produces what is needed in a smooth and efficient manner. The maintenance manager should sign off to show his acceptance of both systems and programming documentation. It should be his responsibility that documentation standards are met and he should have final responsibility for accepting the new system on a maintenance basis. Unless the maintenance manager is satisfied that all requirements for transfer to a maintenance status have been met, responsibility for the system should remain with the new systems development staff.

The programming group within systems maintenance carries the actual programming responsibility for specifications established by the systems analysis and evaluation group. These are the versatile, flexible "pros" who know how to make computers hum. They are experienced in several languages, have good diagnostic abilities, and are the self-starters. They are problem solvers—the backbone of good systems maintenance.

The suggested organization is appropriate to a fairly large systems and data processing function. However, the principles of organization, separation of functions, and assignment of responsibilities apply to smaller companies.

The executive to whom the edp function directed reports is looking for better methods of control and management. As these top executives increase their interest and concern, they will come to realize that management of the company's edp resources is subject to essentially the same management methods which enable them to understand, control and measure the performance of other functional groups. Computer systems and programming activities are not a black art. As in any emerging technology, there are new words and terms being devised to enhance communications among the practitioners. The challenge lies in management looking beyond these new terms and understanding what is going on in the context of traditional management methods. When management achieves this understanding, the systems and programming manager who has failed to think through the problems of computer systems maintenance—and provide the necessary organization, manpower and professional environment to effectively manage this vital function—will find himself continuously, tragically on the defensive with top management. Current failures are contributing to a growing awareness on the part of top management that something must be done about edp systems maintenance.

Experience with Centralized Maintenance of a Large Application System

Stephen K. Stearns

Abstract

Bell Laboratories is developing and installing Business Information Systems in the Bell System operating telephone companies. Centralized maintenance of these large software systems is provided from Bell Laboratories' Piscataway, New Jersey, installation. This paper describes experience gained over the past three years in maintaining an inventory control system, PICS. This experience is applicable to any large software system.

Once a large software system is designed and installed in an Operating Telephone Company environment, Bell Laboratories' involvement does not end. Maintenance, defined as changes and consultation to keep a system functioning satisfactorily, is required for the lifetime of the system. Rather than provide on-site assistance to all Bell System companies, Bell Labs has successfully established centralized maintenance entities for each software product it installs. Staffed with sufficient expertise and testing facilities to duplicate and solve most problems encountered, the Maintenance Control Centers (MCCs) provide total system support to each company.

A single MCC exists for each Business Information System product. To illustrate the concept of centralized maintenance embodied in the MCCs, the operation and evaluation of one will be described. Allowing for minor variation in internal procedures, each MCC is similar. This paper will focus on the one supporting the Plug-in Inventory Control System or PICS.

PICS is designed to provide total inventory control of plug-in equipment within each company. It consists of both batch and on-line teleprocessing portions executing on IBM hardware. The Hyper-FASTER teleprocessing monitor and the AMIGOS access method (both developed and marketed by COMRESS, INC.) are used to support on-line PICS which consists of about 200 programs available to clerical and supervisory staffs for inventory and accounting control. About 300 COBOL programs may be executed in batch mode to provide accounting reconciliation, scheduled investment and inventory reports, and requested management reports. See figure 1.

	On-Line	Batch
Programs	207	314
Source Statements	52K	228K
Object Code	1.6M bytes	6.8M bytes

Figure 1. PICS Program Size Summary

Both on-line and batch programs are supported by extensive user documentation. PICS has been installed and is operating in eight companies as of February 1, 1975. Five additional installations are scheduled for 1975.

To maintain this growing number of users, the PICS Maintenance Control Center was created two and a half years ago at Bell Laboratories' Raritan River location in central New Jersey. The MCC is staffed by people familiar with on-line and batch programs, documentation, Hyper-FASTER, AMIGOS, and IBM systems. The MCC provides 12 hour per day coverage for on-line PICS applications and is on call for batch troubles out of hours. Testing facilities have been provided to ensure that almost any problem encountered by a user can be duplicated at the MCC. While the Bell Laboratories location is a virtual operating system shop, OS can easily be put up should the severity of a problem so dictate. OS and VS system support is provided through the MCC to handle difficulties that might be unique to a user's environment. Similar support for new hardware devices and features is provided.

The ability to quickly diagnose and correct severe system problems is highly dependent on communications facilities. In addition to several telephone lines available over commercial networks, a high speed data transmission facility links each user site to the Bell Labs MCC. This 50 KB line is used for receiving core dumps and data base files and for transmitting new program modules. For those rare cases when data or system dependencies preclude duplication of a problem at the MCC, dial-up terminal arrangements allow the MCC staff to directly access an ailing PICS system. Normal safeguards and security are built in to dial-up facilities to give each user complete control over its data base.

The PICS MCC cannot function effectively without local support at each company. While maintenance is centralized, this in no way absolves the company's computer system personnel from providing a high degree of user support. Three areas of knowledge and expertise—application, computer operation, and system support—must be available in a local MCC before the centralized maintenance concept can work. When a local MCC organization can successfully serve as a buffer between PICS users and the Bell Labs MCC, then the ability to support an installation is measurably increased.

The flow of a maintenance request provides a good illustration of how centralized maintenance functions. A problem is generally identified by a PICS user in a company. Once the problem has been identified, it is forwarded to the local MCC and transmitted to Bell Labs via a telephone call. The PICS Maintenance Control Center then proceeds to assign a unique control number to the maintenance request for future reference. The MCC may request additional information about the problem in the form of a core dump or an entire reference file. These are transmitted via the 50 KB data line.

The majority of these requests are concerned with the software system; few maintenance requests are received for the documentation portion of PICS. See figure 2.

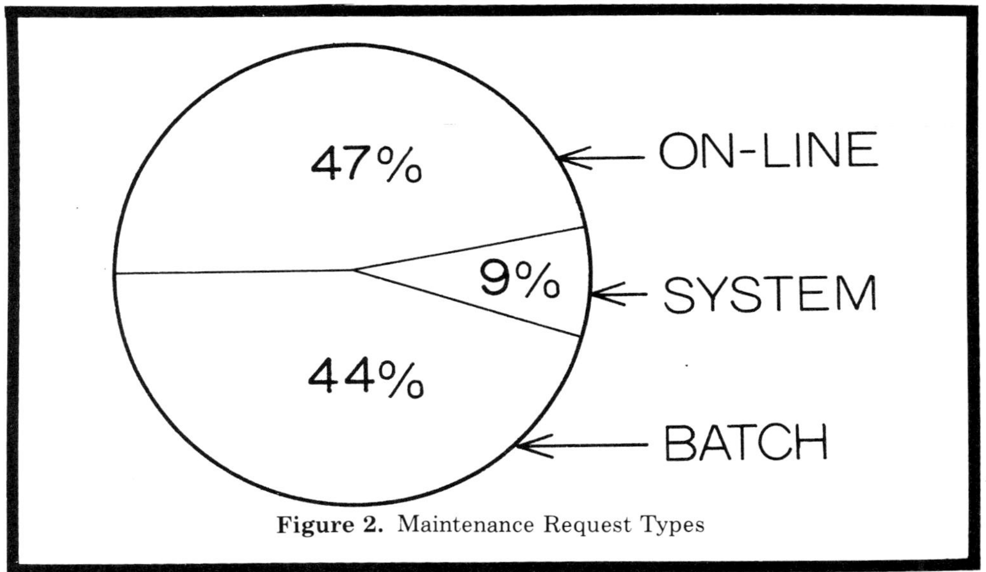

Figure 2. Maintenance Request Types

Figure 2 illustrates the types of software maintenance requests. The Maintenance Control Center next analyzes the request. Approximately 85% of all requests are handled internally by the MCC. Also available, however, are the services of a maintenance group composed of the remainder of the PICS Department, related Bell Labs Departments, and outside vendors such as IBM, the hardware supplier, and COMRESS, the software house which maintains the teleprocessing monitor. Regardless of who provides it, a fix for the original problem is produced. This fix must then be tested to verify its correct operation. An attempt is made during testing to simulate, as closely as possible, the data base environment in which the fix will ultimately reside. A generalized test data universe has been established for this purpose. The fix is then included in a release package which also may contain any updated documentation required and instructions to the company for its installation. The software portion of this release package is transmitted to the local MCC via the 50 KB data line. Any documentary portions of the package are mailed. Once the local MCC has received the entire package, it may then coordinate the installation of the fix. The maintenance request is not closed until the originating user has confirmed that the problem has been resolved to his satisfaction. When verified, the maintenance request may be cleared by verbal confirmation. The MCC is then free to provide this fix to other companies either immediately or in a periodic maintenance release.

To better schedule resources, a severity code structure ranging from 1 to 4 has been defined to apply to all Business Information Systems. This code assigns a high priority (Severity 1) to those problems that cause a total disruption and a low priority (Severity 4) to minor problems and requests for system enhancement to accommodate local practices. Less severe program bugs are assigned between these two extremes. Users are most concerned with response to these problems. Turnaround, defined as the elapsed time from receipt of a maintenance request to its clearance by the user, varies from five hours (average) for Severity 1 to seven weeks (average) for Severity 4. Because of the nature of a Severity 1 trouble, the MCC is prepared to work around the clock until resolution is achieved.

Handling of maintenance requests in this manner is not without problems. Often a lack of thorough knowledge about PICS results in a hand-holding type of maintenance. Here, the system is performing exactly as designed but a user's misunderstanding about its capabilities often requires extensive telephone consultation. A large amount of time (three to four hours per maintenance request is common) is also spent in analysis to simply determine that no real problem exists. Such non-problems account for a large drain on an MCC's resources. Misunderstanding the system can also lead to a more damaging situation: misleading information. When a set of trouble symptoms is incorrectly or incompletely reported to the MCC, considerable time and effort are expended chasing the problem. Unfortunately, for systems as complex as PICS, it is quite easy to dismiss as insignificant (or overlook entirely) the key symptom of a problem. Finally, with a large system completely down, data base integrity unknown, and as many as 80–100 users suddenly idle, there is a strong urge to escalate the call for help to demand immediate on-site support. It is usually more efficient to analyze the problem at the MCC where all of the test facilities and system expertise are located. Only when a severe problem cannot be duplicated should consideration be given to an on-site visit for support.

It should not be construed that the only difficulties in providing centralized maintenance occur at the company interface. Simply coping with the monthly volume of maintenance requests is a time-consuming job.

Figure 3 illustrates a typical company's maintenance request submission profile. Soon after installation, Bell Laboratories' representatives assist a company in initiating PICS operation. During this period of learning, many maintenance requests are generated, a large percentage of which reflect inadequate knowledge of the system. The submission rate declines sharply as the users settle into a routine. With increased familiarity, the rate begins to slowly rise again as a result of enhancements which are provided for a dynamic system such as PICS. A static system, with few or no modifications, would eventually become relatively trouble-free reflecting only problems caused by hardware or operating system changes.

The average total volume has risen from 15 requests per month from two

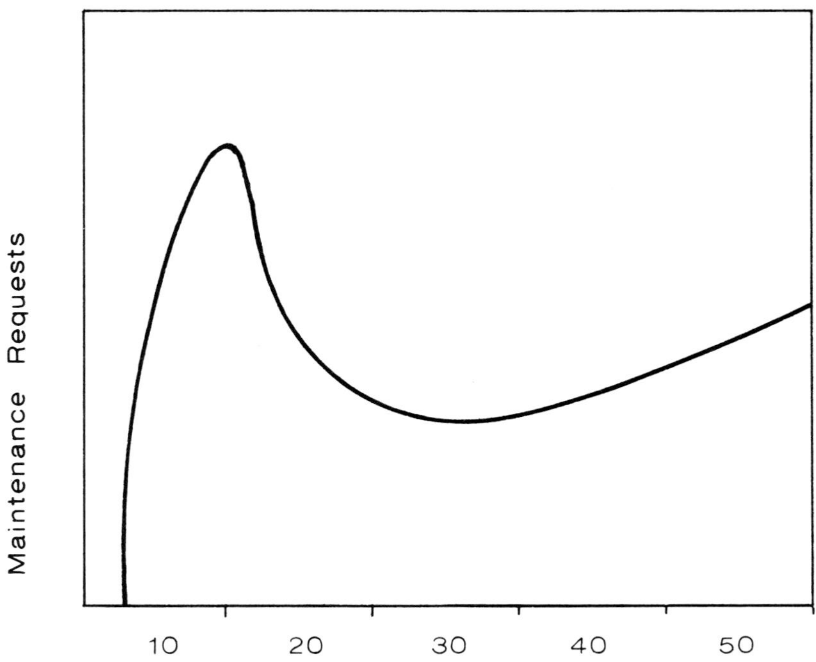

Figure 3. Maintenance Request Submission Profile

companies in 1973 to 40 per month from eight companies (see figure 4). Increases in January, September and November, 1973, and May, 1974 correspond to system installations and subsequent use by new companies. Volume will probably reach 60 per month by the end of 1975 when 13 companies are on-line. Such growth is predictable and can be accommodated through proper planning. Much less predictable (and unexplainable to date) is the monthly variance in volume. With an MCC staff geared for 40 requests per month, an input surge often requires that a choice be made between beginning work on two different problems of equal severity. Care must then be taken to adequately judge the impact of the problems on PICS operation.

Another phenomenon that must be coped with is the propensity of high-runner programs to incur maintenance requests. Especially apparent in on-line programs (figure 5), this is due to bugs being introduced with improved or enhanced versions designed to increase usage even more. Hence, a cycle results that is difficult to control, but can be alleviated through increased testing of new releases.

Testing cannot be stressed too much. In a serious maintenance situation, there is a tendency to "fix" the bug and release the new version immediately. Control must be exercised to avoid this by ensuring adequate testing to prevent other, new, problems from being introduced. Implicit in figure 5, once the high-runner programs

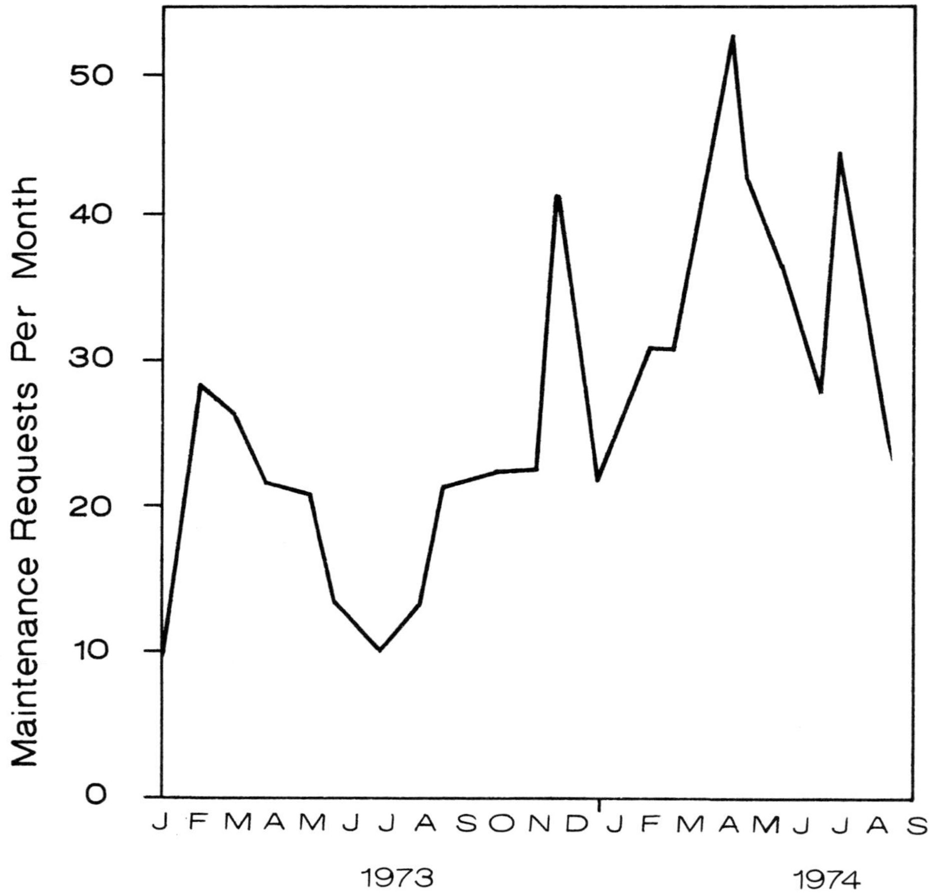

Figure 4. Maintenance Request Volume

are omitted, is a maintenance requests to on-line programs ratio less than one. Stringent pre-release testing permits the MCC to boast of on-line programs for which maintenance has never been requested. A similar situation exists for batch.

The various MCCs serving PICS and other Bell Labs Business Information Systems are functioning. Maintenance request volume and clearances, turnaround time, and user acceptance support the basic concept of centralized maintenance. The Bell Laboratories staff providing maintenance for PICS is a small fraction of the personnel that would be required for individual on-site support. While some expansion will be required to meet new installation commitments as more telephone companies join the ranks of Business Information System users, centralized maintenance will continue to be an efficient, preferable mode of operation.

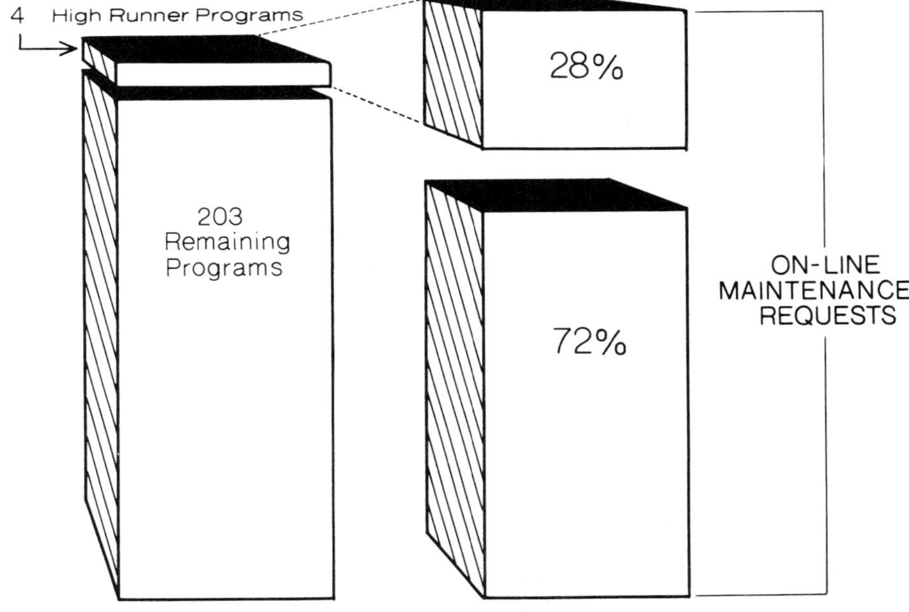

Figure 5. On-line Maintenance Requests

Continuing Development of Centrally Developed and Maintained Software Systems

C. L. Brantley and Y. R. Osajima

Abstract

Field evaluation of DIR/ECT, man/machine white pages telephone book production system, was completed in early 1973; it is currently operating in six Bell System Telephone Companies. Centrally developed and centrally maintained by Bell Laboratories, the system is now entering a stage in the life cycle in which extensive redesign and continuing development are required. Using DIR/ECT as a model, this paper describes long-term requirements for balancing an overall program of maintenance and continuing development of large scale software systems. The latter is emphasized.

Introduction

In a companion paper the impact of maintaining large scale business information systems centrally, and how we at Bell Laboratories have chosen to cope with this problem,was described. Maintenance involvement absorbs a portion (varying, in general, from 50 to 75 percent) of the staff resources available on any given project. Remaining staff resources are dedicated to continuing development, i.e., improving, enhancing, and, in the limit, completely redesigning an existing system in an evolutionary way. Unfortunately, the objectives of centralized maintenance and of continuing development often conflict, and the design agency is then faced with a monumental dilemma. The intent of this paper is to describe some of the processes currently evolving at Bell Laboratories to solve this dilemma. Although DIR/ECT (short for *DIR*ectory proj*ECT*), a man/machine white pages telephone book production system, is used as a model to illustrate these processes, they are equally applicable to a wide variety of software systems. After a brief description of DIR/ECT in terms of its intended functions, some statistics, and its current status, the constraints under which our long term continuing development programs are undertaken are discussed. These constraints are then related to the classical system life cycle; specific characteristics of our processes are discussed, and finally some tentative conclusions are drawn as to the effectiveness of our results.

System Description and Status

Field evaluation and acceptance testing of DIR/ECT was completed in early 1973; it is currently operational in six Bell System Telephone Companies. Market forecasts project an increasing number of clients over the next several years. The system is not new, having celebrated its seventh birthday this year. Born in an era of expensive high speed storage and even more expensive (access time) random access storage, DIR/ECT is a large, people intensive, batch processing system which mechanizes white pages telephone book operations. When coupled with graphic arts devices, it produces white pages telephone books, updated versions of these books for directory assistance, address telephone books and delivery instructions. (See figure 1.)

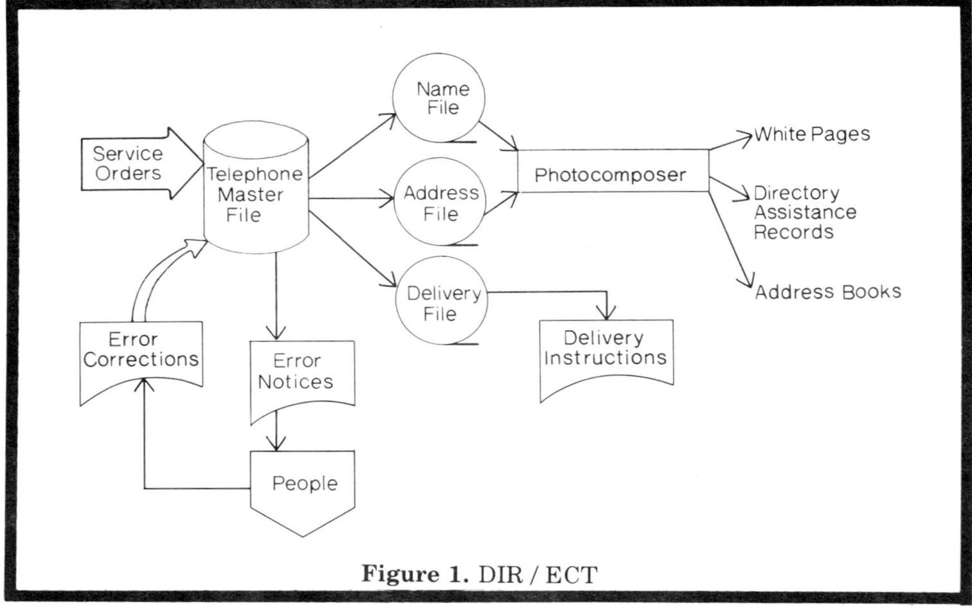

Figure 1. DIR / ECT

Service orders, or customer requests for service, are the primary input to DIR / ECT. The orders are validated against a large, random access Telephone Master File which is organized to optimize validation and updating. Errors are analyzed and corrected by the DIR/ECT people and subsequently reinput. Telephone listings from these orders are also maintained on separate sequential files which are organized to ease the production of the various DIR/ECT products. They are maintained in name order on a separate sequential Name file according to print specifications for each specific telephone book and are output for photocomposition and production of white pages telephone books and directory assistance records. Similarly, listings are maintained in address order and delivery order for subsequent production of address telephone books and instructions for delivering the telephone books.

DIR/ECT is a large system by any measure. Application programs alone run in excess of 800,000 computer instructions. These programs support and operate upon a telephone master file which ranges from 750,000,000 to two billion bytes. Written primarily in a combination of COBOL and BAL for application in an early third generation commercial computer environment, use of the system places heavy people and computer resource demands on the client. Typically, a Bell System Telephone Company having three million listings (a listing is roughly equivalent to an entry in your telephone book) in their telephone master file (approximately a billion bytes) expects to provide the resources of an IBM 370/158 or equivalent and about 100 support personnel.

Since completion of acceptance testing, the DIR/ECT project has primarily been in a centralized maintenance mode, i.e., a mode in which changes have been made to the system to keep it functioning satisfactorily at each of our clients' locations. A maintenance request profile for DIR/ECT is shown in figure 2. While the number of our clients has risen over the years, the number of maintenance requests has not increased. With the current design, we can plan on approximately 50 to 80 requests for maintenance per month. The way we handle these requests has already been described in a companion paper. Design changes have also been incorporated into the system. These changes have been at both our clients' request and of our own initiative in roughly equal measure. They include additional products, interface improvements and performance improvements. There are currently something in excess of 250 design change requests outstanding on the DIR/ECT system.

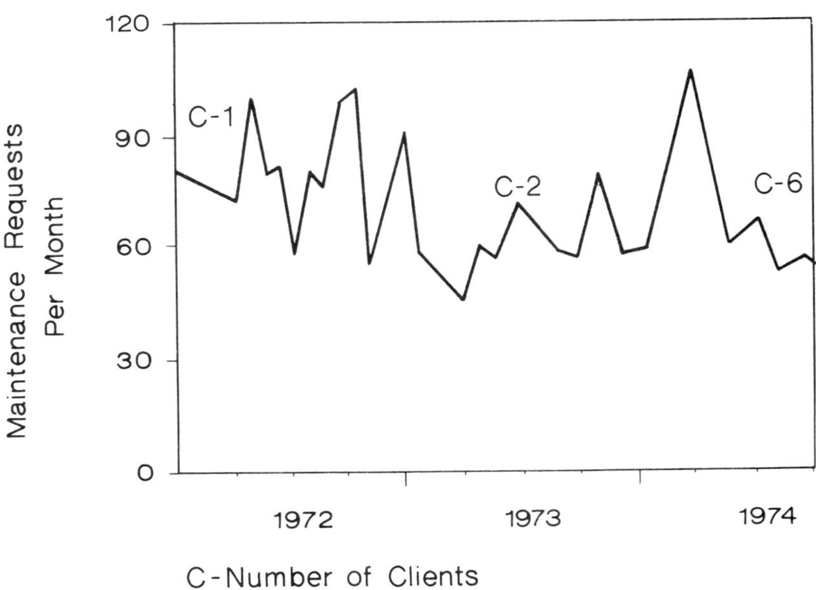

Figure 2. Maintenance Request Profile

While this mode of operation has enabled us to stay afloat, both we and our clients recognize that we are near the point of diminishing returns with the current system design. As indicated before, DIR/ECT, was designed for early third generation computers. Meeting our clients' needs for product flexibility and lower cost system operation requires that we redesign the system to take advantage of emerging technology. We are now implementing a continuing development program to rectify this situation.

Constraints

By far, our most severe constraint in implementing a large scale redesign effort on DIR/ECT is client centered, i.e., we must continue to maintain the current system satisfactorily to our clients, we must accept additional clients, and we must provide advice and consultation when trouble arises. In short, we no longer have the luxury of isolation from our customers and the concommitant high degree of internal control characteristic in an initial development program. If there is to be a new system, it must evolve to minimize the conversion and training impacts on our customers.

Our customers are in various stages of conversion (the process of converting a Bell System Telephone Company's existing records to DIR/ECT compatible format) and operation. Computer architecture varies from one company to the next. Our continuing development program must be compatible with this volatile environment. In figure 3, a staff profile of the life cycle of DIR/ECT is shown. As one may observe, this profile follows the classical structure of most large software systems, i.e., a small number of people during the objectives and requirements phase, increasing rapidly during the design, code and test phase, and tailing off in 1972 during final test and installation. At this point, DIR/ECT departs from the

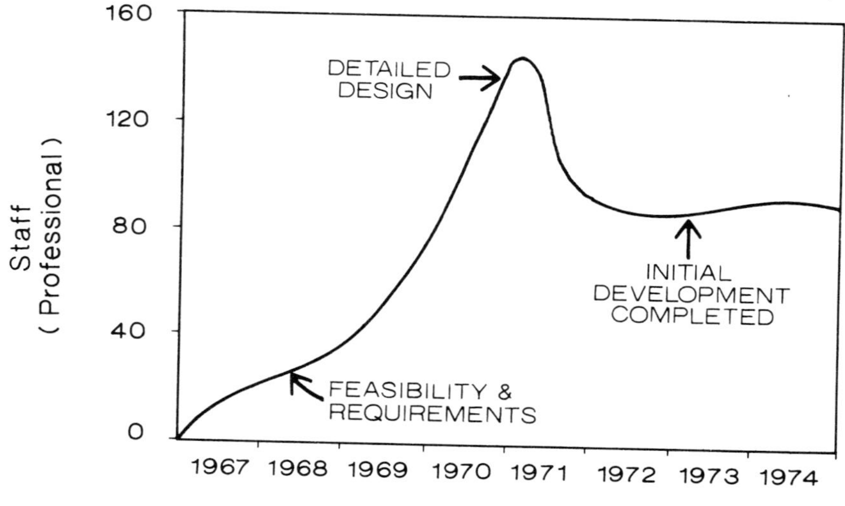

Figure 3. Staff Profile

classical, for it is here that the system is normally turned over to the customer for service and support, while the system developers turn their attention to new horizons. The concept of centralized maintenance and development does not allow the staff parameters to vary much. We currently have 85 staff members to both maintain the current system, and implement our continuing development program, i.e., our capacity to do work is limited. In establishing a meaningful development program, then, the problem we have is illustrated rather simply in figure 4. Here Wi (or Work Input) exists in the form of about 75 requests for maintenance each month, 250 design change requests, and a technical need to redesign an 800,000 machine instruction system. Without limited capacity to do work, Wo, (or Work Output) then must be very selective in nature. This principle, selective determination of work to be done, is the foundation of our continuing development program. With the staff limitation efficient management of resources becomes critical, and participation by our customers in determining what is done is a necessity, since ultimate staff levels available for continuing development are largely dependent on our customers demands (or lack thereof) for service on the current system, i.e., our process is designed to find an effective balance between maintenance and continuing development.

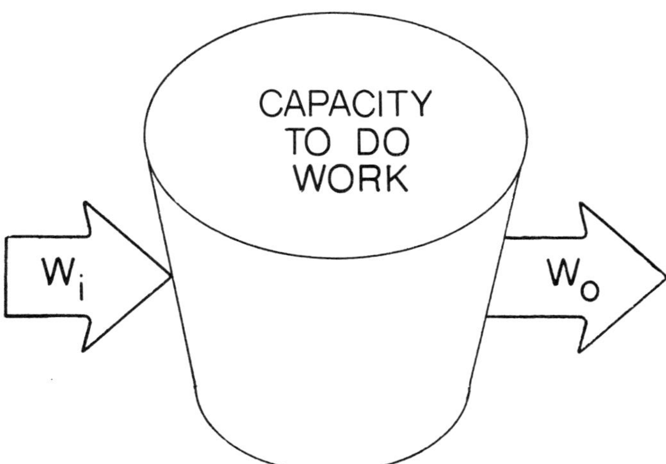

Figure 4. The Problem

Continuing Development Processes

In figure 5, a typical change process is shown in which requests for changes to a system may originate in many places: clients, various stages in the design process, corporate operations, etc. This illustrates the typical mode of operation of a large scale business information system immediately after final test, installation and acceptance. Normally, requests for changes are collected in a large pot, some attempt is made to prioritize the total workload and it is distributed across the design agency. The primary goal of the design agency is to meet the needs of the client. As a consequence, its output is more reactive than active, i.e., very fast response to trouble reports and requests for consultation and planning. As shown before, this process works very well as long as the central focus of the project is maintenance of a current system, and there is no urgency for long term scheduling or planning, or no need to undertake large continuing development programs within the project. The process falters, however, when the focus shifts to continuing development.

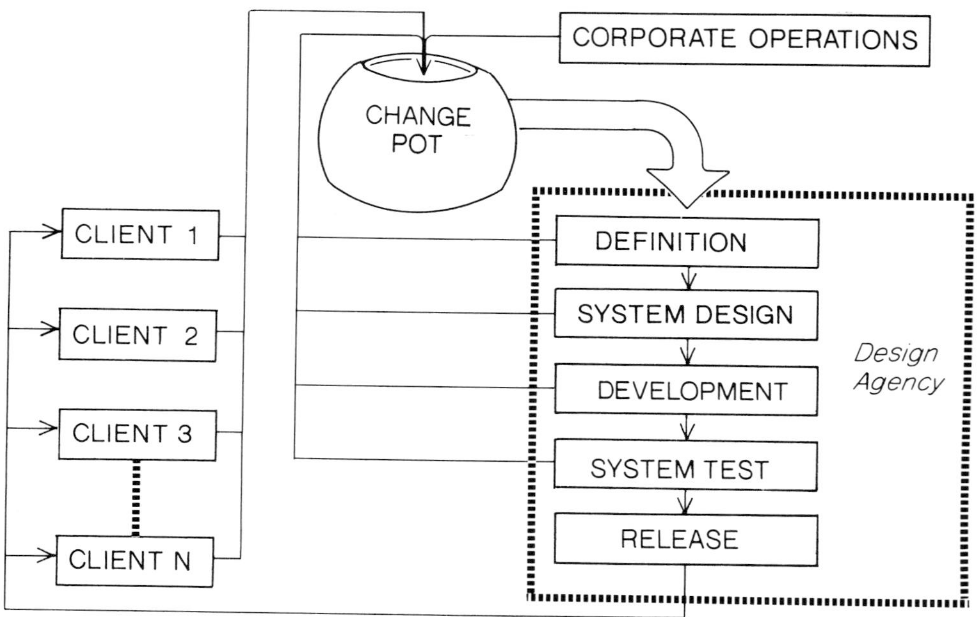

Figure 5. Initial Change Process

In DIR/ECT, institution of a large scale continuing development program meant that a good means of coordinating and managing the staff resources and flow of work within the project had to be found since the project is spread over two departments and eight supervisory groups. In addition, a good means of selectively filtering the flow of incoming work which would deeply involve our clients was required. The latter was necessary, since, as noted above, we do not have the luxury of being isolated from our customers, and as a consequence, the programs we undertake, maintenance or development, are largely determined by our clients. As seen in figure 6, the current DIR/ECT change process embodies these two factors in the form of both alterations in the process and two additional groups, the DIR/ECT Users Group, charged with selectively determining the priority of work to be done by the DIR/ECT project, and the Technical Review Board (TRB), charged with coordination of the flow of work and scheduling within the project. The Users Group is composed of responsible managers (two or three) representing each of our user companies, representatives of corporate operations (AT&T), and two members from the design agency (Bell Labs). The group was formed in November, 1973, and has held four two-day meetings to date. In general, the data with which this group works starts with the change pot described earlier. The change pot, however, is now input to the design agency's definition group which combines high priority design change requests into design packages on the basis of how closely the changes relate—viewed in terms of both user needs and technical design areas. For example, a user need to easily alter the coverage provided by a given telephone book would be in the same package as a user need to easily change the order in which listings appear in the book. The output from the Users Group provides the parent company with consensus input to establish a priority list.

Formed in January, 1974, the Technical Review Board consists of all technical supervisors on the DIR/ECT project and meets weekly. The data they work on are the priority lists for the design packages from the Users Group, incoming requests for maintenance, and the results of technical studies and analyses. Their output is a recommendation for a scheduled program of continuing development balanced with maintenance support for our clients. Normally this program involves significant design releases annually, with intermediate releases scheduled to meet our maintenance requirements.

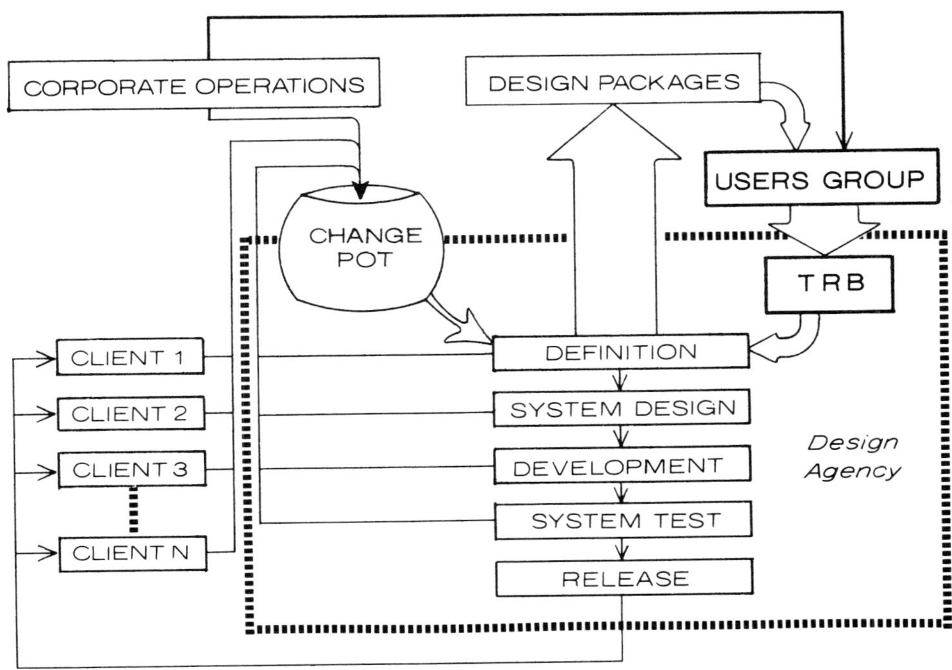

Figure 6. Current Change Process

Results

To date, two major design releases and three maintenance releases have been scheduled. In all cases, the Users Group and Technical Review Board have played their roles well. There has been continued dialogue between the clients, the parent corporation, and the design agency. Besides the priority setting described above, this dialogue includes status updates, design reviews, and performance analysis studies and feedback. As a result each party "owns" a piece of the action, and, in the end, our product has been increasingly accepted as technically sound and in keeping with our clients' needs. As our mutual confidence in the process grows, it is expected that we can, in truth, evolve a new DIR/ECT system which takes advantage of new technology, and proves economically beneficial to our customers.

Program Maintenance

Bob McGregor

Program maintenance, systems maintenance, production monitoring, systems control, application support software maintenance, post implementation development, system tuning.

These and many other familiar phrases have been used throughout the industry to describe a segment of data processing. No matter how you package it, dress it up, color it or whatever else you attempt to do, they all boil down to one basic term—maintenance. And maintenance of ongoing systems and programs is the *raison d'etre* of any operating data processing unit. The programs to be maintained are the foundation on which the data processing organization must build for they represent the justification for the computer and computer personnel. Programs blow up, the users' methods change, outside requirements change and new needs arise. It is essential that the data processing operation be ready, willing and able to respond to these factors on a timely and effective basis.

We all recognize the impact of maintenance on a data processing organization. It is the author's belief that the effective maintenance of systems and programs is by far the largest single weapon in the arsenal of the dp manager. Certainly new systems are needed. Of course, we need to institute and implement new techniques. Surely we must up-grade and enhance. But the question should be posed as to whether these actions are performed for the user department and, in their best interests, whether this is a psychological need on the part of the data processing community to continually prove its worth. New systems development, in my opinion, cannot serve as a justification for lack of maintenance. Effective maintenance creates user goodwill. It gains user acceptance and assistance. It assists the user to perform more effectively. If we provide the user with the tools to meet his business objectives and continually keep them finely tuned, then we have laid the foundation of trust and confidence which is needed to develop the systems of the future.

It is virtually impossible to develop the perfect system. Therefore, the technically adequate program which is effectively used by customers and assists in achieving their goals and objectives is of more overall credit to the industry than that elusive, technically perfect system which we all strive to develop. We are aware of the development cycle. The user often cannot verbalize his management needs. The dp staff guesses or assumes to fill the blanks. Once the system is implemented, we enter the feed-back loop wherein the user is more capable of explaining where the system fails to meet his objectives. This feed-back continues throughout the life of the system, and the data processing staff is obligated to react continually to these changes until something new is developed which the user agrees will better serve his needs. In order to accomplish this task, it is necessary to implement an effective maintenance strategy.

We live in a volatile industry which has as a major thrust the development of new and challenging methods and techniques. We are a young industry. We are a proud industry. And by nature we are continually striving, much as the engineering designer, to develop the perfect answer. In some respects, these factors have created an elitism within the industry which has both a good and a bad effect. The good effect has been the attitude and zeal with which the industry has strived to make itself more professional and develop new and advanced techniques to provide a better service for the user. The bad effect is that we often have a tendency to look towards the new without fully giving credence to that which has gone before in the development of systems. Here is one of the major problems facing many data processing managers.

The data processing manager is most exposed in terms of risk when it comes to ongoing programs and systems. His risk involves amendment and enhancement controls, reliability and security of systems, and reacting quickly to the changing needs of the user. If the data processing manager is to lose sleep at night, he does so over production systems. This problem is compounded when the basic systems and programs are ageing and the character or nature of the business to be monitored is growing and changing. Each of us, depending upon our individual make-up, must accept some degree of risk in dealing with these types of problems. Therefore, minimizing the problems that occur is most important.

Not only is the management of maintenance activities difficult for the data processing manager, but it is compounded by the fact that his staff is not generally interested, from a professional standpoint, in becoming maintenance programmers. Almost everyone wants to be in the vanguard of new system developments and very few programmers are either capable of, or interested in, being firemen. It has been a long standing problem in the industry to interest these specialists with ambitious ideas of improving techniques and methods to be content in maintenance programming. There does not seem to be an appreciation of the need to improve user relationships and to upgrade systems to meet the new challenges of the changing business. Therefore, the dp manager is on the horns of a dilemma. On one hand his staff is interested in development projects while goodwill is to be gained through satisfying the immediate needs of the user. The data processing manager is constantly faced with the problem of rotating staff from development work to maintenance work, dressing up maintenance work to look like it is something else and, in general, paying a very high cost for maintenance control.

Adequate job

To do an adequate job of maintaining systems and programs, an organization must devote a sizeable portion of its staff to this type of effort, particularly as the systems grow older and changes in the user's business occur. This work is normally unscheduled and is often dependent upon the whims of the user department as opposed to any predictable deadlines. The cost of such an operation is generally very high in comparison with the cost of a development project wherein a given task within a specific time frame is prevalent. This is due primarily to the necessity to staff the organization in order to meet the peak needs throughout a given period of time. It is difficult to smooth these curves without adversely impacting the user. Thus, the data processing manager is faced with the problem of balancing the goodwill requirements of the user: with the career development plans of the employee; with the risks involved in operating systems; and with the attendant cost of maintaining a large enough staff to solve peak problems.

Every data processing manager has attempted to solve the particular problems associated with maintenance programming. Some have elected to assign a percentage of every member of the staff's time to maintenance programming. Others have decided to invest a team responsible for continually amending, enhancing and trouble shooting existing systems. Others have used a combination of these two approaches. I propose a different solution to this problem—the use of consultant programmers.

This proposal will provoke an adverse reaction from most dp managers. Having been a data processing manager, the author believes that this would immediately generate a similar emotional response. However, having experienced these problems, some thought to this concept as a possible solution is worthy of discussion. Whether one agrees with the thesis or not is not really important. What is important is that it is considered an alternative to handling a real problem and either accept, modify or reject it on its own merits and not on emotional grounds. I hope that my current position of providing consulting services will not mean that the views presented here will be discarded pre-emptorily, as the proposal is based on having served in both the role of a data processing manager and a consultant.

The first thing to consider is how such a concept could be put into practical operation. First, a position such as maintenance manager must be created. It must be filled by an in-house employee who reports directly to the dp manager. Such action will ensure that overall control resides with the dp staff. Also, the primary interface and liaison with the user organization should be the responsibility of the maintenance manager, together with schedules, completion dates, resource allocation, and other coordinating functions. Sub-manager positions could also be established if the maintenance workload is great enough.

The project team required to perform the work effort should comprise consultant employees. By implication, therefore, the dp organization does not contract for a turnkey service. For a variety of reasons, the dp manager must resist the temptation to include his own employees in these teams, for such action could adversely impact the effectiveness of the work effort. Contractually, the dp manager must be prepared to sign a long term contract with the consultant in order to maximize his benefits. The consultant must warrant that the contracting organization has first call on the services of additional staff to meet peak requirements. Both sides must be prepared to serve the needs of the user.

The dp manager will receive four major benefits from this proposal: career development, personnel smoothing, higher quality work, and reduced costs. In addition, the overall effectiveness of the service provided to the user should be increased.

The appointment of the maintenance manager gives the organization a vehicle for developing individual skills at a prestigious level. Maintenance programming or "fireman" work is an art unto itself, and requires special skills and talents. Rotating more senior staff members through this position will enable them to acquire these skills without feeling they are working beneath their capability.

Let the consultant do it

Personnel smoothing can be achieved by off-setting the peaks and valleys attendant with maintenance on the consultant. Also, depending upon circumstances, the total full-time staff level may be decreased through reduction of the need for maintenance personnel. The organization's staff would be left with the functions of developing new systems, auditing existing systems, and controlling maintenance efforts.

Higher quality work should be produced. One factor that must be mentioned in a discussion of program maintenance is the selection of the personnel for this work. New trainees or junior programmers are often assigned the responsibility of program maintenance. I am not sure that this selection process is valid across the board. The ability to serve as firemen on projects which one has not written is a special art and talent that are based on experience. The selection of junior programmers to fulfill the maintenance role must be challenged. From the standpoint of the data processing manager, the more senior personnel he could assign to such a task the more relaxed he should be with regard to the anticipated results. The junior programmer lacks experience in recognizing the variety of techniques which can be used by different programmers, is less capable of comprehending the inter-relationships of the programs themselves, and is probably weakest at finding the best solution for the problem at hand.

If we couple this problem with the fact that many of our experienced programmers are not interested in doing the mundane maintenance tasks, the weakest link of the chain becomes the effort put forth on program maintenance. Not only is the end result potentially weak but the time to achieve it can be extended severely through the inability of the junior programmer to confidently visualize the problem at hand and then make the most effective solution. The use of outside consulting services to perform this effort would enable the data processing department to acquire a higher level of skill. This in itself should add to the cost effectiveness of using outside programming assistance by increasing productivity. Also, if the client is not happy with the results achieved by the consulting staff members, he can immediately request that an individual be removed from service and be replaced by someone more qualified.

What will it cost?

From a cost standpoint, it is difficult to prove that the concept will be cost effective. This is primarily due to the different character of each data processing organization and its requirements as far as its users are concerned. However, experience indicates that there is a justification from a financial standpoint. How many dp managers have recently gone through the exercise to determine what a man-hour of effort costs? If you have, did you consider that space, rates, recruitment costs, corporate overhead, fringe benefits, idle time, a percentage of accounting and other centralized services, fixed assets such as desks, chairs, filing cabinets, dictating equipment, and so on are all cost additives to the operation of a data processing department? In other words, when examining an internal data processing operation as a business, I have found that actual costs approach those of consulting fees.

One major cost element is non-productive time. As maintenance work fluctuates, the "valleys" will be very costly because the internal hourly rate is fixed. Also, the data processing organization is generally less flexible in adding staff and, therefore, targets staffing at a higher point on the workload curve in order to provide a measure of safety. If you can accept and/or prove that internal costs are within 10 per cent of consulting fees, then you can appreciate that it does not take much non-productive time to increase costs above consulting fees. Also, the consultant should be capable of staffing at a lower basic level, thereby making cost savings possible. Furthermore, since it is accepted that personnel costs will continue to rise, the true value of savings will also rise, even though the percentage difference may remain the same.

We have discussed one side of the equation—the dp organization. The next question which must be answered is why should the consulting software organization be interested in performing these services? The consulting industry faces many of the same problems in terms of personnel and career development as the data processing organization. However, the consultant programmer has accepted a working environment which is more volatile and subject to change. It has often been stated that the creed of the consultant is "if I don't like what I am doing today, wait till tomorrow, and I'll be doing something different." While the consultants have similar problems, I believe they have a better capability to overcome them.

Let us assume that a consultant provides a staff of four programmers to systems maintenance. The team would operate under a project leader assigned by the company, who would in turn report directly to the maintenance manager within the client's organization. The consultant could promise the team that they would never have to spend more than six months in any one capacity within the project team. A rota system could be established where each member of the staff would progressively advance in responsibility with the most senior person removed from the contract and a more junior person brought in. In this way, the consultant can provide a career pattern within a team of programmers that he is incapable of doing in a new development project.

Do it yourself!

The initial reaction of the client should be that we too can provide such a rota system for our employees. Why do we need consultants? While I am sure it is attempted by many organizations, I am not convinced that the volatility of the business of the organization and the changing needs of the users do not disrupt these plans, trapping individuals in maintenance programming. This is particularly true of more junior programmers because of the inherent thought process which places senior, experienced personnel on new development projects. Even if the dp manager decides that he would like to try junior programmers on a development project, he risks creating antagonism within his own staff. The consultant under contract with limited objectives can meet these commitments and provide a fairly firm rota system. Also, any additional staff personnel to be assigned for peak periods would be interested in the change of working environment and appreciate the opportunity to meet a new challenge. All in all, the consultant would have less of a personnel problem in handling a maintenance contract than would the dp manager.

This concept would also be economically viable to the consultant. It only makes sense to undertake this type of association over extended periods of time, similar to the annual maintenance contract on equipment. Further, such a contract would be predicated on a fixed price for the basic team required for the duration of the contract. Any additional staff required to meet peaks in the schedule would be added on a *per diem* basis.

This type of contract would provide the consulting organization with a very stable work load in his business and should enable the consulting firm to reduce its basic prices without destroying its profit picture. Consulting prices must include some provision for down time for billable consultants. Consulting firms use prices based upon a target number of billable hours per annum within the range of 60 to 80% of billable time available. Any contracts which provide stability in the number of billable days per annum is a valuable and profitable one. Therefore, with this assurance of annual billings, the consultant should be willing to pass on some of the savings to the client.

In summary, the proposition is: let consultants assist in maintenance programming. It attacks an industry problem. It is advantageous to the dp manager. It is beneficial to the consultant.

Program Maintenance: Users' Views

It was suggested in the previous article that the use of consultant programmers could provide the optimum solution to program maintenance. The users we spoke to regarding maintenance disagreed, with one exception. A number of reasons were put forward for this. Of particular importance was the fact that, in their view, the consultant could not provide the quality of service that could be expected from in-house staff. However, the one dissenter remarked that if the system is well documented and the proposed changes are properly specified, then the use of outside help is a good way of solving the problems.

The view of several companies on the need for an organized, effective approach to program maintenance echoes that of Bob McGregor. However, discussions with these computer installations, including a large supermarket chain, an insurance company, a county council, a public utility, and a large manufacturing company, revealed, among other things, that the computer user is unlikely to contract out maintenance work and will choose one of two in-house approaches—by involving all programming staff and assigning them to projects requiring both development and maintenance work, or by establishing a separate team whose sole responsibility is the maintenance of all programs.

Program maintenance is not, perhaps, one of the more exciting aspects of computer data processing, but it is a fact which cannot be overlooked. A sound, effective maintenance strategy needs to be implemented if the computer section of an organization is to keep pace with the changing needs of user departments. Although a large proportion of maintenance work is generated by proposals put forward by user departments which request amendments and/or extensions to existing programs designed to improve performance, there are a number of other factors which are sources of program maintenance. These include changes on a national scale such as VAT [Value Added Tax], income tax rates, and grants, and internal policy changes in areas such as trading practice, personnel administration, accounting procedures, and so on. In addition, innovations in computer technology, such as on-line operations and new software releases and operating systems, can create a need for programs to be enhanced in order to implement more advanced facilities. However, these can often be regarded as continuing developments which are funded from savings which may accrue from a new system. The acquisition of new hardware, such as a faster, larger capacity version of disc drive or compatible processor, will usually necessitate changes in areas such as JCL, formats and addressing. Furthermore, any programs which, for some reason, have become inefficient in terms of the time and space required to run them, are subject to maintenance in the form of optimization. The manufacturing company, incidentally, considered that such factors are enhancements to users' requirements and do not constitute maintenance. Bad communication between the computer and user departments, resulting in the latter's needs not being satisfied, and incomplete debugging are relatively uncommon contributors to the need for maintenance.

To what activities does the term program maintenance relate? Most of those we spoke to regard modifications, improvements, or additions made to an installation's productive programs as maintenance. This embraces optimization; extensions to allow the implementation of new hardware/software; updating to make programs compatible with changes in business and/or governmental rulings; the addition of new reports, tabulations, or changes to the format, content and media of existing output, as requested by user departments; developing interfaces between new and existing programs; and updating programs to run under new software, such as a different release of operating system and telecommunication software. In short, any alterations made to programs, apart from total conversion or simulation resulting from the acquisition of non-compatible hardware and software, constitute program maintenance.

Important for management

It is important for computer management to achieve the right balance of effort devoted to systems development and program maintenance. Systems development work should not be carried out at the expense of program maintenance, but resources occupied by the latter should be kept to a minimum. The percentage of time taken up by program maintenance depends, to a large extent, on what stage of development has been reached in a particular installation. In a well-established installation, program maintenance can account for approximately 75% of the programming effort, as the majority of development work has already been carried out. However, the relatively recent acquisition of a new computer probably means that systems development takes priority over maintenance work, the latter's share of resources being as low as 20%. In order to economize on the man-hours and computer resources needed to handle program maintenance, a user can begin by restricting the implementation of non-critical amendments to those which will yield relatively substantial cost and time savings, and improve on the performance of one or more user departments and/or the computer system. Assessing the cost and benefits of proposed amendments at the time they are submitted should avoid wasted effort being spent on trivial modifications. Minor amendments which are found to be of some value can be allowed to accumulate and later be incorporated into the system in a one-shot operation.

The kind of staff assigned to maintenance work is also a contributing factor to the quality and speed of handling maintenance, the ideal being to write programs in modules so that anyone in the team can deal with modifications. The general belief seems to be that program maintenance can, in some ways, require more skill and experience than development work and should, therefore, be left to the experts who have a knowledge of the system and can trace all elements of it which are affected by alterations made to a particular program module, which is all very well if the system is well documented. New recruits, trainees and junior programmers are unlikely to be called upon to do maintenance during their initial period of employment. In some cases, junior programmers may be required to handle some maintenance work, particularly if they are trained in-house and are consequently familiar both with the application and the computer system. A programmer's skill is especially important in dealing with maintenance on applications which are run frequently, say, on an overnight basis. This demands speed and efficiency in locating and correcting sources of error in programs to ensure that normal schedules are not severely disrupted. However, one user remarked that such treatment was not warranted except in the case of an operating system fault, for example.

Accepting that maintenance requires the use of skilled and experienced staff, it is often another matter finding qualified people who are also prepared to do the work. Although there are a few who like the job of program maintenance, the majority of programmers are anything but enthusiastic about the prospect. Computer users, therefore, sometimes operate a rotation system, to make sure that staff are not solely engaged in maintenance work, and assign teams to projects in which development and maintenance work is shared. Another alternative is to offer incentives to encourage volunteers for program maintenance, and set up a separate team comprising people who (might) regard maintenance as a challenge rather than a chore. But to many it is always a chore.

The efficiency of program maintenance can be further improved by establishing a close link between the user department which submits proposals for system changes, and those responsible for implementing the system. If intercommunication between these two is good, user departments are more actively involved in the computing aspects of their procedures, feedback of information is improved, and specifications are less likely to be misinterpreted, thereby enabling dp staff to produce results which conform to the requirements of the user department and avoiding premature revision of the system. Proposals for extension or modifications to programs should be accurately defined and submitted, in the first instance, to the analyst or project leader responsible for the original system. He would normally be in a position to agree or reject proposals, based on an evaluation of the cost of implementing these compared with economies or other benefits which may be gained. In short, it should be a request and acceptance procedure in order to preserve the integrity of the system. Major proposals and optional "extras" may have to be agreed at a higher level, involving a steering committee responsible for decisions on priorities of major projects, as well as extensions or modifications to projects already implemented.

Another factor which undoubtedly pays off in program maintenance is the use of standards in system design, programming and operation. Programs should be written in modules, supported by full documentation. Furthermore, systems which cater for organizations with branches scattered over a wide area should impose rigorous standards to cope with the needs of users. It is also considered that a modular approach to programming also helps in estimating and controlling the cost of maintenance work.

As stated previously, there are two generally accepted ways in which the task of program maintenance is tackled—a combined approach and a separate approach. First, let us look at the combined approach. Because of the unpopularity of maintenance work, some computer users believe that it is better to share the work by assigning teams to projects, any maintenance requirements being the responsibility of the team working on the project concerned. Depending on what stage of development has been reached, a project team may find itself engaged almost entirely on maintaining the project. In this instance, programmers can be switched, from time to time, between teams, thus ensuring that every programmer does a share of maintenance work. Among the advantages claimed for a combined approach is the fact that maintenance is more efficiently carried out by the originators of the project concerned—they are familiar with the system, are less likely to corrupt other routines in the system, and are able to implement changes according to schedule. Speed is particularly important when dealing with statutory rulings and systems which are in constant use. It is also thought that a separate approach encourages too great an effort to be devoted to program maintenance and incurs costly wastage of resources which, during "troughs" in maintenance work, are more usefully applied to development work. Furthermore, by making those responsible for the original project, also responsible for any subsequent maintenance of the project, it is suggested that staff tend to make a better job of programming in the first place in order to avoid having to do maintenance at a later date. Computer users which adopt a combined approach often do this out of concern for the programmer's reaction to a total commitment to maintenance, and the difficulty for members of a separate team to know and understand all aspects of applications running in their installation. By means of a combined approach, together with a rotation system, if required, boredom can be alleviated, the risk of high staff turnover is reduced, employee/management relationships are improved, and a chance is given for all programming staff to work on more interesting development work. Yet, how often does this work in practice?

Short-term requirement

A short-term requirement for a high volume of program maintenance may be necessary for old programs which, until they can be rewritten, are simulated on new equipment. This justifies a separate approach and, perhaps, the best way of achieving this is to appoint programmers on a short-term contract basis to work with a permanent member of staff who has experience of the organization's applications and computer equipment. Program maintenance, however, although it fluctuates according to the progress of development work, is a continuing operation, and it is because of these fluctuations that some users opt for a combined approach.

Other computer users, however, believe that establishing a separate maintenance team is a more logical and efficient way to control and perform program maintenance. Among the benefits claimed for this technique are: it takes the load off people engaged in development work; it ensures that documentation standards are adhered to because otherwise one cannot expect the team to have a full understanding of all systems; it enables more attention to be devoted to development work, while people are still on-hand for maintenance; and it may act as a training ground for less experienced staff who are given an opportunity to become familiar with JCL and programming languages. An argument against the use of a separate team is that its members are faced with the obstacle of having to gain an understanding of a complete system before maintenance work can begin, which may not help to foster initiative. However, if proposals for amendments are initially submitted to the project's team leader, he can act as the interface between the maintenance team and the source of maintenance proposals to ensure correct implementation of any changes to a system. Furthermore, a separate approach is thought to encourage a greater awareness and satisfaction of user department requirements, as the project team leader need no longer reject maintenance proposals out of concern for the pressure this puts on members of his team.

Major operation

Occasionally, what appears superficially to be a simple modification can turn out to involve a major operation. Without a separate team to deal with this, development work could be held up for some considerable time, or the maintenance job might be shelved, or perhaps rushed, and hence be error-prone. This is seen by some as a common pitfall. Regarding "peaks" and "troughs" associated with program maintenance, a separate team can devote its time during "troughs" to optimization of particularly troublesome, inefficient systems. As for difficulties in obtaining staff prepared to be totally committed to program maintenance, this need not necessarily be a problem. This is a question of controlling resource levels and the degree of pressure for the work to be done. Nevertheless some programmers, we were told, actually find program maintenance more interesting than project development work. If current trends continue, development work for programmers is likely to be reduced to a humdrum coding task, with little scope for initiative. Project development is tending to become a job for the systems analyst and very experienced programmer because of the use being made of decision tables, detailed programming specifications, and high-level languages, the logical flow of the system being designed at the analysis stage, rather than the programming stage. If this is the case, program maintenance can be regarded as more challenging work, providing opportunities for some analysis work, troubleshooting and optimization.

Furthermore, the results of development work are often not seen for some considerable time, and perhaps more varied shorter maintenance tasks can be of greater appeal to a number of programmers.

One of the companies we spoke to plans to go a step further and extend the separate approach by splitting the maintenance work between two teams—an operations team and a support group. The operations team, which is already in existence, works on-site and is responsible for keeping productive programs going. The members of the team have to locate and solve run-time problems as quickly as possible in order to avoid delays in the day-to-day running of the system which, in this case, demands that the results of processing are ready at the start of each day. Hence, the team is made up of highly skilled and experienced members who are prepared to be on-call 24 hours a day, and it is important that they be volunteers. In order to compensate for irregular hours and the responsibility for doing someone else's "dirty work", a relatively high salary and other incentives are offered. In addition to this team, it is planned to establish a support group to handle the other aspects of program maintenance which account for a large proportion of the programming effort. Maintenance work is presented to the support group by the team leader responsible for the original project, who states precisely what changes are required and how they should be implemented. The programmers in the support group are given an opportunity of doing some analysis work and, perhaps, original work involving extensions to the system. In order to ensure that aspects of original work are not neglected in the knowledge that maintenance work is handled separately, programmers are responsible for a project until it is fully implemented and, at a later date, they are required to audit the system, checking that it performs exactly as specified. Advocates of the separate approach believe that there can be a greater risk of staff turnover with a rotation system, as members of staff may leave the organization just before it is their turn to do program maintenance.

Controlling costs

Unless an installation adopts a separate approach to program maintenance, assessment and control of the costs incurred by this work are probably more difficult. Some user departments are charged according to their total usage of computer resources, which includes both development and maintenance work. Using a separate approach, resource usage is more readily assessed and departments can be charged according to the number of man-hours worked on implementing the maintenance proposals, plus the cost of testing time on the computer. It is also easier to make an initial cost estimate, and by conforming to this estimate, the cost of maintenance can be kept to a minimum. Another company, which apart from a large central computer operates a number of online terminals in remote locations on a corporate basis, charges the user for all maintenance work unless the service department is at fault, the charges being made according to an agreed budget. The advantage (to the user) is that it makes allowance for certain contingencies, especially one-off jobs, which, although enhancements to the system, constitute maintenance. Thus the importance of controlling a corporate central system from the maintenance aspect is apparent, in order to avoid modification to the system being made at individual locations.

Regarding the arguments posed by McGregor in his article, suggesting that a consultant provides the optimum solution to maintenance, the computer users we approached responded, with one exception, with a definite "NO." A number of reasons were put forward to substantiate this response. Of particular importance was the fact that the consultant could not provide the quality of service that could be expected from in-house staff. The latter are always on-hand (often 24 hours a day), are familiar with the procedure of their organization, and are used to the existing systems and the equipment on which they are run. Those who said no do not think that these qualities could be applied to consultant programmers. Furthermore, it is believed that urgent needs for program maintenance, resulting from run time blow-ups and other critical changes, which must be implemented by a certain date, are problems which the consultant programmer, having no previous knowledge of the system concerned, would be unlikely to be able to solve in time. Although the use of standards goes a long way to making program maintenance more efficient, there are inevitably instances when these are overlooked. To an in-house programmer, with an understanding of the system, this would not prove to be too great an obstacle. Moreover, there is a lack of continuity, as one is not always dealing with the same consultant programmer, and a tendency to lose control over schedules. In addition, it is thought that consultant programmers are not necessarily the best and are expensive. Much is to be gained by handling program maintenance internally, as in-house staff as well as having a knowledge of internal procedures, usually possess a sense of loyalty and responsibility towards their organization. The one dissenting company made the remark that: if the old system is well documented and the proposed changes are properly specified, then the use of outside help is a good way of solving the resource problem. Also, the expert you are looking for could be an outside man.

Number of criteria

To summarize, there are a number of criteria to be taken into account when establishing effective, controlled maintenance procedures including the following: monitor maintenance work as closely as possible; set up a separate team of people who like the work and offer incentives such as higher salaries, or give everyone a share of maintenance work using a rota and a project-oriented approach; use experienced people, regardless of the approach adopted; estimate costs at the outset to avoid trivial changes and ensure estimates are adhered to; evaluate proposals thoroughly to ensure that modifications are cost/effective; closely involve user departments with the computing aspect of the applications which they implement; make sure that specifications conform exactly with the requirements laid down in proposals. Depending on the type of application, volume of maintenance work and stage of system development, a computer user should choose the approach which best meets his individual needs. A combined approach may be better if a low volume of maintenance is anticipated, and for a constant, relatively high volume of maintenance work, a separate approach is probably of more value and is easier to monitor and control.

Control of Program Changes

G. Alexander

No matter how well standards are set up and controlled there is always the chance they will be by-passed under the pressure of immediate business needs. This is true in the area of programming and it is surprising to see programmers who diligently observe all established standards when developing their programs completely by-pass those same standards when effecting a change in a program. This practice is disastrous when the program eventually bears no resemblance to the program listing and has to be completely rewritten, with all the ensuing costs and explanations necessary to a rather less than understanding management.

Program changes do occur and must be taken care of. Unfortunately, they have a tendency to occur at the most inopportune times and require immediate attention. This alone tends to create pressures that will make the most diligent programmers and managers by-pass standards until a more opportune time which, alas, never seems to develop. The manager who is struggling to maintain a schedule most often will orally instruct the programmer to "just take care of this change." The programmer, immersed as he is in the development of a major program, will patch the program to be changed and leave documentation "only" until he has finished debugging the routine he is presently working on. But by then the change has been forgotten; other pressing matters are at hand and, anyway, the program has since been changed again and possibly again by different programmers.

Not many installations are in the fortunate position to be able to maintain a group of programmers for the sole purpose of maintaining and documenting programming changes. How then can the manager of an average installation insure proper documentation without burdening his department with costly and time consuming standards?

It is basic that standards must be established and strictly adhered to in order to maintain an orderly operation. However, standards must be realistic and fit the purpose for which they have been established. They should not be ambitious to the point that they defeat themselves. It should be recognized that for the control of program changes, standards are required which will allow the programmer to maintain them and the manager to control adherence to them regardless of the pressure in work load.

Program changes can be divided into:

1. Major changes which require rewriting and/or additions of large and complicated routines to the program.
2. Minor changes which require addition or changing of some instructions.
3. Changing of an instruction which can generally be accomplished by an absolute patch (changing the instruction on the object card).

In any well managed operation, programs are written only on the basis of detailed written specifications. These specifications together with any other documentation and the program listing are then inserted in a program folder. Rule number one must be, then, that no program change, regardless of whether it is of type 1, 2, or 3 (described above) will be instituted without detailed specifications in writing. These should be in duplicate; one copy will be given to the programmer to effect the change and one copy will be filed in the program folder in chronological sequence. Thus, the folder at all times will have an accurate history of all changes made to the program.

Rule number two must be that no matter how insignificant the change, the source deck must be changed and re-assembled, and the resultant object deck immediately substituted for the patched one. A comments card should be one of the first cards in the program giving the following information: the date of the written specifications this assembly refers to, the number of times the program has been assembled, and the name of the programmer making the change. The object program should be manually marked with the same date specified on the card. This will then establish a complete cross reference between the specifications, program listing, source deck and object deck. The cost of assembling is a small price to pay for the assurance that the program listing will at all times match the object deck in operation. The program should be assembled even if the change was of type three above with an absolute patch. The manager will be more than compensated for the cost of the assembly by not having to spend time retracing absolute patches if any subsequent assembly does not contain the patch.

The third and final rule is to maintain a "schedule of program changes." All program changes will be logged in the schedule but only after the specifications for the change have been completed. Program changes will be assigned to the programmer from the schedule only, thus insuring that no changes will be started before the specifications have been completed. The information to be entered in the schedule includes:

1. Program identification
2. Date of specifications and by whom written
3. Date programmed and name of programmer
4. Date assembled and object deck given to operation
5. Short description of the change and by whom authorized.

Aside from allowing the manager to maintain an orderly schedule and to assign the change to the programmer best qualified, it also serves as a history of all program changes and assures him that each change has been followed up by an assembly.

The above procedure does not eliminate "patching." It does, however, provide that at all times there is a properly assembled program in operation matching the assembly listing.

Responsibility vs. Authority Lying to Management: A Legitimate Solution?

Miles Benson

Clint Ransom was one of your all-time-top software maintenance men.

Well, maybe that's putting it all wrong. Clint didn't wear white coveralls or carry a clipboard or get grease under his fingernails from fixing things. But what he could do with a well-worn program listing, a coding pad and a fast-moving pencil would fairly boggle the mind.

Clint could leap tall data management hurdles in a single bound. He could code his way out of a logical swamp with schedule alligators snapping on all sides. His configurations were so well managed you hardly knew he had any.

And if cleanliness is next to godliness, Clint's solutions were so crisp and clear as to be hallowed.

In short, Clint Ransom was a programmer's programmer. But with a difference. Because where other programmers hate to do maintenance, hate to do debugging, hate to do documentation, Clint ate it all up. Maintenance work was his bread and butter and, like a hot dog, he devoured it with relish.

There was, however, one problem with Clint Ransom: He knew his job too well. No, I don't mean he knew it so well that no one could tell him when he'd done something wrong. He wasn't caught in the ego-full programmer trap, at least not that one.

The problem was that no one could really manage him. He knew his job so well that he functioned best in the total absence of direction from above.

If a manager said, "Here, take over this program and be responsible for correcting all its flaws and implementing all its changes," Clint could go on working with no further direction for several years.

For some managers, those who really understand software maintenance and highly skilled technical people, that presents no problem at all. The manager could gesture vaguely, Clint would take the gesture as sufficient direction and both Clint and the manager would then be free to go off and do what they did best—Clint to maintain the gestured at software, and the manager to—er—do whatever it is managers do.

But this story is about the time Clint Ransom fell among thorns. Symbolically speaking.

There are some managers who just have to do things *their* way. The problem arose when Clint met one of those.

Now, if Farley Snodgrass doesn't know his eraser from his pointy end, he needs to be managed closely. If Bullshot Thunder works up a storm but uses bad judgment at the top of his lungs, he needs to be managed closely. And if Donald Doolittle is a Fulbright Scholar whose favorite workstation is the water cooler, he needs to be managed closely.

But when you have a self-starting, fuel-injected, automatic transmissioned worker like Clint, you do not manage him closely.

Frank Faretheewell couldn't see it that way. When Frank moved in to take over the Balderdash Iron and Steel software maintenance organization, he found both Farley Snodgrass and Clint Ransom in his inherited empire's inventory.

Mumbling something about the manner in which both Farley and Clint pulled on their pants, Frank set about to make sure they both responded the same way to the same kind of harness.

It took a little while for the full impact of the change to hit Clint. After all, he had been maintaining the Balderdash payroll program, its chemical properties analysis program and its real-time input control program for five years without direction.

When Frank started telling him what to do, he thought at first it was a joke. The programs hummed like elegant, finely tuned watches. They were responsive to change, as reliable as the sunrise and as easy to understand as a single-path maze. Why would anyone be telling him what to do?

But Frank was determined to *manage.* Whether he needed to or not.

It's time to digress for a moment. There is more to the Clint Ransom-Frank Faretheewell problem than a simple clashing of personalities. What we have here is a prototype of the whole software power structure dilemma.

Look at the problem generically for a moment. Frank had the authority and the power. Clint had the responsibility and the product control. The question is, what do they each do with their respective attributes?

Tradition seems to say that authority subsumes responsibility and power overwhelms product control. But there are other options.

Product control is in fact the ultimate power. And as long as responsibility resides with product control, the best ends from the corporate point of view can be achieved by ignoring or circumventing authority and power.

Well, that's all pretty heavy stuff. Important, but heavy. And at the moment when the seriousness of his dilemma hit Clint Ransom, he really didn't have time to sort out all the philosophies at stake. He just knew that life had suddenly become intolerable. And that he had to act.

The specific issue around which the clash grew was simple enough. Frank asked Clint for an activity report. No sweat, right? We all do them.

But there was a difference here. Frank wanted all of Clint's activities tied to either a change request or a problem report.

Even that, at first glance, seemed innocent enough. After all, whatever Clint is doing should be traceable to an outside request. Right?

Wrong. Let me try to explain why.

When Clint first took over the chemical properties analysis program, its logic was convoluted and unreadable. To respond to a change request required a six-week learning curve followed by a two-month trial-and-error fix period. The program was ready for the obsolescence heap on grounds of inflexbility.

So Clint dived in—in the total absence of a specific change request or problem report—and began to clean up the program. And the more he cleaned, the better it got. Change responsiveness dropped to two weeks and sometimes less.

In the course of doing that cleanup, Clint began to understand what maintenance of software is all about: Not just force-fitting fixes and changes into an unwilling framework, but lavishing large doses of tender loving care on an awkward framework so that when the time comes to make a change or fix, the framework is in shape to make the job easy. Not just solving specific problems, but writing general solutions anticipating future requirements.

The program was literally rehabilitated off the scrap heap. Problem correction was isolated to relevant modules instead of scattered all over the program.

Not always, of course. Some problems aren't worthy of that kind of ongoing TLC. But chemical properties analysis was. And so were the other programs for which Clint had responsibility.

Now back to the Frank Faretheewell take-charge approach to management. As Clint and Frank began to circle warily around their dilemma, throwing cautious verbal punches at each other, it at first appeared a compromise might be workable.

The obvious one, of course, which Clint suggested, would have him continue to function as he had in the past, reporting his activities in three categories—changes, fixes and cleanup.

Frank, however, would have none of that. There were, he blustered, only two legitimate categories for maintenance activities—and cleanup wasn't one of them. Cleanup was wasted time.

Things escalated rapidly toward an impasse after that. Frank held firm. And it was up to Clint, in response to Frank's authority and power, to bend.

I think the dilemma is clear at this point. But, to be sure, let me state the obvious. Clint has given management his best technical judgment. Management has heard and rejected it.

Clint has only one choice, then—to give in to management and quit cleaning up his programs. And, in the doing, to lessen his sense of responsibility.

Or does he?

Clint could, he saw, continue to do his work as he had in the past and retain his sense of responsibility, if only he would *lie* to his management about the nature of his activities. Some of his cleanup could be reported as changes, others as fixes.

Down at the nuts-and-bolts level of program maintenance, Frank Faretheewell would never know the difference. Only Clint Ransom and his conscience would know what was really happening.

Well, this situation, mired down at this point in balancing deception against irresponsibility, managed to come to a happy ending.

The decibel level from the Frank-Clint verbal fireworks had been loud enough to be heard by Frank's boss. And in this case, the boss was knowledgeable enough to know how to use technical talent, when to override it—and when not to override it.

To make a painful and long story shorter, Frank was eased out of his position of authority and power into another, where his desire to manage his way would do less potential corporate damage.

But Clint was left with the unsettling knowledge that, if necessary, he would have lied to his management to save his sense of responsibility. And that, at the bottom of the hierarchy where the technology resides, he could have gotten away with it.

One area that will continue to prove costly is the maintenance of systems. We have been deluding ourselves if we think that new techniques virtually will do away with the problems of maintenance. Systems theory, especially in the field of cybernetics, has shown that systems must constantly monitor their operations in order to survive. That means continued testing even when things seem to be going smoothly.

We must continually check our operational systems to ensure that they are working correctly. They must be quickly and easily adaptable with change. (We talk a lot about easily maintainable systems, but seem to forget that they still require resources to maintain them.) Obviously, a cost is involved in supporting a maintenance organization whose monitoring function might seem unproductive. But, the price of *not* doing this is even higher. When the unmonitored system finally blows, the cost will be much higher than that of preventive maintenance. Since development does not stop with implementation, I believe we will see a flurry of articles on the subject of structured maintenance.

—Robert T. Atwater

Section IV

Structured Technologies and Maintenance

He that will not apply new remedies must expect new evils.

- Bacon

Structured Retrofit

Jon C. (Cris) Miller

The structured methodologies are now fairly-well accepted for new systems development, although there are differences in interpretation from installation to installation. Their use has rarely been considered, and almost never accepted, in a maintenance environment. Structured Retrofit is the application of today's methodologies to yesterday's systems in order to support tomorrow's requirements.

The typical data processing department spends over half its staff on maintenance coding, maintenance compilations, and maintenance testing. What is needed is a departmental strategy which improves the probabilities of: quick satisfaction of random requests for maintenance, reduction in the number of programs designated incapable of cost-effective maintenance, and increases in the numbers of programs capable of supporting major enhancements without re-writes and extensive testing.

Consider creating a task force using:

1. chief programmer
2. librarian and development support libraries
3. programmer/analysts
4. top-down design
5. structured walk-throughs, and
6. structured programming

in a maintenance support capacity. The chief programmer leads the task force in seeking out candidate systems for Structured Retrofit. In advance, the team must have some scoring system for rating candidates. The system should include both subjective input from users and managers as well as objective data from the program's log. In this latter category, include the age of the program, the number of changes applied since its inception, and the time since last changed.

Each team member conducts some research, and presents the results to task force members in a walk-through fashion, as a basis for proceeding on program changes. Once the high-payoff candidates have been identified, the team members proceed to the next level of research, to be followed by another walk-through before making any changes to program code.

The priorities for changes within a program are:

1. standardization of visual properties (indentation, naming conventions, and paragraph prefixing, in particular)
2. use of libraries for inter-program communication (principally for record formats and standard formulas and algorithms)
3. isolation of I/O routines, with record counts, from in-line processing to one PERFORMable routine per file
4. elimination of PERFORM, GO TO, and ALTER ambiguities, uncertainties, and control pathology
5. elimination of overlapping PERFORM THRUs, and restriction of any residual THRUs to EXIT paragraphs
6. optimization (mechanically) of compiled code to improve program throughput, and
7. flowcharting (mechanically).

The validation mechanism is a file to file compare utility, which may be applied *at any time.* There is no need to complete all retrofit items, but merely to proceed as far as is cost-effective and time-effective. The methodology allows for resumption of retrofit activities at any time that its score on the priority system rises, from information supplied outside the task force.

There is one cardinal restriction: no member of the task force is authorized to make any change to eliminate any revealed error or to satisfy a request for program enhancement. This restriction eliminates time lost to user negotiation, and ensures that there is always a fall-back point, should the file to file compare utility reveal any insoluble problem. It also protects the user from losing an audit trail. The task force members do, of course, record any apparent bugs for review and authorized correction by the normal maintenance group.

The librarian, as in a development team, is the focal point of proven achievement, controlling the retrofit log, the test data used to validate the retrofit, and the mechanized documentation (library materials, flowcharts, and program listings). All migrate back to the normal maintenance area. The librarian may also have the task of researching the literature and marketing materials to find tools which speed up the retrofit activity.

This paper merely introduces the idea of a task force in a maintenance support function. It offers no objective data to support its position. The author contends, however, that existing software packages (library systems, convention enforcing programs, the SORT verb, report writers, structuring engines, and object code optimizers, as well as flowcharters) provide adequate tools for cost-effective retrofit. In closing, simply consider the potential savings from extending the mean time between conversions by months, years, or even decades by having code which can be reliably modified instead of scrapped. Remember that most code scrapped covers conditions undocumented in the old system, and forgotten in the specifications for its successor.

Improved Maintenance Techniques: The Application of Improved Programming Technologies to Existing Systems

Girish Parikh

"How can I use improved programming technologies to maintain existing systems developed without using those techniques?" is the commonly asked question by those exploring or using improved programming technologies. This chapter explores the possibilities of using improved programming technologies to maintain systems developed without using those techniques. I have experience with a librarian, a "mini" walkthrough, and an "informal" chief programmer team. The concepts learned proved extremely successful in maintenance.

The "Improved Maintenance Techniques" (IMT) presented in this chapter propose to use improved programming technologies to maintain and enhance existing systems more effectively and economically.

Improved programming technologies, loosely called structured (programming) techniques, include the following six techniques:

1. HIPO (Hierarchy plus Input-Process-Output).
2. Top-down program development.
3. Chief programmer teams.
4. Development support libraries.
5. Structured programming.
6. Structured walkthroughs.

In using improved programming technologies to maintain existing systems, either of, or both the following two approaches could be taken, depending upon the time and resources available. Improved programming technologies can be used in "direct" maintenance. Improved programming technologies retrofit is for long term benefits. Let us take a closer look at each approach.

Improved Programming Technologies in "Direct" Maintenance

What is "direct" maintenance? Modifying or enhancing the programs and/or system in the affected parts only, without disturbing the rest of the programs and/or system is defined as "direct" maintenance for the purpose of this chapter. The "direct" maintenance solves the problem, sometimes on an emergency basis, either by patching or, if possible, by devising a better, permanent solution. Normally, a better, permanent solution comes later, if done. Some, if not all, concepts of improved programming technologies can be used in "direct" maintenance depending on the situation. The concepts may even need modification. Let us examine how the concepts of improved programming technologies can be used in "direct" maintenance.

The Human Librarian

The librarian, both human and computerized, can be very useful in "direct" maintenance. There will be more about the computerized librarian (library management systems) later, but here, the human librarian would be directly useful. A service bureau where I worked experimented with a librarian among five programmers. The experiment was extremely successful. It released the programmers to concentrate on the technical tasks.

Some of the tasks a librarian can do are:

1. Maintain source, compile and linkage-edit listings.
2. Help create and maintain the test data, JCL decks.
3. Maintain the test listings, dumps, etc.
4. Handle the program moves to production.
5. Maintain the documentation of changes.
6. Maintain the centralized library of programming and system manuals and other pertinent information.
7. Help in the testing of jobs, submit jobs, provide light technical help (particularly JCL) in testing the job streams.
8. Do light keypunching and typing.
9. Act as the centralized information source of project status information, etc.

(Un)structured Walkthroughs

Two or more minds focusing in harmony on the same problem have more chances to come up with a correct or a better solution to a problem.

The purpose of the "mini" walkthrough is to identify and isolate the problems and consider solutions with the help of another programmer.

The walkthroughs need not be formal. The informal "mini" walkthrough is also a powerful method, often giving deep insight into the program and the problems.

Before coding a complex segment for the existing program, a "mini" walkthrough (with analyst and/or programmer) can insure the logic, possibly through pseudo code or a flowchart. The approaches for interfacing of the new routine with the existing program may also be reviewed in a walkthrough. Problem definition should be clear in order to conduct an effective walkthrough. If possible, write it down. The walkthrough can also be effectively used in the testing stage to solve a problem.

The other member in a walkthrough provides the objectivity to the problem solution; the errors not spotted by the programmer may be located by the walkthrough member. If the walkthrough procedure is formally used, the other member may act as the backup programmer. A "dry-run" walkthrough in which one member acts as the computer, while the other helps evaluate the processing of the input data records is also a valuable method.

Chief Programmer Team

The chief programmer team can be implemented as follows. One person having the responsibility of an assignment may act as a chief programmer. The backup programmer, who is also knowledgeable in the system may assist him. Consultation with the analyst can be done as needed. If the size or complexity of the assignment and/or the target date justify, one or more programmers may be added as needed.

The team operation can work very well on large to medium maintenance assignments. A team working in harmony, by some mental chemistry, can produce results unattainable by any single member. The team operation can take the form of a task-force, with a senior responsible programmer acting as the chief in maintenance environment.

HIPO (Hierarchy plus Input-Process-Output)

HIPOs can be used to write the specifications for a maintenance or an enhancement assignment.

Top-Down Program Development

This technique can also be used for adding new routines and enhancing the existing system.

Structured Programming

This also can be used for enhancements and new features and can be called "structured maintenance" or "structured enhancements."

Improved programming technologies retrofit (Miller, Jon C. (Cris), 1976) involves restructuring and reformatting of programs, mechanically and/or manually, to improve their maintainability. It includes standardization of media definitions.

Development Support Libraries

The systematic assignment of program and module names, the standard data names within a record, the standard record and file names, etc., are defined as standard media definitions. If each program has hard coded data names within a record, when the format is changed, the programs that use these formats may need hard changes (changes in program to be done manually by a programmer). Because of different data names or labels used for definitions, it is difficult to determine which programs are affected. Even in recompiling programs, there are changes of coding errors. Misunderstanding may also arise.

By changing the format represented by the member in the library, all the programs that use this format will automatically get this changed format when they are recompiled. By issuing the copy of the listing of the new format to all concerned, effective communication will be established. Also the names will be standardized providing effective documentation. For example, in COBOL, M-LAST-NAME, M-FIRST-NAME, where prefixes "M" is for Master. Use of the library management systems can help in standardizing the media definitions. On time sharing systems, this replacement can be done quickly. Once done, the programs become easier to maintain.

The standard media definitions should be as comprehensive as possible, so that they meet the needs of all the programs that use them. This applies particularly to repetitive fields, hierarchic groups, and fields with both alphabetic and numeric possibilities. As external documentation, a description of each field should be written and kept updated.

The broad view of the development support library is taken here, in the sense that, the contents of the libraries, especially the record format definitions etc., and the library management systems are considered.

A library management system is an automated library system that can manage (add, change, delete, replace, change status to production, etc.) source programs, object and load modules, JCL, test data, etc. Some library management systems are so versatile they may well be called the computerized librarian. The library management system helps the human librarian in many ways, but it does not replace him.

Well organized source program management cannot be overemphasized. The external (human readable) source program and related listings and documentation should be available to the authorized persons whenever they need them.

Source program management should include:

1. The current and previous listings.
2. Program security. Production source program should be always backed up, preferably not on cards but on a reliable library system.
3. An audit trail of program modifications.
4. The facility to copy a production program to create a test version for modifications.

Top-Down Program Development

The hierarchy chart (or the visual table of contents) should give the top down picture of the system. Programs may be converted to top-down structure by using ideas outlined later. After retrofitting, the automated flowcharts may show the top-down structure and may be more useful.

Reformatting and Restructuring the Program

Some COBOL preprocessors with capabilities to reformat the existing COBOL programs are available. In COBOL, by enforcing details like alignment, paragraph numbering, level numbering, common names, etc. through an automatic tool, program maintenance productivity can be improved.

No preprocessing system can correct fundamental logic flaws. It can make programs more "readable," so that logic flaws and other errors are readily apparent.

Restructuring of the programs goes beyond reformatting, so that the programs conform to the structured programming standards. Before undertaking manual restructuring, carefully evaluate the potential gain versus the effort and costs involved.

The unstructured flowchart of the existing program or its parts can be converted to a structured flowchart and then coded to comply with structured programming. The Ashcroft-Manna state-variable technique can be used to convert an unstructured flowchart to an equivalent structured flowchart. Another technique is to duplicate coding to eliminate branching into "common code."

Manual (or automated) routines can be developed to do the following in COBOL programs:

1. ALTER removal.
2. GO TO / PERFORM substitution.
3. Closing sub-routines.
4. Highlighting the control structures.

Guy de Balbine describes results achieved by restructuring the existing FORTRAN programs into a "structured" FORTRAN superset called S-FORTRAN (de Balbine 1975). Examples of restructured programs are easier to understand. Processors exist to translate most FORTRAN programs to S-FORTRAN and vice versa.

The "structuring engine" is a package that transforms unstructured program into a structured program. I do not know of any package that automatically converts the unstructured program in the structured format completely. A "structuring engine" for COBOL (one of the most widely used languages) could be extremely useful if developed (Miller, Jon C. (Cris), 1979).

Structured Walkthroughs

Structured walkthroughs are helpful in making decisions about retrofit projects. Walkthroughs of improved, modified programs with better structure can familiarize the team with the system faster. It is helpful in the evaluation and maintenance of the restructured programs.

A Retrofit Team

A retrofit team can be assembled to carry out the retrofit activities in the installation. It is a formal team for the retrofit activity. A pilot project could be done and then the team could be made permanent if desired. The retrofit team establishes the priorities of action. They do testing prior to and after retrofitting and evaluate the retrofit project or assignments. The team becomes specialized in improved programming technologies retrofitting.

The librarian may act as a "programmer technician" in "Improved Programming Technologies Retrofit" environment. The librarian should keep definitions of media (records, reports, source document) current. It should be automated, but the librarian should see that it is done. Though a librarian is not expected to define a source library, he can contribute to the source library walkthroughs.

The following records kept by the librarian can help in the cost/benefit studies. The record of actual hours spent in retrofitting can be kept. After retrofitting —partial or complete—the hours spent to do the comparative maintenance assignments can be recorded. Though exact measurements may not be possible, the technically oriented manager may be able to fairly evaluate the retrofit project.

Thus, the concepts of improved programming technologies can contribute substantially in improving the maintenance productivity for the existing systems and programs. The management should review the situations and use the techniques described in this report.

HIPO in Maintenance: Documenting Existing Systems with HIPO

Girish Parikh

This article provides guidelines for using HIPO in maintenance, and for creating HIPO documentation for existing systems. HIPO can be used to write specifications for a maintenance or an enhancement assignment.

The heirarchy chart (or visual table of contents) can be created for an existing system using HIPO Method. The detail (hierarchy) charts for the parts of the system that need much maintenance can be created if time permits. If resources and time are available, the overall and detail HIPOs may be constructed for the existing systems.

HIPO or functional documentation developed for the existing system is useful in rewriting the system. Partial HIPO packages may be useful and sufficient for "ordinary" maintenance. It may not be feasible to do HIPOs of programs which are extremely unstructured.

Instead of doing formal IPO (Input-Process-Output) diagrams, functional documentation can be developed by a team. Team operation could also develop effective HIPO for the existing systems. It could work as follows.

If available documentation is not enough, constructing IPO (Input-Process-Output) diagrams may involve studying the entire program—even reading and interpreting the detail code and segments of code. To accomplish this, the chief programmer and backup programmer can divide up the code along major functional breaks, if possible, or by programs for reading. Each concentrates on his assigned part and scans or overviews through the other person's part. The segments are then reviewed in walkthrough sessions and notes made from the programming standpoint. The systems analyst then interprets the findings of the programmers from the systems viewpoint. Thus, the entire program can be covered if necessary.

When the whole program or its necessary parts are thus covered, a meeting between the analyst and programmers (and possibly the users) is needed to complete the function chart and then the HIPO for the program. This method is slow, and some programs may be so unstructured and disorganized that they may not lead into any formal structure chart, but the overall HIPO and functional documentation can be developed. The narration of the program (preferably in pseudocode) should be written down while interpreting the programs. The functional documentation and HIPO can be built in stages as you come across new maintenance activities.

How do you create a program classification by functions? 1) Make an inventory of all the programs and utilities (sort, merge, etc.) in the system. 2) Classify the inventory of programs and utilities by functions and sub-functions relative to the hierarchy chart. Some programs and/or utilities may be repeated in the classified list.

Such a classified list shows the group of programs to accomplish the various functions in the system. The classified list along with the hierarchy chart give a good overall picture of the system. It tells "what" is being accomplished and through "which" programs, and briefly tells "how" through the one-line descriptions of the programs and the utilities. The system hierarchy chart usually does not change much, but with modifications in the system, the program classification may change. It should be updated whenever it is changed. A program could be written to produce an updated list.

Here is how HIPO was used to document existing systems at the University of Illinois.[1]

At the request of Mr. Henard (manager of the financial data systems group at the Urbana campus), staff members of the three data centers documented their existing systems. For this they used traditional flowcharting techniques, mainly because the university had not had time to train all of its personnel in HIPO. Mr. Henard and two of his associates grouped the flowcharts for the procurement and disbursement systems into functional packages. A third member took each package and fitted it into the visual table of contents. The team then expanded the original structure from the 14 functions to include 62 sub-functions listed on procedural flowcharts—a technique they adopted for this, their first major use of the HIPO technique.

The team analyzed each function and prepared HIPO overview diagrams for the functions that could benefit from these charts. The determining factors in the choice were the extent of the information available and the role of the function within the total system. In all, 23 overview diagrams were drawn. Since the team's task was to identify functions rather than to design a system, the development of detailed HIPO diagrams was left for the people assigned to the next phase of the study.

Miss Sandy Dennhardt, senior management methods analyst, describes the way she and her group used HIPO in phase three, starting with the new material developed in the previous phase.

First, they refined the visual table of contents during a thorough review of the system. This review produced a more elaborate structure than was possible during the initial study. The team then reviewed the overview diagrams and developed detailed HIPO diagrams to support each overview.

As the analysts worked on these diagrams, gaps appeared where the interviews had not provided the needed data. The analysts then filled in the material from their general knowledge of the business and marked the item for special review by the user.

Usually, as the analysts embarked on each new level of detail, they saw areas in the level they had just finished that needed further definition. At this point they were able to fill in the necessary information. Miss Dennhardt's experience is that two iterations after the first generally are sufficient to bring any level of diagram to satisfactory completion.

The analysts work in pencil so that they can easily insert modifications. Each page is numbered in a hierarchical fashion to allow rearrangement of the design simply by renumbering and physically reordering pages in the binder rather than redrawing diagrams.

[1]The material in this topic is based on a case study in *Business Systems Planning at the University of Illinois* (Installation Management, GK20–0967–0(4/76), IBM Corporation.

Structured Program Coding: Does It Really Increase Program Maintainability?

Tom Gilb

One of the really strong myths that have become religiously accepted methods is the one about structured programming and its effect on easing our burden of program maintenance.

Let us first limit our discussion to a common, but more well defined variant of structured programming (*all* programs have *some* structure, otherwise they would be unexecutable): some people use the term structured coding and they mean that there are few or no GO TO statements, and only three logical sequences (forward flow, repetition and branching).

Naturally there are lots of other interesting program logic structures such as modules, hierarchies of modules, and dual-but-distinct program code, which can contribute to program maintainability. But let's purposely narrow our vision for the sake of argument here.

If you take a careful look at most of the literature on structured programming, including Jackson's variation, you will notice that there is little or no evidence of better maintainability as a result of using the methods. There are no comparative figures, and certainly none that would stand up to close scrutiny as being even remotely comparable explanations of improved maintenance ease, due entirely to structured coding.

There are people who will put their opinion on record, based on their experience. There are those who think that improved maintenance ease is so self-evident as to need no further discussion. But that doesn't mean they are correct.

There are those who refer to the "New York Times" project as proof, but maintainability was not measured in that project at all. The only measures we have there are of finished statement productivity and operational realiability. That is a different matter. To confuse the N.Y.T. proof there are about eight new methods being tried out at the same time, there are about 3 known super-programmers on the five-man team, and the comparison basis (comparable or identical project type and size) doesn't really exist.

There are at least three researchers who have tried to conduct well controlled experiments in an attempt to assess the maintainability effects of structured code. Their work is not well known yet, but offers some insights, so let's take a look at it.

Laurence Weissman of University of Toronto conducted a series of careful experiments designed to measure several different effects of a few carefully controlled changes in programming style. He measured productivity, accuracy and the opinion of the participants. He used programs which were identical except for being structured (no GOTO) or not structured for example, and about 60 participants were used for each experiment, half of them with each type of program, working in a simulated maintenance situation.

Weissman found that structured programming did not improve results in a statistically significant way, in spite of the fact that all participants were trained and "brainwashed" in structured programming the two previous years! They did however produce a statistically significant opinion that it was better! This is a well measured documentation of the fact that opinions can be misleading; you've got to measure actual results to know.

Weissman did find significant results from paragraphing (or indentation) measured independently from structured code (you do realize that they are two different things, even though almost all structured programming examples also include paragraphing). I began to wonder if much of the credit given to structured programming is really due to indentation, which certainly is simpler to do and capable of compiler automation (example: MetaCOBOL).

Weissman also found that comments gave significant productivity effects (34% to 69% faster rate of reading the program and desk checking it), and that meaningful mnemonics reduced the error rate of desk check output while simulating the running of the program by 48%. I suppose comments aren't academically exciting, so that's why few examples of structured programming include them?

Studies by T. Green and colleagues of Sheffield, and Ben Shneiderman of University of Maryland, do not turn up any significant evidence that structured code helps maintainability. They do show that there are a large number of other factors that may be more important, and that conclusions are difficult to draw for the general case. The experience of the programmer is one factor that must be considered it seems, for example.

Tom Love of General Electric (ACM Software Eng. Notes March 1977) reports experiments designed to test the hypothesis that "structuring a program makes it easier to understand", and uses Sneidermann's "ability to memorize" measure of program understandability. His results showed that graduate students could correctly recall 60% of a program which was of simple structure (GOTO-less) but only 40% could be recalled of complex (with GOTO) programs. There was however little or no difference for beginning Fortran students. Mr. Love performed careful experiments regarding paragraphing and was surprised to see how little effect it had for his subjects. He concluded "Our intuition regarding the benefit of paragraphing was not substantiated by the data, and the seemingly obvious assertion that programs with simplified control flow are easier to understand, was not completely confirmed by the data."

On a larger scale Holmes and Miller of McDonnell Douglas Automation, St. Louis, tried all the IBM improved programming techniques for two years ('73, '74) both with program construction and program maintenance. They reported a net project overflow (excess time compared to previous methods) of up to 85%, the first year.

"We found indentation rules a must for maintaining the readability of nested IF's." "It took us more time to program structured." "As a result of this experience we are recommending that our installation enforce standards to assure the existence of well organized programs, but make Structured Programming optional." They also noted that it takes six months experience subsequent to 80 hours of formal training in the new methods to "develop structured programs top down in about the same time and cost as using traditional practices."

This leads me to wonder whether all the reports of improvements, which others have offered, are more a reflection of their extremely poor set of previously used methods. Any organized methodology is probably an improvement over anarchy in programming. After a substantial modification of IBM's methods and a substantial investment in training in the use of the methods, they reported at a Guide meeting that "Structured Programs are easier to read, but only for programmers trained (in it)."

The only really good quantitative argument I have seen for structured code is that it can result in substantially fewer logical paths to test in the program, which is important if you have decided to have as a test standard "all logical paths." In a 21 statement subroutine the difference can be 144 test cases to 90,000,000,000. But how many installations are even aware of this test criteria yet?

The best news yet is the "Structuring Engine," a 30,000 statement program made by Caine, Farber and Gordon Inc. of California (*Computer,* July 1975) which rewrites unstructured Fortran to Structured and Indented Fortran.

My hypothesis is that structured code probably has some value for program maintainability, but its cost and effect for various purposes are only crudely understood, and there are certainly a large number of alternative and supplementary techniques for doing the same thing or for doing it better.

"Maintainability" is More Than Structured Coding

Tom Gilb

We have become very interested in ease of maintenance of programmed systems. Rightly so when we see the current cost in money, manpower and time.

Prophets have shouted that the answer is "structured": structured programming, structured coding, structured design and structured files (databases?). Maybe some structure is better than none in some cases. But the situation is not a very structured one, from a management point of view. We are throwing claimed solutions at badly structured problems, and it is very hard to find hard evidence that we are making any real progress.

I have a suggestion. Let us structure our approach. Let us organize maintainability technology into a knowledge structure. Let us select appropriate maintainability technology based on a structured decision-making sequence.

Let me define maintainability. It is the probability of our being able to change the "state" of a system, within a given time period. It is best described as a curve of the probabilities of changing the system, plotted against time. But often a single point on the curve can suffice for purposes of specification. For example: Program A is designed to allow maintenance programmers P to repair representative faults B with a 90% probability of completing the change and required post-maintenance testing within two hours. This shall be measured in a controlled acceptance test using artificially embedded errors.

Maintainability technology should not simply be defined as those techniques which "improve" this maintainability measure. We must consider side effects on other quality aspects of our system. It is of little practical interest to get maintenance changes effected which seriously threaten the operational realiability, conversion portability or even later maintainability of our system. Thus we must insist that we are interested in maintainability technology which also leaves us in control of all other critical or interesting qualities of our system. Anything less is to invite problems.

We should not either be so narrow as to (presuppose) a need to "maximize" the maintainability aspect of a system. We may well be interested in a conscious *reduction* of the maintainability level of a planned system when this gives us some other higher priority benefit such as higher work throughput or lower operational cost.

Thus we are primarily interested in knowing the expected multidimensional effects of a set of maintainability techniques, in relation to our system goals. Any maintainability technique where we do not have knowledge (from experience data for example) or at least control (from contract guarantees for example) of these multi-dimensional effects, is a potential danger. It is a threat to our system success.

At this point I know I have "lost" very many readers. For we are not trained yet, as a profession, to handle multidimensional system quality concepts, and to even think of measurable maintainability for programs. Before I continue, I should like to advertise that both a set of techniques for handling this general problem of multidimensional system perception, and the specific problem of maintainability, is described in depth in my book *Software Metrics.* (Gilb, 1977)

Let me now suggest a conscious simplification. We are interested in all ideas (techniques, equipment, management methods) which can improve the *maintainability / cost ratio* in our system, without negatively impacting any other critical quality.

In other words, we are not simply interested in ways of improving maintainability, but we are typically just as interested in the cost of development and of operation of a system, including the life long maintenance cost, which has some predesigned minimum level of maintainability.

As an example of this, a group in Texas reported in *Data Management* (November 1975) that they had performed a controlled experiment, with two program changes carried out by twelve individual programmers, using alternatively written and audio tape program documentation. The total time for twelve maintenance attempts using conventional documentation was 524 minutes, and it was 492 minutes using "audio" documentation, in other words, about the same. The estimated cost of documentation in "audio" format was estimated to be about one fourth (75% cost reduction). So in this example, we see an alternative technique to conventional ones which contribute to maintenance ability, and it is interesting not because it is superior, but because it promises to give about the same results at a substantially lower cost.

The next fallacy about maintainability technology is that it has to do with improving human ability to understand programmed logic. This is only a special case. The important thing is the needed change or repair. We don't have to understand an error, or the old program, if we can successfully replace it with a correct program or a changed program module. This is simply a "spare parts" maintainability concept. It requires understanding of interface specifications for the module, but not of the inner-workings of that module.

Further, as an example, many file reconstruction procedures (back up file reloaded, then rerun all transactions since it was dumped) pertain to maintainability of important parts of the programmed system. Yet this procedure not only makes it unnecessary for us to examine the inner workings of the system being repaired, but it does not require us to look at the programmed logic. Structured program code isn't going to help us a lot when our data base is destroyed. We must stop writing and speaking as though the programs were the only parts of systems which need maintenance effort. A systems oriented maintainability strategy will consider repair and change to all major components of a system to be on an equal footing.

One of the practical consequences of this is that maintainability techniques, like automatic data base audit programs, will get a higher priority than currently popular techniques, because they give some help to the maintainability problem of programs (testing complex files for logical bugs after a maintenance change), files (ensuring compliance with planned record formats and codes) and even hardware (showing the location and extent of hardware failure which has corrupted files.)

In addition the cost of using such a tool is attractive because it is automated. In fact it is really an absolute necessity for current large and complex file systems, in spite of the fact that the majority of us do not initially plan systems with such a maintainability tool. Most of us do not even think of a file audit program as a maintainability tool, which just illustrates the poorness of our conventional professional knowledge.

It is today possible to make a well structured hierarchical list of several hundred "maintainability" ideas which our programmed systems can benefit from. It is also possible to a surprisingly high, but still too low, degree to indicate quantitatively the expected qualities and costs you can expect to experience with each technique. It is difficult, though possible and practiced, to indicate the measurable effects of combinations of these techniques.

Gilb's hypothesis: we can and should "engineer" maintainability into software.

Selections from *Composite / Structured Design*

Glenford J. Myers

Program maintenance

One could easily form the impression that only the programmers involved with the design of new programs need be aware of the ideas of composite design and that others, in particular maintenance programmers, need not be familiar with the ideas. Such an impression is wrong and easy to dispel.

A large portion of budgets for most data processing organizations is spent on program maintenance (defined here as fixing errors in, and making small enhancements to, production programs), implying that maintenance programmers make a substantial number of changes. Because the maintenance programmer typically works under a tremendous amount of pressure, there is an understandable tendency to make a "quick fix," that is, to amend the program in what appears at that time to be the most economical way possible. Such changes (e.g., adding a global data reference or weakening the strength of a module) can quickly undo the original well-designed structure of the program. Spier (1976), for one, graphically illustrates how a program was reduced to shambles by a series of ill-conceived maintenance changes.

If the programs being maintained were designed with composite design, and if the programs are being maintained by people who did not participate in the design of the programs, it is vital that these people (the maintenance programmers) thoroughly understand the ideas of composite design. Not only will they appreciate the programs' increased ease of maintenance, but once they understand the motivations behind the original designs, the maintenance programmers will themselves be motivated to alter the programs in a way that is consistent with the original design.

We can restate this as two key objectives for the maintenance programmer:

1. Have a global view of the program and a long-range view of the consequences of each change to lessen the chances of deteriorating the program's structure.

2. Modify the program in such a way that the resultant program has the appearance of being originally designed and coded that way.

Program Modification

Much of the program development (contrasted with program maintenance) done by data processing organizations involves extensive changes to existing systems and programs, rather than the development of entirely new systems and programs. Since composite design has been presented as applying to only the design of new programs, an obvious question is how, if at all, it can be applied to the modification of existing systems and programs.

If a system is being modified (a system is loosely defined here as a related collection of programs or a set of asynchronously executing subsystems) and the modification entails developing new, or rewriting existing, programs or subsystems, it is relatively easy to apply composite design in the process. However, if the modification entails changes to an existing program, composite design is usually inapplicable.

If the system being modified has some undesirable design characteristics, compromises must often be made when adding a new component to the system. As an example, an experimental attempt was made to redesign a part of IBM's OS / 360 operating system by using composite design. The component selected was the OPEN function for sequential data sets. Because of the existing system design, however, the existing OPEN function was heavily common and stamp coupled to the remainder of the system. This was because of the sharing of a large number of control tables and data structures. Hence, all of the modules in the existing OPEN component were tightly coupled to literally thousands of other modules throughout the system, and redesigning this overall aspect of OS / 360 was beyond the scope of the experiment.

The following compromise was made in the new version. The only coupling among modules of the new version was data coupling. However, since the OPEN function is required to obtain information from some of these system control tables and to build others, there had to be some sensitivity in the new version to these data structures, but it was decided to hide this in only one module—the top module of the new version. Hence, only one module in the new version was common and stamp coupled to the other modules in the OS / 360 system. (This effort was just an experiment and was not incorporated in the OS / 360 product.)

Their maintenance was easy,
Each user wore a grin,
They are not bothered much by bugs,
Who never put them in.

And when they did enhancements,
They found that easy too,
For they had kept the documents,
Which told them what to do.

—David H. H. Diamond

Section V

The Future of Maintenance

Many managers and programmers point out that the structured programming techniques are primarily intended for new development projects; for maintenance of existing unstructured programs they seem to be of limited use (though the librarian concept and the structured walkthrough concept would still be quite useful). This point is basically valid, though it is usually possible to add new sections of code in a top-down structured manner, e.g., when completely new features are being added to a system at the request of a user.

This problem may be solved eventually with the aid of "structuring engines" that will automatically convert unstructured logic into structured form; while such an "engine" cannot magically transform "bad" code into "good" code, it will at least foster some standardization.

Edward Yourdon

From "Making Move to Structured Programming," *Datamation,* June 1975, p. 52.

Structured Maintenance

Edward Yourdon

Part 1: Approach Trains User to Read 'Alien' Code

Structured programming, structured design and structured analysis have revolutionized the development of new computer systems in the past few years. Numerous case studies and surveys have documented impressive gains in productivity, reliability and maintainability of these new systems.

But what about existing systems? It is estimated that at least 50% of all software activity in the U.S. is spent maintaining existing systems—and for many large organizations, the figure is closer to 75% to 80%. Most of these systems were developed long before anyone knew about modular programming, structured programming or any other "modern" development techniques—so it is no surprise that they continue, even after 10 years, to be unreliable and difficult to maintain.

So, what can be done to improve the state of affairs for these wretched old systems, with which we must live for another five to 10 years? Fortunately, there is a new discipline emerging, structured maintenance, which is aimed specifically at the technical problems encountered by maintenance programmers. Those problems are usually such things as:

1. Nobody remembers specifically what the system is supposed to do, nor does anyone really know with any certainty what the system *does* do.
2. It is often difficult to relate specific actions (or outputs) of an existing system to the specific "chunks" of code (we hesitate to use the word module) that produce those actions.
3. If a programmer changes code in an existing system, it is almost impossible to know whether any other part of the system will be affected.
4. It is extremely difficult, frustrating and unpleasant learning to read "alien" code developed by another programmer.

Structured maintenance includes: techniques to document the structure and interconnections of existing systems; guidelines for reading alien code; guidelines for modifying, retesting and debugging alien code; economic models for deciding when existing systems can profitably be rewritten; manual and mechanical techniques of "restructuring" all or part of an existing system; and the use of walkthroughs and teams to decrease the errors and boredom associated with maintenance.

Most of the documentation techniques have been used successfully for the development of *new* systems; what is interesting is that they are now being used to document existing systems. These techniques include Heirarchy plus Input-Processing-Output (Hipo) and structure charts, data flow diagrams and—in the rare cases where complex, decision-oriented logic has to be deciphered—decision tables.

These techniques have been successful in recent maintenance efforts because the existing documentation is usually obsolete; the existing documentation and/or the existing code presents a "low-level" view of the system, without providing the overview that the maintenance programmer needs so desperately; and the existing documentation almost never warns the maintenance programmer of the subtle interconnections between one "chunk" of the program and another.

Structured maintenance also concentrates on techniques for reading alien code—almost as if it were an exercise in archaeology. It is ironic that we train most programmers in "write-only" mode—that is, we train them to *write* computer programs without ever teaching them the nontrivial art of *reading* computer programs. Imagine what things would be like if we taught English, French and Spanish that way!

What does a programmer have to learn to be able to read programs successfully? Perhaps the most important thing to learn is the importance of taking notes. Reading a program usually raises questions that can't be answered immediately or it suggests modifications that the programmer would like to make "some day."

In our work, we recommend that the maintenance programmer keep five "diaries": bugs, maintainability issues, usability issues, efficiency issues and mysteries and unanswered questions.

Part 2: Cost to Reshape User System Can Be Forecast

I would appreciate some feedback on the concepts of structured maintenance and some ideas on the guidelines needed to give it form as an approach to improved programmer productivity.

In the above, I suggested some of the things a programmer has to do to be successful and effective in reading "alien" code.

The other important part about reading programs is knowing what to look for. As many programmers know, most maintenance problems are associated with loops, decisions, logical expressions, subscripting, numerical operations, error-handling, data structures or input/output operations. For each of these areas, a number of specific "what-to-look-for" guidelines can be given.

Some of the other important pieces of structured maintenance are also the result of several years' experience with the structured development of new systems. For example, many of the "pilot projects" that have been used to demonstrate the effectiveness of structured techniques have been *conversions* of old systems to their new structured equivalents.

As a result, we now have a growing body of evidence with which we can estimate several factors:

1. How much it costs to reanalyze, redesign and/or recode an existing system. For example, it usually turns out that such efforts can be carried out at the rate of 20 to 25 debugged statements per day instead of the usual 10 to 15 statements per day. And it is reasonable to estimate, in the absence of any other evidence, that the new structured system will be approximately the same number of statements as the old version.
2. How much more reliable the new system will be. This depends largely on whether the old system has "settled down" or whether it continues to be unstable.
3. How much more maintainable the new system will be. In most cases, it is reasonable to assume that maintainability will improve by at least a factor of two, and possibly by as much as a factor of 10.
4. How much more CPU time/memory will be required by the new system. A reasonable "worst case" estimate is that a new structured system will require no more than 5% to 10% additional hardware resources. In addition, in a surprisingly large number of cases, the new system is considerably more efficient than the old system, since the new designers are, in a sense, able to stand on the shoulders of the original designers and see a better way of approaching the problem.

Another structured maintenance technique involves the "restructuring" of existing programs. This, too, is based on techniques that were originally developed for structured programming. There are a number of techniques that can be applied either manually or mechanically to restructure code (Baker 1977).

While there is considerable controversy about the merits of mechanically restructuring whole programs and systems (remember when we tried to mechanically convert 1401 Autocoder programs to Cobol?), there is no question that these techniques can be useful as a guideline for rewriting small chunks of existing logic that, in their present unstructured state, are impossible to understand.

All in all, structured maintenance is based largely on common sense and on techniques learned in structured programming and structured design. So why all the fuss about it?

Partly because, as Will Rogers once said, "Common sense isn't common." Remember, structured programming is still dismissed by some skeptics as trivial "common sense"—and yet it's evident that all of us need some rigorous, disciplined guidelines to ensure that we don't forget our common sense in the excitement of coding.

Also, it's evident that the structured design / programming movement has, to a large extent, been ignored by a large group of maintenance programmers. And who can blame them for ignoring discussions about the virtues of *future* systems when they're still responding to midnight phone calls about their *old* systems? So, it's time we developed a package of guidelines and techniques specifically tailored to the needs of such people—and that's what structured maintenance is all about.

Guaranteeing Program Maintainability

Tom Gilb

Do you know how to write a systems specification, or a contract guarantee which will help you be sure that the resulting programs are really easy to modify and understand once they have gone into the operational phase?

Some people fool themselves that they know how. They write specifications like "Standard COBOL," "Structured Programming," and "Small Modules." Probably these things do contribute to a certain degree to ease of program maintenance. But they do not guarantee any known level of maintainability.

The system can be delivered by the software house or your own people, it can formally meet your specifications, and it can be much more difficult for your maintenance programmers to find their way around in than you had hoped.

What we need is a way of motivating the program producer, and the program designer, to create a specific level of ease of understanding the program. From our point of view it shouldn't really matter *how* this is achieved, the important thing is *that* it is achieved.

There are many different techniques for increasing the maintainability of a program, and a lot of them are much more effective than the three techniques mentioned above. We should not therefore limit our suppliers by constraining them to a specific set of techniques, because we then become the ones responsible for lack of sufficient maintainability.

Let's learn to judge by results, not by techniques.

Engineers have long had a language for describing the maintainability of any system. Briefly they speak about the "probability of repairing the system within a specified time, under specified conditions," more popularly this amounts to the same thing as the Mean Time to Repair (MTTR). I firmly believe that this concept is applicable for "soft" systems such as programs and databases.

The practical technique which we use to measure the degree of maintainability is called the "*b*ebugging" technique.[1] Various other terms are used such as artificial bug insertion, which is close to the concept of artificial insemination.

This technique has been used extensively by researchers such as Gould and Drongowski of IBM to study debugging behavior. It measures the effect of various people and various program documentation levels on the work of identifying bugs.

Learning from these experiments I have for the past two years made use of the following system and contract specification in a variety of applications:

The program maintainability shall be at least 90% probability (in half an hour) for the assigned and trained maintenance programmers to identify (without fixing and retesting) undesirable program results ("bugs"). A practical test for system acceptance may be carried out by insertion of at least ten artificial program bugs at random by an independent party, one at a time. The qualified maintenance programmers must demonstrate that they can correctly identify the statements causing the bug in at least nine out of ten cases within a time limit of under one half-hour ("each," or "on the average," depending on how lenient you are feeling that day).

In one case, a Scandinavian bank online system, the contracts were already written, and the only specification for the supplier of the 180 intelligent cashier machines, and their programs to be supplied, was that the bank's people "should be able to maintain the programs."

We got agreement immediately from the supplier to an acceptance test based on the above formulation. At first he was skeptical, until I pointed out that such a formulation actually *limited* his responsibility to the bank. His other objection was, "How can I know if my programmers are making high enough quality programs until it is all finished?" To which the reply was, perform the test on the first module (of 200 planned). If you pass it, you are on the right track, if not, you have an opportunity to change your programming methods and documentation methods.

One immediate result of the agreement on the maintainability acceptance test in the case above was that the supplier agreed to get his programmers to write extensive comments in the modules (something that they had not practiced at all up to that point).

Since that time I have gotten contract agreement using this formulation for both remote job entry software and multiterminal software for a nordic microcomputer supplier from a nordic software house, and am currently working on getting such a clause in a contract for development of an automated warehouse mini-computer project where my client is going to take over maintenance from the software house which will develop the system.

[1] For more information, see "*B*ebugging and Maintainability" in Tom Gilb *Software Metrics,* (Cambridge: Winthrop), 1977.

Spare Parts Maintenance Strategy for Programs

Tom Gilb

You are responsible for the on-line project, or its maintenance. When the inevitable system breakdowns occur due to program bugs, you know that it is important to all users of the system that the programming team can diagnose the source of the error, correct it, retest the entire system, and then at the end of two to 20 hours, with luck, you can put the "real time" system back on the air again. With the best available technology and a lot of luck this will only happen once a week or once a month.

I know this will sound incredible but I recently received technical papers from software specialists who are responsible for the safety systems of atomic power plants. They clearly thought that the solution to their reliability and maintenance problems was through structured programming. Anti-pollution forces take note! Needless to say, in panic (my own life was at stake) I offered to visit them at my own expense and set them straight. I am much relieved to say they accepted, and part of what I told them is the idea below.

The basic idea is very simple. Write two programs to perform the *same* function. One acts as a spare part for the other. The basic assumption is that both are well tested and that whenever a bug does occur in one of the program versions, then exactly the same bug will not usually be present in the spare part version.

We do this with computer hardware, and with the software known as "files," and if you think about it we have actually been practicing this technology on a wide scale with programs for years. You don't believe me, do you? Think about what a systems programmer does when he unexpectedly encounters a bug in the new update of the supplier's software. He goes back to the spare part with different bugs, the old version. Similarly, when converting to new programming languages on the same system, we are naturally prepared to revert back to the old version (even if it does run slower and is less portable) when we hit unexpected bugs on the recently coded version.

So in fact, what I am talking about is making conscious use of the concept of spare part programs when planning a new system. The most immediate objection is cost. However, before you discard the idea on cost grounds, ask yourself whether the dual computer system you have planned (for graceful degradation to one of the CPUs, when the other fails) is really well planned. Half the breakdown causes are hardware, but half of them are from software, including user written programs. Is it really consistent economics to buy hardware spares and not to buy software spares? The myth that programs don't break down ("once they are right") and therefore need no spare parts, is difficult to break down, because the people who believe it have not been listening to the widespread experiences in the software field which tell their clear story. Software is as error prone as hardware. There is no known way of guaranteeing error-free software which is practical, and in any case a spare part is much cheaper than a perfect program. Two Volkswagens are probably a more reliable transport alternative than one Rolls Royce, and a lot cheaper.

For some real-time on-line installations, particularly the ones who feel they can afford to have a mostly idle standby computer, even a doubling of the application coding cost would be an acceptable increase in the project budget, if it resulted in almost immediate repair of software faults, using the spare part method.

Fortunately for the rest of us, there is good reason to believe that we can afford the spare part software too. Experience plays surprising tricks on our intuition. Would you believe that writing two programs can be cheaper than writing one of them? That is the experience of a large number of those who have tried. And even when it hasn't been cheaper, there are reports of "only ten percent more." The reason is that dual but distinct software can be used in a variety of ways to reduce the total cost of software production and maintenance, so that the effort of coding it twice (coding being only 5 to 10 percent of a real time project anyway) may be a profitable investment.

One example is the kind of thing that Rault of Thomson-CSF in Paris has practiced. He codes electronic design programs in APL, as a cheap model (one tenth the cost of FORTRAN) and then recodes, from the model as a plan, in FORTRAN, to get a program with one tenth of the operational cost. In order to test the system he feeds the same inputs into both "models" and checks to see if they produce the same outputs. This amounts to automating the desk checking and automating manual validation of test cases.

If you are planning on thorough testing (like, "all test paths") this results in a considerable saving of human time, which more than pays for the APL model. The APL model was already paid for since it replaced flow charts and non-machine readable pseudo-code. Also it can be used during maintenance phases both as documentation and as comparison for retesting of a large amount of test cases. And who among you can automatically verify that your flow charts are correctly updated along with the program? (Gilb 1977)

Should We Specialize in Hiring and Training of Application Program Maintenance Technicians?

Tom Gilb

In November 1978, a New York client described a pressing problem to me. The maintenance people they had for their most critical on-line system (one with 1,800 terminal operators) kept quitting on them faster than they could be replaced.

The client was hiring recent computer science graduates, training them in Assembler and the "system," only to find that they then decided that the pressure of 400 or more backlogged change requests, and a critical on-line system upon which hundreds of employees were dependent and with which the general public came into regular contact, was too much of a pressure.

They quit in six months.

This led me to wonder aloud to them if they had similar problems with their maintenance people for the company's electrical systems in the field. Or for that matter does their supplier, IBM, experience similar problems of instability with their field maintenance people?

Maybe if we recruited atomic physics graduates to paint atomic reactor power stations, they would quit their job too? Maybe if IBM took experienced computer wiring technicians and asked them to do field maintenance on their computer systems, there would also be some difficulties.

In the case of my New York client, I had the strong feeling that the candidates they recruited were not particularly trained or motivated for the job they were given. They only took the job because it gave them a start in industry, and they did not understand the nature of the work.

A month later I was visiting an old professional colleague at a Norwegian technical training college with a recently started two year training course in computers. My colleague had a simultaneous commitment to graduate computer science students at the University of Oslo, so it was natural that we asked the question of what difference there was between the technical college and university students.

There were several: in length-of-study, practical-versus-academic, and even quality of recruitment. But, the basic syllabus and orientation was not substantially different from what we have seen all over the world.

I raised the question of whether this technical college could consider training a specialist in program maintenance. Either as a directly recruited two year study, or as a third year specialization.

In almost any well established company using a computer, from 30% to nearly 100% of the programming staff are engaged in maintenance of some sort or other. There would seem to be a real need for people especially trained and motivated in this area. Yet I have never heard of a training program especially for program maintenance.

It is possible that maintenance requires a particular type of person, who might be very different from those who lead projects, design systems, or code someone's pseudocode into COBOL.

It is possible that the vast array of tools and techniques which has surfaced to analyze program actions, aid changes, and help with testing, requires in depth study and orientation by specialists.

In today's immediate climate in several parts of the world, the demand for programmers is artificially high. This state cannot last, and we might well again see over-production of computer specialists. This might be the time for both centres of training and employers to ask if some of the over-production should be guaranteed useful employment by being recruited and trained especially to solve the demanding problems of program maintenance.

The specialization is necessary now. In the long run it is inevitable. I suspect our profession will be unusually slow in responding to our need.

Better Manpower Utilization Using Automatic Restructuring

Guy de Balbine

Introduction

Our intent is to introduce the concept of automatic restructuring as a powerful method for improving the quality of software developed before the advent of structured programming. The quality improvements we are concerned with are neither execution time efficiency nor core size requirements but, rather, higher readability and clear structured code. These, in turn, should improve the reliability and reduce the maintenance costs by making human verification more efficient.

The fact that arbitrary flow diagrams can be mapped into equivalent structured flow diagrams by introducing new Boolean variables has been established by Bohm and Jacopini (1966) (see Ashcroft, Manna, 1971 for an example of a program that cannot be restructured without additional Boolean variables). The first steps toward systematizing this mapping are taken in (Peterson, Kasami, Tokura, 1973: 503–512).

In practice, however, we have found that adding Boolean variables (whose names are meaningless since they would have to be program generated) makes the code often harder to read. Thus Djikstra's comment (Djikstra 1968: 147–148) that the exercise to translate an arbitrary flow diagram more or less mechanically into a jumpless one is not to be recommended because "the resulting flow diagram cannot be expected to be more transparent than the original one."

On the other hand, if we allow certain constrained forms of the GO TO statement, many of the difficulties vanish and readability can be enhanced. One form of the constrained GO TO, which we call UNDO is used to exit from nested structures when necessary, the jump always being a forward jump to the end of a DO group. This is similar to the LEAVE statement in BLISS. (Wulf 1972: 63–69)

Figure 1 shows an example derived from Ashcroft and Manna, 1971. With the UNDO construct, a natural straightforward representation can be obtained.

Based on the hypothesis that the restructuring process could be applied systematically to existing unstructured programs and enhance their clarity, we have designed and implemented a software tool known as the "structuring engine." We shall now describe in more detail some of our motivations and the experimental results that we have obtained while using the "structuring engine."

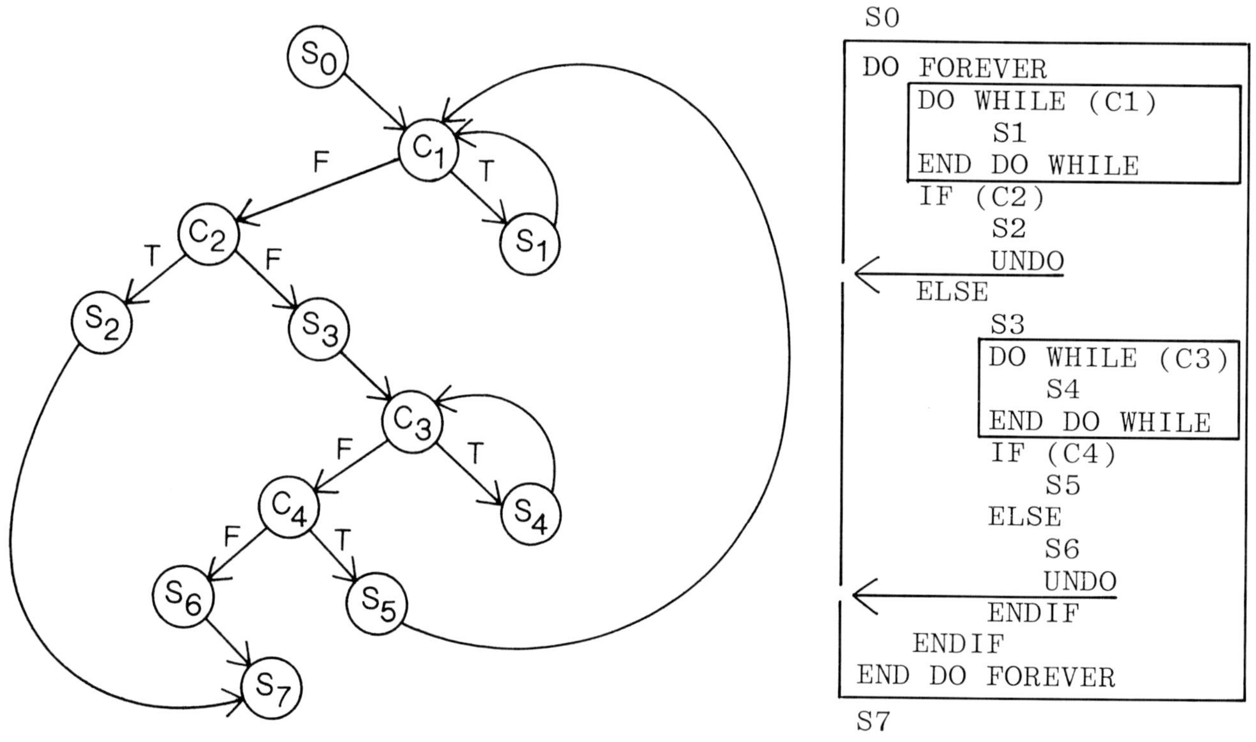

```
S0
DO FOREVER
   DO WHILE (C1)
        S1
   END DO WHILE
   IF (C2)
        S2
        UNDO
   ELSE
        S3
        DO WHILE (C3)
            S4
        END DO WHILE
        IF (C4)
            S5
        ELSE
            S6
            UNDO
        ENDIF
   ENDIF
END DO FOREVER
S7
```

Figure 1. Example of UNDO Usage

Improving the Human—Software Interface

Most production software in existence today was developed using no precise design methodology. The programming languages generally used (FORTRAN, COBOL) were invented over a decade ago and have hardly evolved due to the severe binds imposed by upward compatibility. Maintaining and extending the huge software inventory is a difficult and inefficient task which is becoming even more so year by year. The software documentation is poor, the logic is often obscure, and the authors are most likely to be gone or assigned to other projects. Operational programs still break down with bugs that have managed to escape the most careful scrutiny. Modifications and extensions are dreaded and postponed since they are likely to cause perturbations whose far ranging effects cannot be easily and reliably assessed.

We do not claim to have a panacea that can cure all of these problems instantly. However, the experience gained while developing large scale software using structured programming has shown some of the important factors that influence software reliability and maintenance costs. In our experience, the quality of the human—software interface is one such factor since it influences the efficiency of all manhours invested at the program level, both during development and maintenance.

To benefit from a better human—software interface applicable to future software development, as well as to current software, we suggest extending commonly available programming languages, imposing some constraints to ensure proper language usage, emphasizing the need for visual improvement of programs, and providing transitional tools to assist in the conversion of existing software to meet the new interface specifications.

Language extensions

The only precise, and by definition up-to-date, source of internal documentation for most software in existence today lies in the programs themselves. Understanding what programs accomplish implies an understanding in the formalism and at the level of detail imposed by the programming language used as a vehicle for implementation. Thus, any shortcomings of the implementation language have a direct impact on the effort needed to understand what the programs do and to modify and extend them successfully.

The two most widespread programming languages, FORTRAN and COBOL, do not contain adequate mechanisms to support structured coding. The limited facilities they provide can be exploited very cleverly to look somewhat like structured code. However, a substantial effort is needed to maintain proper indentation and the legibility is never as good as that obtainable with a structured language.

The obvious step is to build preprocessors to provide the necessary syntactic extensions and perform some of the manual chores such as automatic indentation.

Several dozen preprocessors have already been built to translate various brands of structured FORTRAN into pure FORTRAN (Miller 1973). Our effort along these lines has led to the design and implementation of the S-FORTRAN language and translator. S-FORTRAN embodies a small but powerful set of structured constructs. S-FORTRAN was designed to serve both as a target language for restructured programs and as an implementation language for new programs. It is not only simple but easy to remember unambiguously. The S-FORTRAN language is succinctly described in the Appendix.

We do not wish at this point to discuss at length the individual merits of each S-FORTRAN feature and whether LOOP is a better term than DO FOREVER or should DO UNTIL test first rather than execute first. These decisions are mostly conventions. Let us simply express the hope that a consensus will soon develop so that a "de facto" standard will prevail. Structured FORTRAN programs will then be unambiguously understood by all.

Language usage

Providing extended languages to permit structured coding is not sufficient to guarantee software clarity. Programmers can still misuse structured languages to follow their traditional thought processes, the result being obscure programs under the guise of structured code.

Rather than resort to building enforcement tools, it is our belief that the simplicity and intellectual appeal of a well formed program will generate the necessary motivation among programmers to adopt a new standard of quality.

Visual improvement

Structured coding techniques require that programs be systematically indented to stress the relationships between code segments. This hierarchical arrangement allows a quick grasp of the global as well as the local structure of the code. Understanding the code no longer requires keeping track of many scattered items such as labels and transfers. Rather, it means perceiving visual patterns that can be precisely mapped into our analytical understanding of the solution. Each part and subpart corresponds to a block of code, carefully delimited to facilitate its verification. Systematic indentation makes it easy to collect the conditions controlling the execution of each indentation level down to the code segment being examined.

The power of visual perception can be readily tapped by developing patterns whenever feasible. Symmetry, lack of symmetry, block indentation, regularity, recurring patterns, aligned similar items, . . . are characteristics that can be detected at a glance by the eye. Interestingly enough, these are characteristics whose global nature is usually hard to detect and utilize automatically with software tools.

How to benefit from the new interface

Formulating a better human—software interface is clearly valuable for software that has not yet been written. The important point is that such an improvement can also be applied to a large part of the software inventory in existence today. It is our belief that this should lead to a significant reduction in the maintenance effort by better utilizing the available manpower.

Until very recently, the main route for modernizing existing unstructured software was to start over with a clean top-down design and structured implementation. Needless to say, such complete manual reprogramming should not be undertaken without a very careful evaluation of the potential gain versus the effort involved. We have found that the major obstacles to manual reprogramming are the need for top talent during the redesign phase, the manpower expenditure, the elapsed time before a new system is up and running and the penalty for having to go through a full testing and debugging period again.

As an alternative, we have developed a method which is much easier to apply in practice. It consists in keeping the global design as is, in particular the data structures, and in automatically transforming every program into an equivalent structured program, visually improved to make its reading easier and its understanding more thorough. This method is supported by a software tool known as the "structuring engine." We have applied this tool to a variety of FORTRAN programs. We shall now describe the characteristics of the tool and some of the experimental results that we have obtained so far.

The "structuring engine"

Capabilities

The "structuring engine," as it now exists, is a large task running on an IBM/370 under VS. It consists of over 30,000 lines of structured PL/1 code. It will restructure programs written in FORTRAN including any language extensions acceptable by IBM, Univac, CDC and Honeywell compilers.

Each program or subprogram is restructured independently. The complete flow graph of each program or subprogram is analyzed to determine the best strategy for obtaining a well structured program. Machine dependencies are taken into account when building the flow graph because the interpretation of some statements depends on the particular compiler that the program was intended for. For instance, values outside the range of a computed GO TO can be handled in three distinct ways depending upon the particular compiler implementation. Such variations are taken into account by the "structuring engine" which generates the necessary statements to guarantee consistency in the restructured output.

In general, the restructured programs will bear little resemblance to the original unstructured ones, particularly if the logic was complex and somewhat twisted to start with. In the output, the logic flows from top to bottom, from the single entry to the single exit.

Figure 2 is an example of a simple program before and after restructuring. Similarly, figure 3 shows what happens in the case of a heavily folded program.

STRUCTURED SFORTRAN PROGRAM

```
CORRESPONDING   LINE
FORTRAN LINE    NUMBER                    OUTPUT SFORTRAN STATEMENT

                  1     C      ************************* FORIT    ENTRY **************************

                  2     C****************** M S I N C    12 **********************************
      2           3            SUBROUTINE FORIT (FNT,N,M,A,B)
      3           4                 IMPLICIT REAL*8 (A-H,O-Z)
                  5     C
      5           6                 DIMENSION FNT(1),A(M),B(M)

                  7     C      *************************** LOGIC START **************************

                  8     C
                  9     C                                                        ... SET CONSTANTS
      8          10                 COEF=1.0/(N+0.5)
      9          11                 CONST=3.141593*COEF
     10          12                 S1=DSIN(CONST)
     11          13                 C1=DCOS(CONST)
     12          14                 C=1.0
     13          15                 S=0.0
     14          16                 FNTZ=FNT(1)
     15          17                 J=1
     16          18                 M1=M+1
     17          19                 N2=N+N+1
                 20                 EXECUTE (AFR PROCEDURE001)
                              ------------------------------------------------------------
                               |
     30          21            |DO WHILE ((J-M1) .LT. 0)
     31          22            |     Q=C1*C-S1*S
     32          23            |     S=C1*S+S1*C
     33          24            |     C=Q
     34          25            |     J=J+1
                 26            |     EXECUTE (AFR PROCEDURE001)
                 27            |END DO WHILE
                               |------------------------------------------------------------

     36          28                 A(1)=A(1)*C.5
     37          29                 RETURN
                        <---------
```

```
CFC, INC.          PROGRAM  FORIT                         18:83:30      C1 DEC 74          PAGE  14

                                                   STRUCTURED SFORTRAN PROGRAM

CORRESPONDING    LINE
FORTRAN LINE    NUMBER                              OUTPUT SFORTRAN STATEMENT

                  30    C     ****************** AFR PROCEDURE001 PROCEDURE *******************

                  31          PROCEDURE (AFR PROCEDURE001)
                  32    C
                  33    C                            ... COMPUTE FOURIER COEFFICIENTS RECURSIVELY
      20          34               U2=0.0
      21          35               U1=0.0
      22          36               I=N2

                                  ------------------------------------------------------------
                                  |
      27          37              |DO UNTIL ((I-1) .LE. 0)
      23          38              |     U0=FNT(I)+2.0*C*U1-U2
      24          39              |     U2=U1
      25          40              |     U1=U0
      26          41              |     I=I-1
                  42              |END DO UNTIL
                                  |-----------------------------------------------------------

      28          43               A(J)=COEF*(FNTZ+C*U1-U2)
      29          44               B(J)=COEF*S*U1
                  45          END PROCEDURE
```

Figure 2a. Sample Program FORIT Before & After Restructuring.

```
CFG, INC.          PROGRAM                        18:83:30     C1 DEC 74        PAGE   1

                                      FORTRAN PROGRAM INPUT

        LINE
        NUMBER                        INPUT FORTRAN STATEMENT

      C***************** M S I N C    12 ************************************
            SUBROUTINE FORIT (FNT,N,M,A,B)
            IMPLICIT REAL*8 (A-H,O-Z)
      C
            DIMENSION FNT(1),A(M),B(M)
      C
      C     ... SET CONSTANTS
            COEF=1.0/(N+0.5)
            CONST=3.141593*COEF
            S1=DSIN(CONST)
            C1=DCOS(CONST)
            C=1.0
            S=0.0
            FNTZ=FNT(1)
            J=1
            M1=M+1
            N2=N+N+1
      C
      C     ... COMPUTE FOURIER COEFFICIENTS RECURSIVELY
         70 U2=0.0
            U1=0.0
            I=N2
         75 U0=FNT(I)+2.0*C*U1-U2
            U2=U1
            U1=U0
            I=I-1
            IF (I-1) 80,80,75
         80 A(J)=COEF*(FNTZ+C*U1-U2)
            B(J)=COEF*S*U1
            IF (J-M1) 90,100,100
         90 Q=C1*C-S1*S
            S=C1*S+S1*C
            C=Q
            J=J+1
            GO TO 70
        100 A(1)=A(1)*0.5
            RETURN
            END
```

Figure 2b.

The restructured programs are equivalent to those from which they are derived in the sense that they behave identically at run time. That is, they carry out the same sequence of operations on the data structures, great care being taken that the ordering of operations not be modified. For instance, a three way arithmetic IF cannot be simply converted into two nested S-FORTRAN IF statements because the arithmetic expression would then be evaluated twice. In that case, incorrect results might be obtained if the arithmetic expression contains calls to abnormal functions i.e., functions which do not always produce the same results from a given set of inputs.

One of the basic processes used in restructuring is known as node splitting. If a node of the subgraph can be reached from two different paths that must be separated, the node is split into two identical nodes so that each path can have its own copy of the node.

If the node splitting operations were carried out indiscriminately, the resulting S-FORTRAN programs would often become so large as to be virtually useless. Not only would clarity be lost but the object program would be likely not to fit in the target machine. To circumvent that difficulty, the "structuring engine" tries recognizing proper subgraphs that can be turned into procedures instead of being duplicated in line. A procedure is simply a section of code with one entry and one exit. This concept corresponds to the PERFORMed group in COBOL, but with additional constraints to guarantee a clean invocation and a clean return. Once a procedure has been extracted and given a name, it can be referenced from many locations within the restructured program, including from other procedures. The example in figure 2 contains one procedure, the one in figure 3 contains two. The decision whether to expand code in line or create procedures can be externally controlled using a threshold which indicates how complex a subgraph must be before it becomes a procedure. Procedures are not separate subprograms. Rather, they are segments of code that can be executed from various locations within a particular program or subprogram. The EXECUTE command hides the ASSIGNed GO TO linkage that a FORTRAN programmer would have to set up otherwise.

To visually improve the resulting code, every statement is laid out according to its logical indentation level. This stresses its relationship with other statements in the same program unit. A box is built around each complete DO group to enhance the scope of the DO statements. Statements such as UNDO, CYCLE, and RETURN are followed by an arrow that attracts the attention of the reader and shows him immediately what implications these statements have on the logic flow. Consecutive comment cards are right adjusted by block in order to make them as unobtrusive as possible.

Of course, if the modules to be restructured contain logic errors, the same errors will be found in the structured output. In general, the "structuring engine" is incapable of detecting errors except for some obvious language violations. The input programs are supposed to have compiled correctly so that the errors we are really trying to eliminate are errors in the logic that cannot be identified without an intimate understanding of the problem. Only a programmer aware of the problem being solved can discover and correct these errors.

Emphasis in building the "structuring engine" has been on reliability rather than efficiency. This has been achieved through a combination of structured design techniques, self identifiable data structures and dynamic assertion verification at run time i.e., the constant verification that the assumptions underlying the design are never violated during production runs.

Experimental results

We are currently applying the "structuring engine" to a wide variety of unstructured FORTRAN code. Although our analysis is far from complete, we would like to comment on some of the experimental results that we have obtained so far.

Clarity of the restructured programs. A reliable assessment of clarity improvements is obviously quite difficult to obtain until we get some figures on maintenance costs. The familiarity of the end user with structured code is a factor as noted in Holmes and Miller, 1973. The cleverness of the "structuring engine" in making the right choices is obviously another important factor since there are not one but many solutions to the restructuring problem. So far, we have found that:

1. the majority of the programs (about 90 percent) will come out extremely clear, at least in our opinion and in that of end users that have worked with restructured programs.

2. the rest (about 10 percent) will either remain complex or become lengthy or both. In this group, we find a number of programs that could be handled more cleverly by the "structuring engine" and, therefore, move into the above category. We are obviously building the necessary improvements into the "structuring engine." Still, there are some programs that will probably never look very good. They are ill-designed. The problem that they are supposed to solve should be reexamined and a complete redesign and reprogramming of these programs may be necessary.

Execution characteristics of the restructured programs. Let us now try to answer some of the most common questions regarding this automatic restructuring process. What price do we pay for the improved clarity of the restructured programs? In particular, how do the restructured programs execute compared to the original ones?

To answer these questions, we must first examine the various components in the processing chain as shown in figure 4. The "structuring engine" transforms unstructured FORTRAN into structured S-FORTRAN. The resulting S-FORTRAN programs are then translated back into FORTRAN using the S-FORTRAN to FORTRAN translator. At that point, we have pure FORTRAN source code again which can be compiled, loaded and executed. Thus, the characteristics that we are reporting on involve not only the "structuring engine" but also the translator and a compiler.

```
C...... REF: LSTAT            ALIAS  ORDB
C****** ELEMENT NAME:ORDB                             ***************************
        INTEGER FUNCTION LSTAT(LINE,FLAG)
        IMPLICIT INTEGER (A-Y)
        DATA NIV/5/
        COMMON/ARRAY/C,LINOWN,CLCARD(80),PICTUR(1320),BUFFER(15,200)
        COMMON/DEBUG/DEBUG
        COMMON /EFNARR/LENGTH,NREF,REFMAX,MAXLIN,EFNLIS(1567),CREF(3000)
        COMMON/RANGE/K1,K2
        LOGICAL FLAG
        L=LINE
        TARGET=LINE
        SWITCH=1
     65 KOUNT=1
     70 L=MOD(L    -1,LENGTH)+1
        LINOLD=FLD(0,18,EFNLIS(L))
        IF (LINOLD.EQ.TARGET)GO TO(115,180,140,150),SWITCH
        IF (LINOLD.EQ.0)GO TO 255
        IF (KOUNT.EQ.LENGTH)GO TO 255
        IF (KOUNT.EQ.1)LINC=MOD(L-1,LENGTH-1)+1
        L=L+LINC
        KOUNT=KOUNT+1
        GO TO 70
    115 LINEW=FLD(18,18,EFNLIS(L))
        LTEMP=K1*LINEW+K2
C     FLAG IS TRUE IF LINE IS A STATEMENT EFN
C              FALSE IF LINE IS A REFERENCE TO AN EFN
        IF (FLAG.OR.NREF.LT.0)GO TO 260
C     BUILD CROSS REF LIST
        IF (NREF.EQ.REFMAX)GO TO 235
        IF (LINOWN.GE.MAXLIN)GO TO 195
C     OLD EFN FOR CURRENT LINE IS LINOWN
        IF (SWITCH.LT.4)SWITCH=SWITCH+1
        TARGET=LINOWN
        L=LINOWN
        GO TO 65
    180 CURLIN=FLD(18,18,EFNLIS(L))
        CURNEW=K1*CURLIN+K2
        GO TO 200
    195 CURNEW=K1*(LINOWN-MAXLIN)+K2
    200 NREF=NREF+1
        FLD(0,18,CREF(NREF)) =LTEMP
        FLD(18,18,CREF(NREF))=CURNEW
        IF(DEBUG.GT.NIV)PRINT 220,NIV,LTEMP,CURNEW,NREF,CREF(NREF)
    220 FORMAT(' NIV',I3,': ORDB LTEMP=',I5,' CURNEW=',I5,
       1' CREF(',I4,')=',O12)
        GO TO 260
    235 PRINT 240
    240 FORMAT(1X,10(1H*),28H CROSS REFERENCE TABLE FULL ,90(1H*))
        NREF=-NREF
        GO TO 260
    140 CURNEW=CURLIN+K2
        GO TO 200
    150 CURLIN=FLD(18,18,EFNLIS(L))
        GO TO 140
    255 LTEMP=0
    260 LSTAT=LTEMP
        IF(DEBUG.GT.NIV)PRINT 270,NIV,LINE,FLAG,LTEMP
    270 FORMAT(' NIV',I3,': ORDB LINE=',I5,' FLAG=',L1,' LSTAT=',I5)
        RETURN
        END
```

Figure 3a. Sample Program ORDB Unstructured (Part I)

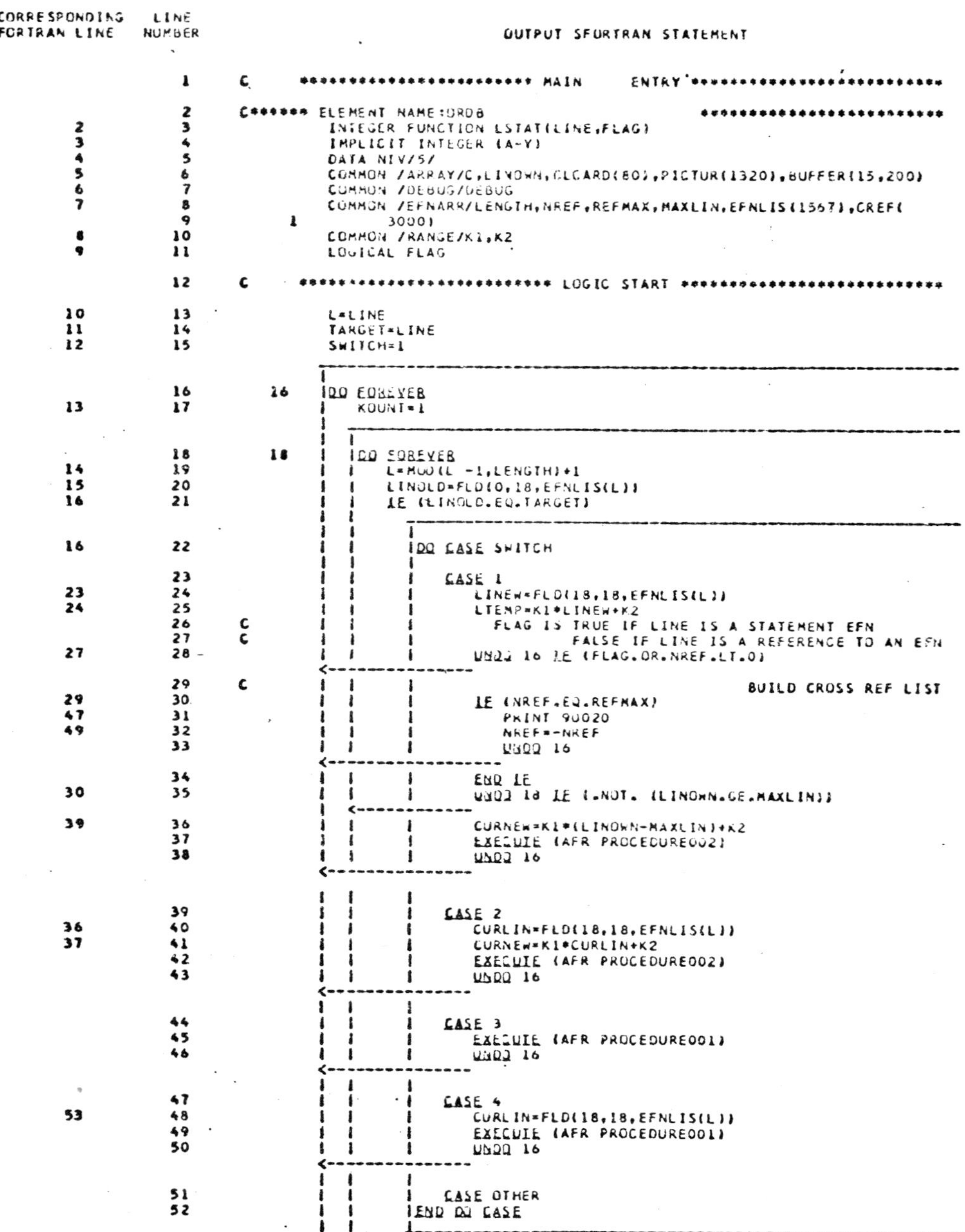

```
CORRESPONDING   LINE
FORTRAN LINE    NUMBER                        OUTPUT SFORTRAN STATEMENT

                  1     C       ************************* MAIN      ENTRY ***************************

                  2     C****** ELEMENT NAME:ORDB                              *************************
      2           3              INTEGER FUNCTION LSTAT(LINE,FLAG)
      3           4              IMPLICIT INTEGER (A-Y)
      4           5              DATA NIV/5/
      5           6              COMMON /ARRAY/C,LINOWN,CLCARD(80),PICTUR(1320),BUFFER(15,200)
      6           7              COMMON /DEBUG/DEBUG
      7           8              COMMON /EFNARR/LENGTH,NREF,REFMAX,MAXLIN,EFNLIS(1567),CREF(
                  9           1       3000)
      8          10              COMMON /RANGE/K1,K2
      9          11              LOGICAL FLAG

                 12     C       *************************** LOGIC START ****************************

     10          13              L=LINE
     11          14              TARGET=LINE
     12          15              SWITCH=1
                                ------------------------------------------------------------------
                                |
                 16         16  |DO FOREVER
     13          17             |    KOUNT=1
                                |
                                |  ---------------------------------------------------------------
                                |  |
                 18         18  |  |DO FOREVER
     14          19             |  |    L=MOD(L -1,LENGTH)+1
     15          20             |  |    LINOLD=FLD(0,18,EFNLIS(L))
     16          21             |  |    IF (LINOLD.EQ.TARGET)
                                |  |
                                |  |      --------------------------------------------------------
                                |  |      |
     16          22             |  |      |DO CASE SWITCH
                                |  |      |
                 23             |  |      |   CASE 1
     23          24             |  |      |      LINEW=FLD(18,18,EFNLIS(L))
     24          25             |  |      |      LTEMP=K1*LINEW+K2
                 26     C       |  |      |        FLAG IS TRUE IF LINE IS A STATEMENT EFN
                 27     C       |  |      |                FALSE IF LINE IS A REFERENCE TO AN EFN
     27          28             |  |      |      UNDO 16 IF (FLAG.OR.NREF.LT.0)
                                <---------------
                 29     C       |  |      |                                 BUILD CROSS REF LIST
     29          30             |  |      |      IF (NREF.EQ.REFMAX)
     47          31             |  |      |         PRINT 90020
     49          32             |  |      |         NREF=-NREF
                 33             |  |      |         UNDO 16
                                <------------------
                 34             |  |      |      END IF
     30          35             |  |      |      UNDO 18 IF (.NOT. (LINOWN.GE.MAXLIN))
                                |  <-----------
     39          36             |  |      |      CURNEW=K1*(LINOWN-MAXLIN)+K2
                 37             |  |      |      EXECUTE (AFR PROCEDURE002)
                 38             |  |      |      UNDO 16
                                <---------------

                                |  |      |
                 39             |  |      |   CASE 2
     36          40             |  |      |      CURLIN=FLD(18,18,EFNLIS(L))
     37          41             |  |      |      CURNEW=K1*CURLIN+K2
                 42             |  |      |      EXECUTE (AFR PROCEDURE002)
                 43             |  |      |      UNDO 16
                                <---------------
                                |  |      |
                 44             |  |      |   CASE 3
                 45             |  |      |      EXECUTE (AFR PROCEDURE001)
                 46             |  |      |      UNDO 16
                                <---------------
                                |  |      |
                 47             |  |      |   CASE 4
     53          48             |  |      |      CURLIN=FLD(18,18,EFNLIS(L))
                 49             |  |      |      EXECUTE (AFR PROCEDURE001)
                 50             |  |      |      UNDO 16
                                <---------------
                                |  |      |
                 51             |  |      |   CASE OTHER
                 52             |  |      |END DO CASE
                                |  |      ---------------------------------------------------------
```

Figure 3b Sample Program ORDB Restructured (Parts II and III)

```
      |  |   END IF
17    |  |   IF (LINOLD.EQ.0)
55    |  |      LTEMP=0
      |  |      UNDO 16
<---------
18    |  |   ELSE IF (KOUNT.EQ.LENGTH)
55    |  |      LTEMP=0
      |  |      UNDO 16
<---------
      |  |   END IF
19    |  |   IF (KOUNT.EQ.1)
19    |  |      LINC=MOD(L-1,LENGTH-1)+1
      |  |   END IF
20    |  |   L=L+LINC
21    |  |   KOUNT=KOUNT+1
      |  |END DO FOREVER
      |  L--------------------------------------------------
      |
   C  |                         OLD EFN FOR CURRENT LINE IS LINOWN
32    |  IF (SWITCH.LT.4)
32    |     SWITCH=SWITCH+1
      |  END IF
33    |  TARGET=LINOWN
34    |  L=LINOWN
      |END DO FOREVER
      L-----------------------------------------------------

56       LSTAT=LTEMP
57       IF (DEBUG.GT.NIV)
57          PRINT 90030, NIV,LINE,FLAG,LTEMP
         END IF
59       RETURN
```

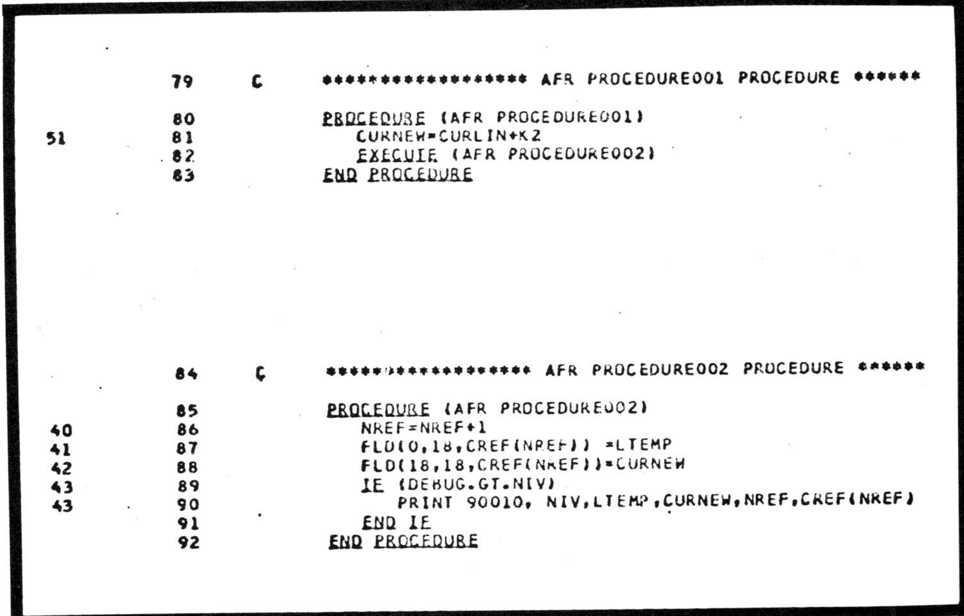

```
      C   ******************* AFR PROCEDURE001 PROCEDURE ******

          PROCEDURE (AFR PROCEDURE001)
51           CURNEW=CURLIN+K2
             EXECUTE (AFR PROCEDURE002)
          END PROCEDURE


      C   ******************* AFR PROCEDURE002 PROCEDURE ******

          PROCEDURE (AFR PROCEDURE002)
40           NREF=NREF+1
41           FLD(0,18,CREF(NREF)) =LTEMP
42           FLD(18,18,CREF(NREF))=CURNEW
43           IF (DEBUG.GT.NIV)
43              PRINT 90010, NIV,LTEMP,CURNEW,NREF,CREF(NREF)
             END IF
          END PROCEDURE
```

Figure 3. Continued

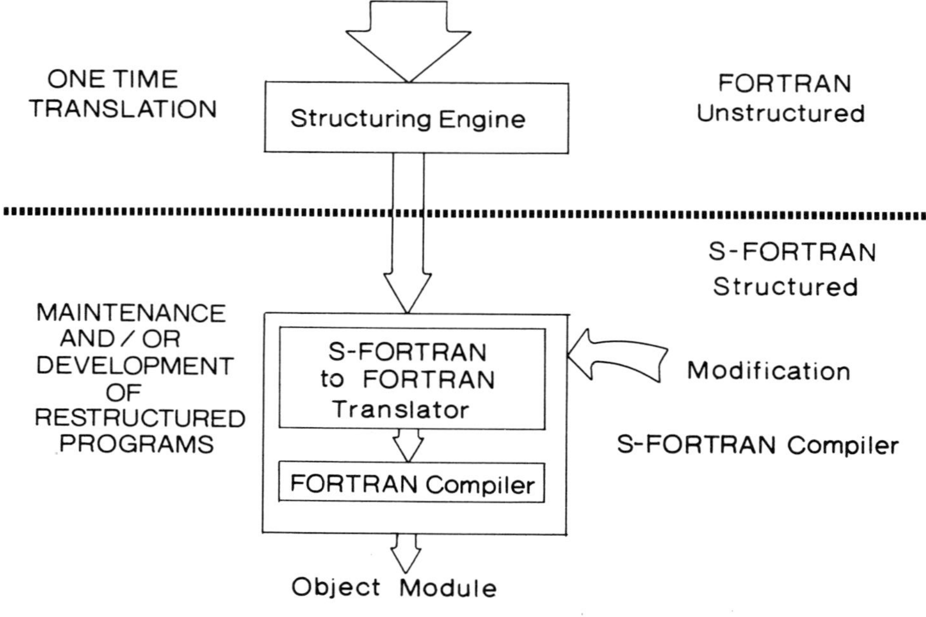

Figure 4. The Restructuring Chain

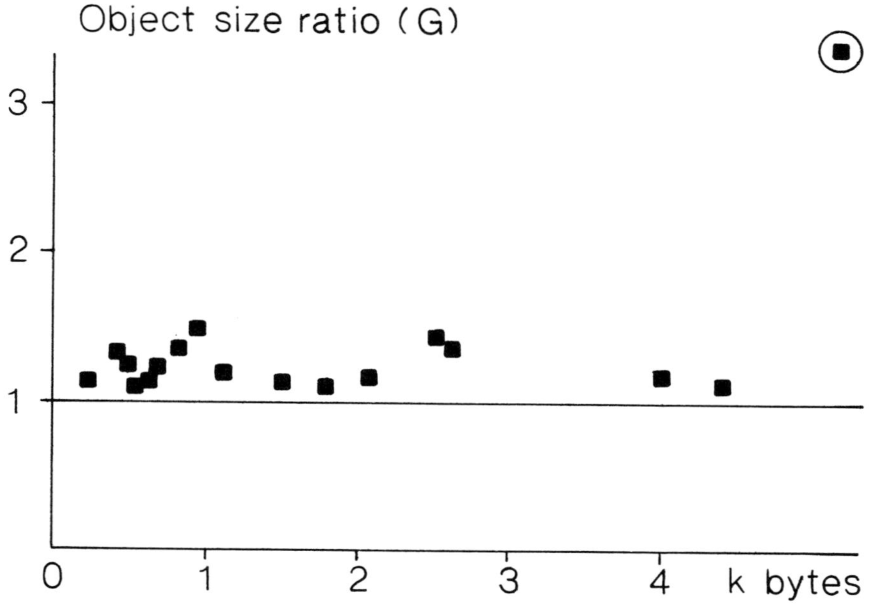

Figure 5. Core Size Expansion Ratios

The core size of the object modules produced from the restructured programs has been found to always be larger than that of the original modules, typically by about 20 percent.

We know from Peterson, Kasami, and Tokura, (1973) that arbitrary programs cannot be restructured without increasing their running time or their core size. In the present case, we have chosen to accept a limited increase in memory size. The creation of internal procedures is our method for preventing a program from growing beyond an acceptable point.

Figure 5 shows a typical distribution of core size expansion ratios (1 would mean no increase) as a function of the size of the object module for the unstructured program when compiled with IBM's FORTRAN G compiler. The circled data point corresponds to a program that the "structuring engine" could not structure without producing three times as many S-FORTRAN cards as there were FORTRAN cards. This "abnormal" expansion factor was caused by a deeply nested section of code that could not be turned into a procedure because it would then have contained an UNDO outside its scope. Such an UNDO outside the scope of a procedure is not permitted in S-FORTRAN. Consequently, the same section of code was duplicated 18 times throughout the program.

Data on the execution speed of the restructured programs has been harder to get because most of the programs we have restructured so far were components of much larger systems which we could not run ourselves. Preliminary results show that we should expect slight variations in the running time with a trend toward a reduction rather than an increase. This may seem paradoxical at first but can be explained as follows. There are two major factors that influence the running time in opposite ways:

1. the size of the basic block: the restructuring process cannot decrease the average size of the basic block and in general will increase it. Thus, an optimizing compiler should generate better code within each basic block of the restructured programs.
2. the control flow statements produced by the translator to support branching, looping and procedure referencing: These require, in general, more instructions than needed to implement the original control logic.

The first factor tends to make restructured programs run faster whereas the latter tends to slow them down. This means that with a translator generating very good code we should be able to have programs run faster restructured than unstructured. In fact, we have now built more sophistication into the translator than had been originally planned in order to make full use of the capabilities of optimizing compilers. For instance, with IBM's FORTRAN H (OPT = 2) compiler, changes in the translation of IF statements have reduced in one instance the core size by 12 percent and the running time by 8 percent when compared with earlier versions of the translator.

Conclusions

Automatic restructuring as implemented by the "structuring engine" is proposed as a method to modernize existing programs. It should prove much more practical than manual reprogramming, particularly with regards to manpower requirements, conversion time and the reliability of the conversion process itself.

Manpower requirements are reduced since no major human effort is invested redoing what already exists. On the contrary, programmer time is devoted to perusing restructured programs, implementing improvements wherever deficiencies show up, and correcting errors. In particular, any program which still appears to be overly complex after restructuring compared to what it is supposed to accomplish, becomes a good candidate for an in depth investigation of the reasons underlying its apparent complexity. Poor algorithms may be pinned down fast and replaced accordingly. The overall result is that the programmer understands the structured code more rapidly and can, therefore, allocate more time to difficult areas. Consequently, his error detection rate increases, thus justifying our claim to improved software reliability.

Conversion time is negligible compared to that required for manual reprogramming. In particular, the project's clock is not set back since the restructuring process does not introduce any new errors.

Of course, there may still be cases where complete redesign and reprogramming appear to be absolutely necessary. Under those circumstances, the "structuring engine" can still play an important role. Indeed, no matter how unstructured and clumsy the original software may be, it represents an approximate solution to the problem, correct in most if not all of the cases. As such, it acts as a repository for a wealth of details that were added throughout the life cycle of the software to handle unusual and certainly unforeseen cases. Starting from this rich data, the "structuring engine" becomes a very valuable tool since it produces an up-to-date structured picture of the solution currently implemented. This picture may then be used to base a thorough evaluation of the status of the project, including any needs for manual redesign and reprogramming.

The main characteristics of S-FORTRAN are:

a. S-FORTRAN is a superset of FORTRAN (including the FORTRAN language extensions provided by various manufacturers).

b. Any construct with a scope has both an opening and a closing delimiter. If the opening statement is XXX, the ending statement is of the form END XXX. (e.g., IF . . . END IF, DO WHILE . . . END DO WHILE).

c. The IF includes any number of ELSEIF clauses and an optional ELSE clause. ELSEIF's are often convenient to prevent very deep indentation levels (and the so-called "wall to wall" ENDIF's).

d. *Repetitive DO groups* include a DO FOR analogous to the FORTRAN DO loop, a DO WHILE, a DO UNTIL (which is in fact a DO AT LEAST ONCE UNTIL), and a DO FOREVER (an infinite loop).

e. *Non repetitive DO groups* include a DO for bracketing statements, a powerful DO CASE, a DO CASE SIGN OF which is the equivalent of a three way arithmetic IF, and a DO LABEL to handle abnormal returns from subroutines and functions and end and error exits from I/O statements.

f. UNDO is a mechanism to exit from a DO group prematurely. We have found this multilevel exit mechanism to be superior to introducing switch variables which tend to clutter the program and make its logic harder to follow. UNDO is applicable to any DO group, repetitive or not. It can be followed by a label if another DO group besides the innermost one is to be exited from.

g. CYCLE is similar to UNDO but implies skipping any statement until the closing delimiter of a DO group is found. The test controlling the repeated execution of the DO group is then performed to determine whether to exit or repeat. CYCLE is only applicable to repetitive-DO groups.

h. Internal parameterless procedures can be defined using PROCEDURE . . . END PROCEDURE. Their execution can only be triggered by an EXECUTE (proc-name) statement. Premature termination of a procedure can be accomplished by an EXIT statement. Procedures share the same data space as the program in which they are contained.

Structured Programming Perspective

Introduction

What is structured programming? A panacea to cure all programming ills? A solution to the rising costs of program preparation and maintenance? A set of rigid rules and no "GO TO" statements that removes all the creativity from the art of programming? Or is it just a bunch of new names for old ideas and procedures that have always been around? Procedures that you've more or less been using anyway, in your programming.

And, structured programming versus what? Unstructured programming? What's that? Or just versus "however you used to program"? Maybe that was already structured. What is programming anyway? Take a moment to formulate your own brief definition of programming.

Well, Webster says programming is "to work out a sequence of operations to be performed by (a mechanism)." Of course, that's a pretty generalized description. Since we are specifically discussing computer programming, a more appropriate definition would be "the design, writing and testing of a program." Then, by adding the definition of "structured," we obtain as a formal definition of structured programming, "the design, writing and testing of a program made up of interdependent parts in a definite pattern of organization".

It is obvious, of course, that a computer program is composed of interdependent parts. The crux of this definition is the "definite pattern of organization". Sure, there are a set of "rules", or guidelines, to follow in attempting to structure your programming. But, from a philosophical standpoint, the idea is not just to follow some rules blindly, not just to eliminate GOTO's[1] without exception, but rather to include more "structure" in your programming.

Art or Science?

The skill of programming is still in relative infancy, being only some quarter of a century old. This art/science has grown, along with computer development, from simple machine language to extremely sophisticated, high-level programming languages. And, unfortunately, for the most part it has remained more of a black art than a science.

In the past, good programmers were thought to be those who could write a given routine in fewer steps than anyone else; and cute, tricky, concise programs were marvelled at. There was good reason for this in the "old days," since storage space was at a premium and computers then were much slower than today. The result, however, was programs that were very difficult, if not impossible, for someone else to read and maintain. In fact, many programmers freely admit to great difficulty in reading their own programs six months later, or even one month, or one week later.

Another problem with past programs has been their bugs; the difficulty in locating and correcting these bugs, and avoiding the creation of other problems while so doing. Techniques such as interactive computing, checkout compilers and so forth have enhanced a programmer's ability to find errors. However, while machine testing can be used to prove the presence of bugs, it cannot be used to prove their absence. Thus, the old programmer's adage, "There are no programs without bugs, only programs in which the next bug has not been found yet."

Error free code?

All this leads to a defeatist attitude. Since there will be bugs anyway, why make a concerted effort to write bug-free code? But, the times they are a-changin'! There are growing numbers of people asking why programs should not be composed correctly, instead of being debugged into correctness. It turns out that it is much easier, and less expensive in terms of time and money, to keep errors out of a system to start with, than it is to remove them after they have been introduced into the system.

Why should you as a programmer be interested in structured programming? Several reasons. Structured programming is one of a number of interrelated disciplines which, when grouped together, can be referred to as "improved programming technologies." The related techniques are team operations, top down program development, code reading and walkthroughs, HIPO documentation technique, and program development support libraries. More and more installations are turning to these techniques as a means of doing their jobs better.

Then too, there is the matter of keeping up with the state of the art. As a programmer, you should be familiar with new techniques and new approaches to solving data processing problems. In this way, you become more valuable, not only to yourself, but also to your employer. Also, as in any other trade, you should take pride in doing your job in the best possible way.

And the people cost is not just for the writing of programs. The cost of testing and correcting (debugging) programs, and the cost of maintaining and updating these programs is taking a bigger and bigger chunk of the budget.

While all of these improved programming techniques are not mutually inclusive, experience has shown that their combined use can result in a significantly more efficient data processing operation. Although we will touch briefly upon the related techniques, the major attention of this course will be focused on the technique of structured programming.

Before structure

Suppose, for a moment, that you have been assigned the task of updating an existing program. Maybe you have to adjust a tax rate; we can always depend on taxes going up! As you try to trace your way through this program, you find a branch to a label several pages away (figure 1). So you hold a finger in the second page and start through the new routine. In a very short time, not only do you run out of fingers, but also your attention span begins to suffer. As you get several levels removed from the starting point, it becomes very difficult to hold all the previous information in your mind concurrently. And, assuming you find the routine and make the change, you may not be sure how many other locations branch to the label of that routine. Therefore, you may not be sure of what type of cascading effect this change might have on other parts of the program.

This program in figure 1 was unstructured. It had undisciplined GOTO's that branched us hither and yon, and it was difficult to read and to follow clearly and logically. The big plus for structured programs is that they are easy to read; easy to trace our way through and follow logically. This, in turn, makes them easier to debug and easier to maintain. And that's what it's all about! That's the answer to the big "why" of structured programming. In fact, a good, informal definition of structured programming is "a method of programming according to a set of rules that enhances a program's readability and maintainability."

After structure

Let's say that the program you have to update is a structured program as shown in figure 2. The first thing you notice is the dearth of branches or GOTO statements. Instead you see CALL'S or PERFORM's.[2] So any time another routine is referred to, say by the CALL at arrow (1), you can depend upon a return being made to that point, with confidence that there will be no random paths not returning. This, even though at arrow (2) you see within the second routine a PERFORM of another subordinate routine. That routine will also return, and so on, as with arrow (3).

Although we go out from page one on arrow (1), and part way through the second routine we go out on arrow (2), and part way through the third routine we go out on arrow (3), we then see that upon completion of the fourth routine we return to the third routine on arrow (3R). Next we finish the third routine and return on arrow (2R). Here we complete the second routine and then return to the main routine on arrow (1R). No wild paths that run off and never return.

Next, still on figure 2, you notice there are not a bunch of labels and GOTO statements. Then you notice that each page is complete unto itself; enter at the top, exit at the bottom, one coding segment per page. No long rambling on of a routine for page after page. Although not noticeable in figure 2, closer inspection would show special indentation and nestling of functions, as well as the use of intelligent data names: names that convey information about the data.

Further close examination would show a very limited number of statement types being used throughout the whole program, as well as minimum use of "comments."[3] All of these things together would make a very readable program, a very well-organized program; thus, an easily modifiable, correctable, and maintainable program.

All of these things together also make up a structured program. These attributes, just mentioned, comprise a set of guidelines which, when understood and followed, result in the creation of so-called structured programs.

By the way, it's entirely possible that you have been organizing your programs into good logical structure already, without using some of these new descriptions. In that case, you are already using a form of structured programming. Now, if we can all agree on a set of conventions, or guidelines, then it will be easier for us to read and understand each other's work. [Figure 3 illustrates a traditional and a structured program.]

The goal

The goal of structured programming is to change the process of programming from a frustrating, trial and error activity to a systematic, quality controlled activity. However, to attain this goal of precision programming, the ideas of structured programming must be used constantly; not simply treated as good ideas to be used when convenient, but as basic principles which are always valid.

A good example of a technical standard occurs in engineering logic circuit design. There, it is known from basic theorems in Boolean algebra that any logic circuit, no matter how complex, can be constructed using only AND, OR, and NOT electronic circuitry. Of course, if you were to imagine engineering in its infancy, as programming is today, it undoubtedly was a far cry from the well-organized science that it now is.

However, if programming is to become more of a science and less of an art, then it behooves programming to follow the lead of engineering. The technology of computer engineering has progressed by leaps and bounds while that of programming has not. This is reflected in the reliability and reduced cost per computation of "hardware" versus that of "software."

The Work of Experts

As long ago as 1966, Böhm and Jacopini showed how to prove that relatively simple structured program control logics were capable of expressing any program requirements, no matter how complex they might be. In addition, Edsger W. Dijkstra of the Netherlands has originated a set of ideas and a series of examples for clear thinking in the construction of programs. These ideas of Dijkstra, who is generally considered to be the first name in structured programming, are powerful tools in mentally connecting the static text of a program with the dynamic process it invokes in execution. This correspondence between program and process permits the new level of precision in programming mentioned previously as a goal.

If we are to accept technical standards in programming procedures, it is essential to have mathematical assurance that these standards are sound and practical. Harlan D. Mills of IBM has provided this assurance in his Mathematical Foundations for Structured Programming (1971). Dr. Mills has been instrumental, also, in successfully applying all of the interrelated improved programming technologies to practical applications, through his experience with the Federal Systems Division of IBM.

Dr. Mills points out that initial practical experience with structured programming indicates there is more than just a technical side to the matter. There is a psychological effect, as well, when programmers learn of their new power to write programs correctly. This new power motivates, in turn, a new level of concentration which helps avoid errors of carelessness. Also, there is a contagion to precision programming—a confidence in also being able to accomplish something that others have achieved. For example, when the typewriter was first invented, imagine suggesting to someone that they should try to type at least 50 words a minute. And, by the way, do it without even looking at the keys! This would have been considered a ridiculous, unattainable goal. Yet today, students walking into typing school are not only expected to achieve this goal, they don't even think it ridiculous or unattainable. All about them they see others reaching or exceeding this goal, and realize it is not beyond their capability. Is error-free coding beyond a programmer's capability?

It is universally accepted today that programming is an error-prone activity. Any major programming system is presumed to have errors in it. Only the very naive would believe otherwise. The process of debugging programs and systems is a mysterious art. Indeed, more programmer time goes into debugging than into program designing and coding in most large systems. But there is practically no systematic literature on this large undertaking.

Can we do better?

Yet, even though errors in program logic have always been a source of frustration, even for the most careful and meticulous, this does not necessarily have to be so in the future. Programming is still very young as a human activity. As technical foundations are developed for programming, its character will undergo radical changes. Those who have worked with improved programming technologies contend that such a radical change is possible now: that in structured programming the techniques and tools are at hand to permit an entirely new level of precision in programming.

The contention is that this new level of precision will be characterized by programs of large size, from tens of thousands to millions of instructions, which have mean time between detected errors of a year or so. Note that the objectives of such precision in programming deal with execution, rather than assembly/compilation.

Some improvement may be noticeable in reducing syntax errors, but assemblers/compilers can find syntax errors already. It is the program logic errors at the system level which can be practically eliminated from programming. However, to accomplish this proposed new level of precision, a new attitude toward programming expectations will be required in programmers.

[1]A GOTO, pronounced as "go to," is merely a branch statement. It is used as a device to have program execution "jump" out of the normal sequence, to a location specified in the label in the operand of the GOTO statement.

[2]The CALL and PERFORM are macro-type program statements that, during execution, transfer program control to the specific closed subroutine identified in the operand of the particular statement. Upon completion of the subroutine, control is returned to the program statement immediately following the CALL or PERFORM.

[3]Excessive use of comments has frequently been the penalty paid for the sin of poor logic and confusing code. Proponents of structured programming point out that the coding used is so readable that the need for explanatory comments is greatly reduced.

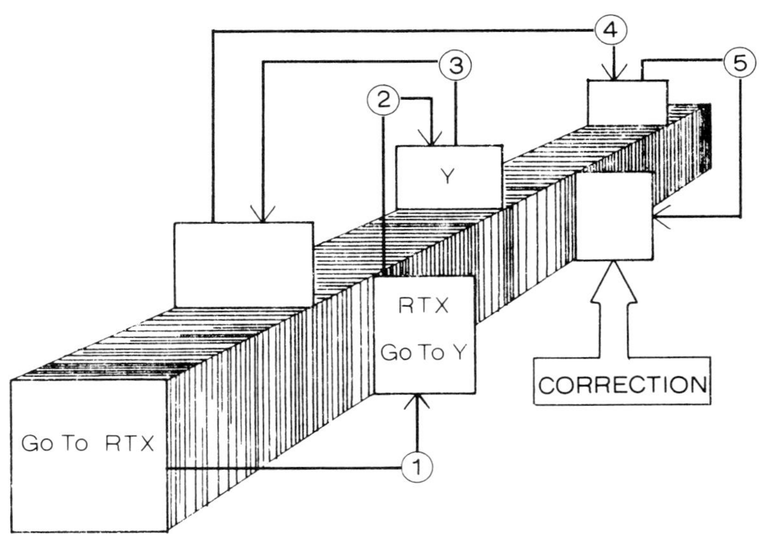

Figure 1.

"redrawn from original IBM illustration"

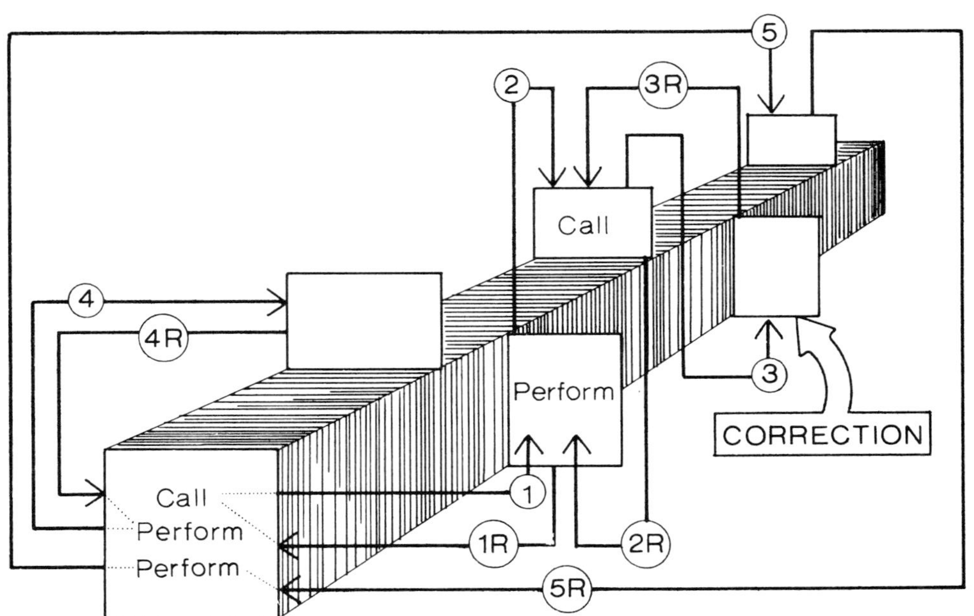

Figure 2.

"redrawn from original IBM illustration"

```
          IF p GOTO label q
          IF w GOTO label m
          L function
          GOTO label k
label m   M function
          GOTO label k
label q   IF q GOTO label t
          A function
          B function
          C function
label r   IF NOT r GOTO label s
          D function
          GOTO label r
label s   IF s GOTO label f
          E function
label v   IF NOT v GOTO label k
          J function
label k   K function
          END function
label f   F function
          GOTO label v
label t   IF t GOTO label a
          A function
          B function
          GOTO label w
label a   A function
          B function
          G function
label u   IF NOT u GOTO label w
          H function
          GOTO label u
label w   IF NOT t GOTO label y
          I function
label y   IF NOT v GOTO label k
          J function
          GOTO label k
```

TRADITIONAL

```
IF p THEN
   A function
   B function
   IF q THEN
      IF t THEN
         G function
         DOWHILE u
            H function
         ENDDO
         I function
      (ELSE)
      ENDIF
   ELSE
      C function
      DOWHILE r
         D function
      ENDDO
      IF s THEN
         F function
      ELSE
         E function
      ENDIF
   ENDIF
   IF v THEN
      J function
   (ELSE)
   ENDIF
ELSE
   IF w THEN
      M Function
   ELSE
      L function
   ENDIF
ENDIF
K function
END function
```

STRUCTURED

Figure 3.

"Courtesy of IBM"

. . . maintenance is merely the continuation of development by other means.

Moreover, if development is done in a systematic, stepwise manner, the "other" means are neither more nor less than the *same* means. With proper maintenance and development, we shouldn't be able to tell whether the program is in one stage or the other. Each "patch" becomes just another substage in the refinement process—bringing us closer and closer to the true needs of our customers.

Initial development gets us off on a sound footing—a footing that acts as both foundation and guide for further development or maintenance. . . .

From *High Level COBOL Programming* by Gerald M. Weinberg, Stephen E. Wright, Richard Kauffman, and Martin A. Goetz, p. 182.

Section VI

Annotated Bibliography

Annotated Bibliography

The entries marked '***' are reprinted in entirety. An entry marked '*' is excerpted, quoted, or a chapter based on it appears in the book. We thank the publishers/authors of these entries for their kind permission to reprint.

Alexander, G.

*** 1968 "Control of Program Changes." *Data Management* Dec. pp. 35–36.

This article sets down three rules for program changes which allow the programmer to maintain established standards and the program manager to control adherence to them regardless of time or workload pressures.

Aron, J. D.

1974 *The Program Development Process—Part I: The Individual Programmer.* Reading, Mass.: Addison-Wesley.

This book emphasizes the importance of maintainability and modifiability of programs, and briefly covers the topic of maintenance.

Ashcroft, E., and Manna Z.

1971 "The Translation of 'GO TO' Programs into 'WHILE' Programs." Proc. IFIP Cong., pp. 250–255.

This paper presents, by examples only, the concepts of two different algorithms for converting programs with GO TO's into WHILE programs.

Atwater, Robert T.

*1977 "The Further Reaches of Structured Development." *The Yourdon Report,* Oct.–Nov. pp. 2–3.

In the concluding paragraphs of this article, maintenance of systems is considered one area that will continue to prove costly. The new techniques will not do away with the problems of maintenance. Since development does not stop with implementation, a flurry of articles on structured maintenance will be seen, Atwater predicts.

Baker, Brenda S.

1977 "An Algorithm for Structuring Flowgraphs." *Journal of the ACM,* Jan. pp. 98–120.

Balzer, R. M.

1975 Imprecise Program Specification. Univ. Southern California, Los Angeles, rep. ISI/RR–75–36, Dec.

Belady, L. A., and M. M. Lehman

1975 The Evolution Dynamics of Large Programs. IBM Research, Sept.

Benson, Miles

*** 1978 "Responsibility vs. Authority, Lying to Management: A Legitimate Solution." *Computerworld,* Sept. 11, pp. 30, 31.

The thought-provoking statement of this story of a super maintenance programmer who functioned best in the total absence of direction from above, is: "Product control is in fact the ultimate power. And as long as responsibility resides with product control, the best ends from the corporate point of view can be achieved by ignoring or circumventing authority and power."

Boar, B. H.

1976 *Abend Debugging for COBOL Programmers.* New York: John Wiley.

Using the ANSI COBOL under the 360/370 OS/MVT as the case study, it provides approaches to Abend (Abnormal Ending) debugging. It also contains information about the compiler, linkage editor, and operating system.

*** 1978 "Abend Debugging and the COBOL Programmer." *Computerworld,* Oct. 2, pp. 19, 21–23.

The testing and debugging tasks represent the major cost component of the maintenance budget, but they are addressed minimally in COBOL courses and the professional literature. This article describes some abend debugging techniques and tools for COBOL programmers.

Boehm, B. W.

1971 "Some Information Processing Implications of Air Force Space Missions in the 1980's." *Astronautics and Aeronautics,* Jan., pp. 42–50.

1973 "Software and Its Impact: A Quantitative Assessment." *Datamation,* May, pp. 48–59.

This article includes the topics of software productivity and software reliability. Regarding software modifications, it reveals that after a small modification, the chance of successful first run is about 50%.

1974 "Some Steps Toward Formal and Automatic Aids to Software Requirements Analysis and Design." *Proc. IFIF Cong.,* pp. 192–197.

*1976 "Software Engineering." *IEEE Transactions on Computers,* Vol. C–25, No. 12, Dec. pp. 1226–1241.

This excellent paper provides a definition of "software engineering," and a survey of the state of the art and likely future trends. It covers the technology available in the various phases of the software life cycle, including maintenance, and in the overall area of software management and integrated technology management approaches. 104 references are provided.

Boehm, B. W., J. R. Brown, and M. Lipow

1976 "Quantitative Evaluation of Software Quality." *Proc. IEEE/ACM 2nd Int. Conf. Software Eng.,* Oct.

Böhm, C., and G. Jacopini

1966 "Flow Diagrams, Turing Machines and Languages with Only Two Formation Rules." *Communications of the ACM,* May, pp. 366–371.

Brantley, C. L., and Y. R. Osajima

*** 1975 "Continuing Development of Centrally Developed and Maintained Software Systems." *IEEE Computer Society Conference Proceedings (COMPCON) Spring 1975,* pp. 285–288.

Using DIR/ECT (a man/machine white pages telephone book production system, centrally developed and centrally maintained by Bell Laboratories) as a model, this paper describes long-range requirements for balancing an overall program of maintenance and continuing development of large scale software systems.

Braverman, Philip H.

1976 "Managing Change." *Datamation,* Oct., pp. 111–113.

He suggests ways to handle changes during the project development. "The Project Change Request" form illustrated in this article can be adapted for change requests to operational programs.

Brooks, Frederick P.

1975 *The Mythical Man-Month.* Manlo Park, California: Addison-Wesley.

This classic book authored by the "father of IBM System/360," includes passages on debugging and structured programming. Brooks warns against using maintenance as a training ground for junior programmers.

Brown, A. R., and W. A. Sampson

* 1973 *Program Debugging.* New York: American Elsevier Publishing.

Though this is not a book on maintenance, it gives excellent suggestions and some useful techniques for maintenance.

Caine, Stephen H.

1971 Reference Guide to the XXX Language, CFG 70–8–001, Feb.

Canning, R., ed.

1972 That Maintenance Iceberg. *EDP Analyzer,* Oct., pp. 1–14.

A "definitive" report that made the dp industry aware of the maintenance "iceberg." It reveals that about 50% of the programming expenses of most business users of computers go for maintenance and enhancements of existing programs. The case studies of B. F. Goodrich Chemical Company, General Motors Oldsmobile Division, and General Motors Truck & Coach Division are included. Some causes of maintenance changes and the problems associated with them are described. A plan for "more maintainable" systems is given. It comprises of designing for change, (tools for) design changes, configuration policies, control and audit, organizing for maintenance, and converting to more maintainable systems.

1978 Progress in Software Engineering: Part 1 & Part 2, *EDP Analyzer,* Feb., pp. 1–13 & March, pp. 1–13.

An excellent overview of the state of software engineering. Software engineering seeks to impose a methodology and a discipline on 1) the development and modification of software, and 2) the management of software development and modification. The reports point out that software maintenance needs more attention.

Carnegie, Dale

1948 *How to Stop Worrying and Start Living,* New York: Simon & Schuster (pbk.)

An excellent antidote to one of the worst problems of the maintenance programmer/manager—worry!!!

Chapin, Ned

1978 "Semi-Code in Design and Maintenance." *Computers and People,* June, pp. 17–27.

Semi-code is a method for describing program or system design in words. For maintenance visibility into the system after it has been implemented, semi-code offers both a convenient means of documentation and a way of working. It is congenial to the thinking needed in maintenance, in implementing, and in design. Semi-code can be easily modified on-line in computer libraries.

Daly, E. B.

1977 "Management of Software Development." *IEEE Transactions on Software Engineering,* May, pp. 229–242.

This paper describes four major aspects of software management: development statistics, development process, development objectives, and software maintenance. It has some excellent ideas about maintenance, such as: ". . . design maintenance programmers are more efficiently employed if approximately 50 percent of their working hours are spent in new design." . . . Design maintenance group should contain at least 30 percent senior programmers. . . . Invite the maintenance programmer, who will be later responsible for maintenance in the walkthroughs during development. . . . Establish an Attack Team to handle critical problems.

Data Processing

*** 1973 "Program Maintenance: Users' Views." Sept.–Oct., pp. 314–317.

Describes adverse reaction from most users to the proposal, presented in (McGregor 1973): Use consultant programmers for maintenance.

Data Processing Digest

1971, 1972 "COBOL Support Packages . . . Programming and Productivity Aids."

An excellent and detailed overview of the whole area of Cobol aids, by the editors and staff of DPD. July 1971, "Introduction"; August, "Cobol Subset"; September, "Cobol Manual"; October, "Cobol Shorthands"; November, "Decision Table Translators"; January 1972, "Data Management Systems"; February, "Test Data Generators"; March, "Debugging Systems"; April, "Documentation Aids"; May, "Summary."

de Balbine, Guy

*** 1975 "Better Manpower Utilization Using Automatic Restructuring." *Proc. AFIPS 1975 National Computer Conf.* Vol. 44, Montvale, N.J., AFIPS Press, pp. 319–327.

This excellent paper describes results achieved by restructuring existing FORTRAN programs into a "structured" FORTRAN superset called S-FORTRAN, using a proprietary package that operates as a "structuring engine." The examples of restructured programs are easier to understand.

1975 "Using the FORTRAN Structuring Engine." *Proceedings of Computer Science & Statistics, 8th Annual Symposium on the Interface,* UCLA, Feb., pp. 297–305.

The "structuring engine" is a transitional tool designed to perform the automatic conversion of arbitrary FORTRAN programs into structured S-FORTRAN programs. Sample runs and an analysis of the execution characteristics of sample restructured programs are included.

1975 "The Structuring Engine: A Transitional Tool." *Computer,* June, pp. 64–65.

Briefly describes the "structuring engine" that restructures FORTRAN programs into equivalent structured S-FORTRAN programs. An example of unstructured and automatically restructured code is included.

1975 "Design Criteria for the 'Structuring Engine.'" *Proceedings 2nd USA Japan Computer Conference,* Tokyo, August, pp. 422–426.

The "structuring engine" is a software tool that rewrites unstructured FORTRAN programs into equivalent structured programs. The purpose is to help maintain existing programs by making them easier to read and understand. This paper describes the selection of an adequate target language (S-FORTRAN), and the use of visual aids to enhance control structures and flow paths. The major design and implementation choices dealing with the reliability of the restructuring transformation are examined, and the extension of the restructuring concept to other languages is discussed.

1976 "Procedure Extraction for Automatic Restructuring." *Compcon '76 Proceedings,* Feb., pp. 225–227.

This paper examines some of the difficulties encountered in practice when automatically restructuring FORTRAN programs. Experimental gains as well as the need for further developments are discussed.

Defense Management Journal

1975 Special Issue on Software Management, Vol. II, Oct.

Dijkstra, E.

1968 "GOTO Statement Considered Harmful." *Communications of the ACM,* Vol. 11, No. 3, March.

This classic "Letter to the Editor" contains the famous quote ". . . the quality of programmers is a decreasing function of the density of GO TO statements in the programs they produce. . . ." The concluding statement is: ". . . The exercise to translate an arbitrary flow diagram more or less mechanically into a jump-less one, however, is not to be recommended. Then the resulting flow diagram cannot be expected to be more transparent than the original one."

1968 "A Constructive Approach to the Problem of Program Correctness" BIT, Vol. 8, No. 3, pp. 174–186.

1969 "Complexity Controlled by Hierarchical Ordering of Function and Variability." *In* Software Engineering: Concepts and Techniques. Naur, Peter, Brian Randell, and J. N. Buxton, eds. (see this entry in the bibliography), pp. 114–116. (Originally published in Software Engineering, Nato Science Committee Report, Naur, Peter, and Brian Randell, eds., Jan.)

1969 "Structured Programming." *In* Software Engineering: Concepts and Techniques. Naur, Peter, Brian Randell, and J. N. Buxton, eds. (see this entry in the bibliography), pp. 222–226. (Originally published in Software Engineering Techniques, Nato Science Committee, Buxton, J.N., and B. Randell, eds.)

1972 "The Humble Programmer." Communications of the ACM, Vol. 15, No. 10, Oct., pp. 859–866.

Ditri, Arnold E., John C. Shaw, and William Atkins

1971 *Managing the EDP Function.* New York: McGraw-Hill.

This book covers software maintenance at various places. A separate group for maintenance is favored.

Donaldson, James R.

1973 "Structured Programming." *Datamation,* Dec., pp. 52–54.

Elliot, R. W., and E. R. Story

1975 "Audio Techniques for Program Documentation." *Data Management,* Nov., pp. 32–35.

This article describes the economics of audio documentation (about one-fourth the cost of conventional techniques) along with a test of its effectiveness for maintenance purposes.

Elshoff, J. L.

1976 "An Analysis of Some Commercial PL/I Programs," *IEEE Transactions on Software Engineering,* June, pp. 113–120.

An analysis of 120 commercial PL/I programs of several DP installations at General Motors Corporation. The programs were scanned manually and automatically, to identify areas in which a better programming job could be done. The programs were considered with respects to five attributes: 1) the size of the programs, 2) the readability of the programs, 3) the complexity of the programs, 4) the discipline followed by the programmers, and 5) the use of the programming language. The users of other programming languages have also found the findings typical. Includes seventeen references.

Fagan, M. E.

1974 Design and Code Inspections and Process Control in the Development of Programs. *IBM, rep. IBM-SDD TR–21.572, Dec.*

Freedman, Daniel P., and Gerald M. Weinberg

1977 *EthnoTECHnical Review Handbook.* Lincoln, Nebraska: Ethnotech, Inc.

Describes dozens of variations of technical review, such as structured walk-throughs, inspections, and round-robin reviews. Technical reviews now cover every phase in the program life cycle, including maintenance. Written in question and answer format, this excellent handbook is based on the experience of dozens of Ethnotech clients who have used technical reviews to bring sense and sanity to programming.

Gause, Donald C., and Gerald M. Weinberg.

1976 *Are Your Lights On? A Treatise on the Definition of Diverse Problems.* Lincoln, Nebraska: Ethnotech, Inc.

A series of lively, casually written essays, built on anecdotes. They provide approaches to problem definition and solving. This is not a heavy textbook for solving problems. Only two problems in the book involve computers. However, the principles suggested from the examples can be applied to highly technical problems, including, I believe, maintenance. The illustrations are entertaining.

Gerhart, Susan L., and Lawrence Yelowitz

1976 "Observations of Fallibility in Applications of Modern Programming Methodologies." *IEEE Transactions on Software Engineering,* Vol. SE–2, No. 3, Sept.

The overriding goal of this paper is to cast a more realistic perspective on the methodologies, particularly with respect to older methodologies, such as testing, and to provide constructive recommendations for their improvements. Includes thirty-one references.

Gilb, Tom

1977 *Software Metrics.* Cambridge, Massachusetts: Winthrop Publishers.

Provides many practical techniques for estimating program reliability and efficiency. Gilb also presents his own "MECCA" method, and details the experiences of leaders in the field like TRW–Systems and Lockheed.

1977 "The Measurement of Software Reliability and Maintainability: Some Unconventional Approaches to Reliable Software." *Computers and People,* Sept., pp. 16–21.

It presents a selection of technological and management approaches to the production and maintenance of more reliable software. The emphasis is on the two software attributes of reliability, in the sense of operational correctness, and maintainability. It addresses four major areas: 1) quantification of reliability, 2) management of reliability, 3) automation of the reliability and maintainability tasks, and 4) redundancy-based reliability technology.

*** 1977 "Guaranteeing Program Maintainability (Gilb's Mythodology)." *Computer Weekly,* Sept. 22.

A practical technique to measure a degree of maintainability is a "*b*ebugging" technique (also called "artificial bug insertion"). It measures the effect of various people and various program documentation on the work of identifying bugs. The following system and contract specification for maintenance may be used: The program maintainability shall at least be 90% probability (in half an hour) for the assigned and trained maintenance programmers to identify (without fixing and retesting) undesirable program results ("bugs"). The article then describes the practical application of the technique. A revised version of this article is published in this book.

*** 1977 "Spare Parts Maintenance Strategy for Programs (Gilb's Mythodology)." *Computer Weekly,* Dec. 15.

Gilb suggests the writing of two programs to perform the same function. One acts as the spare part for the other. The dual but distinct software can be used in a variety of ways to reduce the total cost of software production and maintenance, so that the effort of coding it twice (coding being only 5 to 10 percent of a real time project) may be a profitable investment.

*** 1978 "Why Structured Programs Don't Always Ease Maintenance (Gilb's Mythodology)." *Computer Weekly,* Jan. 15.

This article is titled "Structured Program Coding: Does It Really Increase Program Maintainability?" in this book. The literature on structured programming contains little or no evidence of better maintainability as a result of using the methods. This article describes the works of the researchers, including Laurence Weissman of the University of Toronto, who have tried to conduct experiments to assess the maintainability effects of structured code. Gilb's hypothesis for this article: Structured code probably has some value for program maintainability, but its cost and effect for various purposes are only crudely understood, and there are certainly a large number of alternative and supplementary techniques for doing the same thing or for doing it better. A revised version of this article is published in this book.

1978 "Structured Program Coding Mythodologies." *ComputerData,* March, p. 11.

This is a slightly abridged article from "Why Structured Programs Don't Always Ease Maintenance."

*** 1978 "Maintainability is More than Structural Coding (Gilb's Mythodology)." *Computer Weekly,* June 1.

Suggests to organize maintainability technology into a knowledge structure. Maintainability is defined as the probability of being able to change the "state" of a system, within a given time period. Maintainability technology should also leave us in control of all other critical or interesting qualities of the system. The article mentions the concepts of multidimensional system quality and measurable maintainability for programs. It also introduces the spare parts maintainability concept. The concluding "Gilb's hypothesis" is: We can and should "engineer" maintainability into software. A revised version of this article is published in this book.

1978 "Documentation Standards Are Less Important than Standard of Documentation." *Computer Weekly,* Sept. 7.

"Gilb's hypothesis" for this article: Most of the currently common documentation techniques for program maintenance can now be replaced by more effective technology, the reason is mainly that the cost relationship of people and machines has changed dramatically since they were developed. More automation is needed.

1978 "Audio Documentation (Gilb's Mythodology)." *Computer Weekly,* Dec. 14.

This article is primarily a summary of the experiment described in Elliot, R. W., and E. R. Story, 1975.

*** 1979 "Need for Training in Program Maintenance (Gilb's Mythodology)." *Computer Weekly,* March 15.

This article is titled "Should We Specialize in Hiring and Training of Application Program Maintenance Technicians?" in this book. If the candidates recruited for maintenance are not motivated for the job, the result may be a high turnover. A question is raised whether a technical college could consider training a specialist in program maintenance, either as a directly recruited two year study, or as a third year specialization.

1979 "Controlling Maintainability: A Quantitative Approach for Software." Published by Infotech International Limited, Maidenhead, Berks, U.K. in *State of the Art Report on "Structured Software Development."*

Here is the abstract of this paper:

"The process of maintenance can be broken down into eleven steps or events, each of which deserves separate design specifications if we want to control total maintenance effect on the user of the system, instead of merely optimizing the program readability.

"A couple of the design methods used within a larger design method framework, known as the goal integrated logic building method, are used to illustrate the systematic engineering approach to the design of software.

"A hierarchically explodable goal specification method (Metrics Matrix) allows us to see the detailed design goals for maintainability, and the design specification overview method, known as the Function Attribute Component Table is used to build up the design specification.

"The multiple, and often conflicting attributes of the alternative maintenance-design specification alternatives are shown to be important to know and collect for future use if we are to progress from intuitive to engineering methods."

Gunderman, Richard E.

*** 1973 "A Glimpse Into Program Maintenance." *Datamation,* June, pp. 99–101.

It offers suggestions, techniques, and concepts which may aid in the necessarily customized implementations of maintenance philosophy.

Gunther, Richard C.

1978 *Management Methodology for Software Product Engineering.* New York: John Wiley.

Chapter 12 of this book on software engineering management is "Managing Software Product Maintenance."

Hetzel, William C., ed.

1973 *Program Test Methods,* Englewood Cliffs, New Jersey: Prentice-Hall.

Based on the proceedings of the Computer Program Test Methods Symposium held at the University of North Carolina, in June, 1972. Includes bibliography containing 375 references selected and grouped into sixteen topical areas.

Hilb, R. C.

1977 "A Pre-processor for a Structured Version of COBOL." Available from NTIS, 5285 Port Royal Rd., Springfield, VA 22161.

A thesis submitted to the Graduate Faculty of Auburn University, Auburn, Alabama. Includes source listing of preprocessor written in PL/I, and examples of processed and unprocessed COBOL programs.

Holmes, Charles E., and Leslie W. Miller

1973 "Chief Programmer Experience." Guide 37, Nov.

IBM Corporation

* 1974 *Structured Programming,* Independent Study Program, Textbook (SR20–7149), Workbook (SR20–7150). Poughkeepsie, New York.

Assignment 3 of this course is "Structuring Unstructured Flowcharts."

1974 *Hipo—A Design Aid and Documentation Technique (GC20–1851).* White Plains, New York.

This manual is a technical bible for HIPO users throughout a development cycle. It also includes a chapter on maintenance phase. The topics covered are: reviews of the maintenance HIPO package, and uses of the maintenance HIPO package.

1974 *Improved Programming Technologies—An Overview (GC20–1850).* White Plains, New York.

This excellent document briefly describes the six techniques designed to improve the program development process, and help develop error-free maintainable software: structured programming, top down program development, chief programmer teams, development support libraries, HIPO, and structured walkthroughs.

1975 *An Introduction to Structured Programming in COBOL (GC 20–1776).* White Plains, New York.

This excellent text describes and illustrates the use of structured programming. The technique and its supporting practices are described, the implementation of the technique in COBOL is illustrated, and two sample programs are presented.

Infosystems

* 1977 "Non Standard COBOL Programs Get Treatment (Users Report)." July, pp. 82–83.

Describes how a paper manufacturer, using a preprocessor (ADR's MetaCOBOL), solved the problem of re-doing 1,000 non-standard COBOL programs with half of its original staff.

Jones, Capers

1978 "Measuring Programming Quality and Productivity." *IBM Systems Journal,* Vol. 17, No. 1, pp. 39–63.

This engineering article includes discussion of the usefulness of separating quality measurements into measures of defect removal efficiency and defect prevention. Regarding the maintenance costs it states ". . . the smaller the change, the larger the unit cost is likely to be. This is because it is necessary to understand the base program even to add or modify a single line, and the overhead of the learning curve exerts an enormous leverage on small changes. Additionally, it is often necessary to test the entire program and perhaps recompile much of it, even though only a single line has been modified. . . ."

Jones, Robert R.

*** 1978 "Creativity Seen Vital Factor, Even in Maintenance Work." *Computerworld,* Jan. 23, pp. 25, 30.

The concluding statement of this article is: ". . . at least as much talent and creativity as is required in an original system development group is also required in the maintenance group. This will no longer be the case when the group that developed the original system is flawless and develops the ability to anticipate all future user requirement changes."

Kepner C. H., and Tregoe B. B.

1965 The Rational Manager: A Systematic Approach to Problem Solving and Decision Making. New York: McGraw-Hill.

Khan, Z.

1975 "How to Tackle the Systems Maintenance Dilemma." *Canadian Data Systems,* March, pp. 30–32.

One method suggested for controlling the extent of maintenance work is to limit the manpower resource allocated for this purpose. It discusses and illustrates four ways of organizing for maintenance: 1) maintenance function as separate activity within systems and programming, 2) Maintenance function integrated with new applications development, 3) Separate maintenance function, and 4) maintenance function as part of the data center organization. The prime determinants in the organization structure should be the availability of staff and their willingness to perform this type of work. A suggested solution to the maintenance prolem: "Strive for and design systems which are easier to maintain."

Lane, R.

1975 *An Introduction to Utilities.* New York: Petrocelli/Charter.

Describes the eight major IBM System 360/370 OS utilities: IEHLIST, IEHDASDR, IEBCOPY, IEHMOVE, IEBGENER, IEHPROGM, IEBPTPCH, and IEBUPDTE.

Larson, Harry T.

1974 "EDP: A 20 Year Ripoff!" *Infosystems,* Nov., pp. 26–30.

This hard-hitting article includes complaints against costly ongoing maintenance because of EDP applications being put into operation before they are ready. Also, there are too many incompetent people in EDP, producing programs with errors which need continuing maintenance.

Lientz, B. P., and E. B. Swanson

1978 "Discovering Issues in Software Maintenance." *Data Management,* Oct., pp. 15–16, 18.

A preview of a 2-year study. (The preliminary results of this study were presented at DPMA New Orleans '78, see next reference). It surveys the literature in the maintenance of computer application software. The basic issues covered in the literature are in five groups: conceptual issues, scale-of-effort issues, organizational issues, productivity techniques issues and problem area issues. It includes a list of nineteen references.

1978 "A Survey on Application Software Maintenance." A paper presented at the Annual Conference of the Data Processing Management Association (DPMA), New Orleans.

This paper reports preliminary results of a survey conducted on the characteristics of application software maintenance.

Lientz, B. P., E. B. Swanson, and G. E. Tompkins

1978 "Characteristics of Application Software Maintenance." *Communications of the ACM,* June, pp. 466–471.

A pretested questionnaire was submitted to 120 organizations to analyze the problems in the areas of maintenance and enhancements. Respondents totaled sixty-nine. Responses were analyzed with the SPSS statistical package. The paper presents some of the analysis results of that exploratory survey. It includes a list of twenty-three references.

Lindhorst, W. Mike

*** 1973 "Scheduled Maintenance of Applications Software." *Datamation,* May, pp. 64, 67.

Describes the implementation of a policy whereby maintenance of each installed application is deferred until a predetermined month.

Liskov, B. H., and S. Zilles

1974 "Programming with Abstract Data Types." *SIGPLAN Notices,* April, pp. 50–59.

Liu, Chester C.

*** 1976 "A Look at Software Maintenance." *Datamation,* Nov., pp. 51–55.

Provides an excellent introduction to "the world of maintenance."

McCracken D, D.

1973 "Revolution in Programming: An Overview." *Datamation,* December, pp. 50–51.

This article introduces a four-article group on structured programming. The structured programs using only the three structures (sequences, conditional statements, and a loop-control mechanism) can be read from top to bottom, without ever branching back to something earlier. Structured programming makes it easier to write and maintain programs and increases programmer productivity.

1975 "International Conference on Reliable Software." *Datamation,* June, pp. 93–94.

A brief review of the conference held in Los Angeles in April, 1975. Among the sponsors were the Association for Computing Machinery, and the IEEE Computer Society. The review includes many stimulating quotes.

McGregor, Bob

*** 1973 "Program Maintenance." *Data Processing,* May–June, pp. 172–174.

Advocates the use of contract programmers to do maintenance under the project leader assigned by the company. The project leader reports to the maintenance manager within the company.

Martin, W. A., and M. Bosyj

1976 "Requirements Derivation in Automatic Programming." In *Proc. MRI Symp. Comput. Software Eng.,* April.

Miller, E. F.

1972 Extentions to Fortran and Structured Programming—An Experiment. General Research Corp., RM–1608, Feb.

Miller, Jon C. (Cris)

1975 "Some Thoughts on Structured and Traditional Programming." Unpublished paper. Montgomery Wards Corporate Systems Division.

1976 "Improved Programming Technologies Retrofit (A Study of the Application of Improved Programming Technologies to Systems Developed Without Improved Programming Technologies)." Unpublished report. Montgomery Wards Corporate Systems Division.

This pioneering study may open a new field in software maintenance. (Miller's chapter in the book includes some of the ideas from this report.)

1977 "Sow's Ear: The Structuring Engine (COBOL)." *Yink, The Weekly Memo to Yourdon Instructors,* Nov., 18.

This short article outlines assumptions, objectives, transformations, methodology, and possible extensions for a COBOL structuring engine, that would mechanically structure original unstructured code.

1979 "S.E.—The Structuring Engine." Unpublished paper.

Describes the background, and some of the concepts of a COBOL Structuring engine that is being developed. The paper is available from The Catalyst Corporation, 5827 West Race Avenue, Chicago, Illinois 60644.

Miller, Larry K., and David Ostrom

1976 "Source Program Management." *Datamation,* Dec., pp. 67–70.

A good source program management system can go a long way in helping the maintenance programmer. This article describes the system (developed in-house) used by a medium size shop supporting the administrative functions of Washington State University.

Milligan, L.

1976 "Structured Programming—The After Effects." *Proceedings of the 42nd Meeting of GUIDE International.* New York: Guide International Corp., pp. 601–612.

It briefly mentions how the improved programming techniques benefited maintenance, the area where seventy to eighty percent of the effort was expended.

Mills, Harlan D.

1971 Mathematical Foundation for Structured Programming. IBM Federal Systems Division, Gaithersburg, Maryland, Feb.

1973 "On the Development of Large Reliable Programs." *IEEE Symp. Computer Software Reliability,* pp. 155–159.

* 1976 "Software Development." *IEEE Transactions on Software Engineering,* Vol. SE-2, No. 4, Dec., pp. 265–273.

This paper contends that beginning with ad hoc heuristic methods of design and implementation of software systems, problems of software maintenance and changes have become unexpectedly large. The improvement is possible only with more rigor in software design and development methodology.

Mooney, John W.

*** 1975 "Organized Program Maintenance." *Datamation,* Feb., pp. 63–64.

Describes the planning, staffing, and organizing a new approach to program maintenance at Spring Mills, Inc., a major Fort Mill, South Carolina-based textile manufacturer.

Myers, Glenford J.

1976 *Software Reliability: Principles and Practices.* New York: John Wiley.

Part 3 covers software testing. The topics covered are: testing principles, module testing, function and system testing, and debugging. Regarding maintenance, it states: ". . . The best way to dramatically reduce software costs is to reduce the maintenance and testing costs. This is achieved not by devising methods to make programmers program faster, but by devising means to allow software to be designed with more precision and accuracy."

* 1978 *Composite / Structured Design.* New York: Van Nostrand Reinhold Company.

The design of highly reliable, maintainable, and extensible programs is the aim of composite/structured design. The last chapter includes some thoughts on program maintainability, maintenance, and modification.

1979 *The Art of Software Testing.* New York: John Wiley.

Naftaly, Stanley M., Bruce G. Johnson, and Michael C. Cohen.

1972 *COBOL Support Packages: Programming and Productivity Aids.* New York: John Wiley.

A "definitive" book on COBOL aids. The excellent series of articles on COBOL aids published in the July, 1971 through May, 1972 issues of *Data Processing Digest* was re-edited and published as this book. At the time of this writing, this book was out of print.

Naur, Peter, Brian Randell, and J. N. Buxton, eds.

1976 *Software Engineering: Concepts and Techniques (Proceedings of the NATO Conferences),* New York: Petrocelli / Charter. The reports of the two NATO Science Committee Conferences, "Software Engineering" (Garmisch, Germany, October 7–11, 1968), and "Software Engineering Techniques" (Rome, Italy, October 27–31, 1969) have been combined and republished in this volume.

"This book points the way to the future of software. It examines our shortcomings in software practice and technique and suggests alternatives that could overcome many of the problems. But most important, it lays out, by implication, the frame of mind that we take to produce dependable software," says the series editor Ned Chapin. It includes Dijkstra's two landmark papers on structured programming.

Ogdin, Jerry L.

1972 "Designing Reliable Software." *Datamation,* July, pp. 71–72, 75, 78.

"The designed program has at least a five-to-one edge over programs that are simply 'coded' in the ease with which major and minor changes can be made," reveals this article. It also distinguishes between maintenance and modification. "Maintenance is the continuing process of keeping the program running, or improving its characteristics . . . program modification has its objective, the adaption to a changing environment."

Orr, Ken

1979 "Warnier-Orr Technology and Systems Maintenance." *Future(s)* (A newsletter published by Langston, Kitch & Assoc., Inc., 715 East 8th, Topeka, KS 66607), Vol. 3, No. 2, Spring, pp. 1–3.

Orr's long term goal in structured maintenance is to replace the existing system over time piece by piece, from the output back. I think Orr's following suggestion for redesigning an exiting system is excellent: "As time allows, we should attempt to redesign our exiting systems, starting with a systematic structuring of the existing outputs, and including a serious review of each output with the appropriate users. Then we should go through logical and physical systems design to determine what our system should look like. After doing this, we will be in a position to develop a long-range plan for replacing the existing system."

In my opinion, every DP manager concerned with software maintenance should carefully consider Orr's concluding comment: ". . . Structured maintenance, like structured development, is not impossible, just difficult. But I suspect it is much less difficult than what we are doing now."

Parikh, Girish

* 1977 Improved Maintenance Techniques. Published in the series "Programmer Productivity Reports." Chicago: Shetal.

Describes the use of Improved Programming Technologies to maintain and enhance existing systems and programs developed without using those techniques. The two approaches described for using these techniques are: "direct" maintenance (for immediate problems), and/or "retrofit" (for long term benefits). In the "direct" maintenance approach, a librarian, (un)structured walkthroughs, chief programmer teams, HIPO, top-down program development, and structured programming are used. The "retrofit" method includes extensions to development support libraries (standard media definitions, and library management systems), HIPO, program classification by functions, reformatting and restructuring programs, team operations to develop functional documentation and HIPO, and librarian (as a "programmer technician"). Also includes capsule descriptions of selected software packages that aid maintenance, and a list of fifteen references.

1978 How to Document Program Changes and Enhancements Internally. Published in the series "Programmer Productivity Reports." Chicago: Shetal.

A new tested technique presented in this report can help increase programmer productivity in maintenance and in new developments. It provides instant identifications of program changes. A concise, chronological record of the changes is also preserved. For further reference, it also includes identifications of the external specifications for the changes. The technique can be learned and applied in a few minutes. Examples from the real world COBOL and BAL programs are included. The technique can be easily adapted for almost any programming language on any computer system. Moreover, its use generally does not take any additional core storage.

* 1978 How to Increase COBOL Programming Productivity Using a Preprocessor. Published in the series "Programmer Productivity Reports," Chicago: Shetal.

Shows how COBOL preprocessor(s) can help increase programmer productivity in maintenance and in new developments. The preprocessor functions described are: shorthand, macro preprocessor, reformatter, Data Management System (DMS), decision table preprocessor, program analyzer, conversion package, and restructuring program are also covered. Also includes capsule descriptions of fourteen selected COBOL preprocessors, and a list of eighteen annotated references.

* 1978 How to Make the Most of HIPO. Published in the series "Programmer Productivity Reports." Chicago: Shetal.

Tips, trends, ideas, sources, and case studies to help make the most of HIPO in new developments and in maintenance. Also includes a list of twenty-seven reference sources, most of them annotated.

1980 A Powerful Structured Tool: The Warnier-Orr Diagram (Published in the series "Programmer Productivity Reports"). Chicago: Shetal.

This report includes the use of the Warnier-Orr diagram in maintenance—primarily its use to document existing systems/programs.

1980 How to Measure Programmer Productivity. (To be published in the series "Programmer Productivity Reports"). Chicago: Shetal.

This report, while focusing mainly on measuring programmer productivity in new developments, will briefly cover the measurement of software maintenance (and conversion) programming productivity.

1980 How to be Egoless (To be published in the series "Programmer Productvity Reports"). Chicago: Shetal.

Here's one guideline from this report: Do you know an egotistic programmer? Challenge him to maintain an almost unmaintainable system/program in your shop and see what happens!

1980 How to Make the Most of Pseudocode (To be published in the series "Programmer Productivity Reports"). Chicago: Shetal.

This report will include the use of pseudocode in system/program maintenance.

1980 How to Make the Most of Pseudocode (To be published in the series "Programmer Productivity Reports"). Chicago: Shetal.

The effective use of a program cross-reference listing can not only make a maintenance programmer more productive, but also help him reduce costly mistakes. This report will explore some of the techniques of using cross-reference listing in maintenance and in new developments.

1980 "How to Make the Most of Top-Down Development" (To be published in the series "Programmer Productivity Reports"). Chicago: Shetal.

This report will briefly include top-down development of program enhancements.

Parnas, D. L.

1972 "On the Criteria to be Used in Decomposing Systems into Modules." *Communications of the ACM,* Dec., pp. 1053–1058.

Peterson, W. W., T. Kasami, and N. Tokura

1973 "On the Capabilities of WHILE, REPEAT and EXIT Statements." *Communications of the ACM,* Aug., pp. 503–512.

Pomeroy, J. W.

1972 "A Guide to Programming Tools and Techniques." *IBM Systems Journal,* Vol. 11, No. 3, pp. 234–254.

Programming tools and techniques facilitating program development and maintenance under OS/360 and 370 are collected and discussed. These aids are categorized and defined according to their function. Abstracts of some of the programs are also presented.

Punter, M.

*** 1975 "Programming for Maintenance." *Data Processing,* Sept.–Oct., pp. 292–294.

Maintenance considerations are usually ignored in the system development stage. This leads to problems later. Program designers should remember that all programs need modifying sooner or later.

Reifer, Donald J., and Stephen Trattner

1977 "A Glossary of Software Tools and Techniques." *Computer,* July, pp. 52–60.

This paper provides a comprehensive listing of the software tools and techniques. It describes the three major stages of a typical software life cycle (conceptual and requirements, development, and operations and maintenance) and the six categories of software tools (simulation, development, test and evaluation, operations and maintenance, performance measurement, and programming support). A table relates the life cycle areas to the various categories of software tools, and a matrix relates the specific tools/techniques listed in the glossary to categories of software tools of which they are a part. The glossary of aids briefly describes seventy tools/techniques. It includes a list of sixty-one references.

Riggs, Robert

*** 1969 "Computer Systems Maintenance." *Datamation,* Nov., pp. 227, 231–232.

It describes a systems maintenance group to control and improve the maintenance of EDP systems.

Rindfleisch, Daniel H.

1976 *Debugging System 360/370 Programs Using OS/VS, Storage Dumps.* Englewood Cliffs, New Jersey: Prentice-Hall.

One of the most frustrating problems of a maintenance programmer is to work with program dumps. This book provides dump debugging procedures. It includes graphic COBOL, FORTRAN, PL / I, and generated Assembly and Machine language examples resulting in abnormal terminations.

Rustin, Randall, ed.

1971 *Debugging Techniques in Large Systems.* Englewood Cliffs. New Jersey: Prentice-Hall.

This is the first book in the series of books based on the computer science symposium series presented by the Courant Institute of Mathematical sciences of New York University since the summer of 1970. It is an important addition to the scanty literature on debugging.

Sackman, H., W. J. Erickson, and E. E. Grant

1968 "Exploratory Studies Comparing Online and Offline Programming Performance." *Communications of the ACM,* Jan., pp. 3–11.

Shooman, M. L., J. C. Dickson, J. L. Hesse, and A. C. Kientz

1972 "Quantitative Analysis of Software Reliability." *IEEE Symposium on Software Reliability,* Jan.

Sibley, E. H., ed.

1976 *ACM Computing Surveys* (Special Issue on Data Base Management Systems), March.

Spier, M. J.

1976 "Software Malpractice—A Distasteful Experience." *Software Practice and Experience.* Vol. 6, No. 3, pp. 293–299.

Stearns, Stephen K.

*** 1975 "Experience with Centralized Maintenance of a Large Application System." *IEEE Computer Society Proceeding.* (Compcon) Spring, pp. 281–284.

Describes the experience gained over three years in maintaining an inventory control system.

Swanson, E. B.

1976 "The Dimensions of Maintenance." *Proc. IEEE/ACM 2nd Int. Conf. on Software Eng.,* Oct., pp. 492–497.

This excellent paper presents the "dimensionality" of the maintenance problem for practitioners and researchers. "Some measures are suggested for coming to grips with this dimensionality, and problems of utilization associated with these measures are explored."

Trainor, W. L.

1973 Software From Satan to Savior. In *Proc. NAECON,* May.

Van Tassel, Dennie

1978 *Program Style, Design, Efficiency, Debugging, and Testing.* 2nd ed., Englewood Cliffs, New Jersey: Prentice-Hall.

Warnier, Jean-Dominique

1978 *Program Modification.* Leiden, the Netherlands; and Hingham, Mass.: Martinus Nijhoff Social Sciences Division.

This book on the modifications of programs constructed according to Warnier's method Logical Construction of Programs (LCP) is the translation of his book in French, titled La Transformation des Programmes; originally published in 1975 in France.

Weinberg, Gerald M.

1971 *The Psychology of Computer Programming.* New York: Van Nostrand Reinhold.

A classic study of computer programming as a human activity. The author challenges the myths and half-truths of the profession. He offers surprising and challenging ideas about the roles and relations of human beings within the programming environment. The relaxed, anecdotal style makes the book delightful to read. It includes many case histories and annotated bibliographies.

*** 1978 "The Mid-City Triangle. *Datalink.*

This story of a curious circulation of programmers amongst the Big Three of Mid-City, USA, brings home the eternal maintenance problem!

*** 1978 "The Worst-First Maintenance." *Datalink.*

This essay reveals how the maintenance cost and effort can be dramatically reduced by dealing with the worst part of a system first.

1978 "Disposable Programs." *Datalink.*

What are the species of disposable programs? Ever wonder whether to dispose of, or not to dispose of a program? This essay provides some enlightening ideas. "It costs much more, in the end, to run a one-time program N-times than to run an N-time program N times," it reveals.

* 1980 *Essays on Programming.* Lincoln, NE: Ethnotech, Inc. To be published.

This book will cover some of the major problem areas in programming, of which maintenance is near the top. (The two chapters in this book: "The Mid-City Triangle" and "Worst-First Maintenance" will be included in this book). Other areas include Debugging, Design, Writing (and Documentation), Training, and Professionalism. Mostly, it will be adapted from Weinberg's columns published during 1979, in the Ethnotech newsletter *Bullseye,* and in *Datalink.*

See also Freedman, Daniel P., and Gerald M. Weinberg; and Gause, Donald C.

Weinberg, Gerald M., Stephen E. Wright, Richard Kauffman, and Martin A. Goetz.

* 1977 *High Level COBOL Programming.* Cambridge, Massachusetts: Winthrop.

This book must be read and digested by every (COBOL) programmer and (COBOL) programming manager. The chapter headings are: The Programming Business. Managing High Level Programming. Critical Program Reading. High Level Control. Style and Workmanship. Modularity. Refinement. Verification. Sheltering. Maintenance. Putting Theory Into Practice. Appendix 1: The Meta COBOL System. Appendix 2: The LIBRARIAN System. This book contains many gems for a maintenance programmer. It is significant that a whole chapter is devoted to maintenance, the subject is almost always ignored in such books.

Wulf, W. A.

1972 "A Case Against the *GO TO.*" *SIGPLAN Notice,* pp. 63–69.

1974 "ALPHARD: Toward a Language to Support Structured Programs." Carnegie-Mellon Univ., Pittsburgh, PA, Internal Rep., April 30.

Yourdon, Edward

1972 *Design of On-Line Computer Systems.* Englewood Cliffs, New Jersey: Prentice-Hall.

1972 "Reliability of Real Time Computer Systems." *Modern Data,* Jan.–June.

* 1975 "Making Move to Structured Programming." *Datamation,* June, pp. 52–54, 56.

Regarding the use of structured programming techniques in maintenance, this excellent article suggests that the librarian concept and the structured walkthrough concepts can be useful. Also, new sections of code can be added in a top-down structured manner. Eventually, a "structuring engine," automatically converting unstructured logic into structured form may solve the problem.

* 1975 *Techniques of Program Structure and Design.* Englewood Cliffs, New Jersey: Prentice-Hall.

In addition to the excerpts on maintenance that are reprinted in this book, it includes a section on converting unstructured programs to structured programs, using the duplication of coding, the state-variable, and the Boolean flag technique. Included are testing techniques to eliminate program errors—from logic, documentation and timing errors to throughput, fallback and recovery errors. It also includes techniques for implementing the DDT (Dynamic Debugging Techniques) package. Other topics covered in separate chapters include characteristics of "good" computer program, top-down program design, modular programming, structured programming, programming style—simplicity and clarity, anti-bugging.

*** 1977 "Structured Maintenance—Part 1: Approach Trains User to Read 'Alien' Code," "Structured Maintenance—Part 2: Cost to Reshape User System can be Forecast." *Computerworld,* Sept. 12, p. 38 & Sept. 19, p. 33.

This article introduces the emerging discipline of "structured maintenance."

1978 *Structured Walkthroughs,* 2nd ed. New York: Yourdon Inc.

Walkthroughs in a maintenance environment, according to Yourdon, is a question of trade-offs. Maintenance of a large product, developed in an "unstructured" fashion is likely to benefit most from walkthroughs. Also, when staff is too small to assign each programmer his own program to maintain, working in a team, and walkthrough of the change and modified code, help maintain many programs.

1979 "Choosing a Pilot Project." *The Yourdon Report,* Feb. Mar., pp. 3–4, 7.

This article is adapted from Yourdon's revised book *Managing the Structured Techniques.* Note the use of the term "unstructured program," to denote a program developed without using structured techniques.

* 1979 *Managing the Structured Techniques,* 2nd ed. (Formerly, *How to Manage Structured Programming, 1976).* New York: Yourdon Press.

An excellent management summary of structured programming, structured design, structured analysis, chief programmer teams, and other productivity techniques. It contains some enlightening flashes on maintenance.

Yourdon, Edward, and Larry L. Constantine

1979 *Structured Design: Fundamentals of a Discipline of Computer Program and Systems Design,* 2nd ed., Englewood Cliffs, New Jersey: Prentice Hall.

Constantine is considered to be one of the pioneers of the structured design concepts. The book discusses maintenance at several places. Originally published in 1975 by Yourdon Inc.

Section VII

Index

INDEX

A

B

C

D

M

N

O

P

R

S

T

U

V

W

Y

Z